Forever
Fulfilled

The Eternal Wisdom of Everlasting Happiness

Jay Gardner

1st WORLD PUBLISHING

Forever Fulfilled

The Eternal Wisdom of Everlasting Happiness

Jay Gardner

Copyright © 2012 Jay Gardner

Published by 1st World Publishing
P.O. Box 2211, Fairfield, Iowa 52556
tel: 641-209-5000 • fax: 866-440-5234
web: www.1stworldpublishing.com

First Edition

LCCN: 2011916382
SoftCover ISBN: 978-1-4218-8623-7
HardCover ISBN: 978-1-4218-8624-4
eBook ISBN: 978-1-4218-8625-1

This material has been written and published for educational purposes to enhance one's well-being. In regard to health issues, the information is not intended as a substitute for appropriate care and advice from health professionals, nor does it equate to the assumption of medical or any other form of liability on the part of the publisher or author. The publisher and author shall have neither liability nor responsibility to any person or entity with respect to loss, damages, or injury claimed to be caused directly or indirectly by any information in this book.

CONTENTS

INTRODUCTION

I did not plan to write this book. A few times in my life I had in the back of my mind that someday I would like to write one, but had no idea when. The idea first came to me when I was in my late teens. But I really didn't feel I was the person to write a book on happiness back then. I didn't know enough yet. Over the years I would have moments of insight regarding other topics to write about, but I never felt inspired enough to actually take the time to write at length on them.

Then one morning about a year ago, while sitting at the foot of my bed, the idea of a book on how to be happier began to resurface. I was surprised that the idea came up when it did, because I was going through some difficulties, and they were beginning to wear on me. But as my troubles grew, something happened.

All at once I gained a much deeper understanding about why we experience difficulties. I realized more clearly than ever before that our problems are really only lessons about what needs attention in our lives. Not just some of our difficulties—but every single one of them, regardless of who seems to be to blame for bringing them to us. I suddenly recognized that life's hardships are simply trying to move us in the direction of greater fulfillment in our lives.

Even as my difficulties continued to grow, I was seeing how these experiences were revealing to me in every moment all that I needed to know to gain lasting happiness in my life. It was all there, not hidden from view, but plain as day. It seems that my spiritual practices had been, year by year, edging me ever closer to this realization. But my ultimate understanding about exactly how it works culminated and became completely clear to me within just a few days, in a way that would change me forever.

As these new understandings began to settle into my awareness, the thought came that this knowledge could be helpful to others too, because of the ongoing problems that were playing out on the world stage, like the continuing conflicts in the Middle East and elsewhere, as well as a badly faltering world economy. I felt that others could also use a way to maintain greater contentment in their lives, regardless of what was going on around them.

Within 24 hours of this idea crystallizing in my awareness, I had the thought that I should write a book about how to maintain happiness in life. I was intrigued that this was the same book idea I had so many years before as a teenager. Within 48 hours of having the first idea of writing it, I sat down at my computer to see what came. After a few minutes I stopped to fix a sentence that I had just written, but something inside of me said to just write and don't worry about the details, so that's what I did.

The words came quickly, one paragraph and then another. Soon I had a few pages. My enthusiasm began to grow. All that I had learned in my life began to pour out of me as fast as I could type it. Before I knew it, I had 20 pages and it was obvious there was much more to come. I only stopped that first day when I became too tired to go on. The next day I did the same thing; I just typed as fast as I could to try to get all my thoughts down. This continued day after day without me having to stop to think about what to write next. In 14 days I had written nearly 250 pages.

I then spent a number of days refining and organizing the text. After a total of 90 days of working on it, sometimes a couple of hours a day and other times many hours, I looked at my calendar to count the days I had left before I had to stop writing completely to put my attention on another project that I was putting off. I counted 18 more days left to write.

In 108 days, I wrote the manuscript to this book. All the ideas included here were written as they flowed out of my heart and mind. I never would have believed a manuscript could come out of me so easily without any preparation or struggle to bring it to completion.

When I was done writing, I just kind of sat and marveled at what had happened.

Now that the manuscript was completed, I needed to find the sources I wanted to reference. I thought this would be finished quickly—something I could do on the weekends while handling the other responsibilities that now needed my attention. But as the weeks passed it became apparent that the sources I wanted to include, some of them quite obscure, were going to take a year to assemble on my current schedule.

This began to weigh heavily on me, because a sense of urgency to complete the research was growing in my awareness. It seemed that this book wanted to be completed, and soon. I was feeling torn. I asked God for guidance about what I should do, which is my practice. Within moments, a powerful thought came that I needed to leave work immediately so I could finish my research, and strong emotions started to fire in me in a way I had never felt before.

As I stopped resisting the joyful inevitability of it all, my heart started to rapidly expand. The expansion was so great that it was all I could do to put my hand over my heart as waves of joy welled up inside of me. Within a short time of fully acknowledging and accepting that the decision was made, my heart became calm, warm, and contented.

I left work early that day to contemplate how best to approach the remaining research and to arrange for some time off. I initially wrote the manuscript completely from my personal experiences, but as I immersed myself in the details, I was surprised at how much the field of science continues to catch up with spiritual thought and is more and more confirming the age-old spiritual principles included here.

For this reason, I have whenever possible sourced scientific research to verify the spiritual truths that are included in this book. I know that some of you will appreciate seeing and reading these sources as validation of the underlying principles presented here. Similarly, even though much of what appears in this book is drawn from my own spiritual insights, wherever possible I have referenced the spiritual masters who first elaborated on many of these truths to show the universality of the knowledge expressed herein.

With that, I think you're ready to be on your way to greater fulfillment in your own life. I am profoundly confident that the knowledge in this book will bring peace and contentment to all who are willing to read and use it with an open heart and mind. The great spiritual wisdom of the ages lasts because it has value. Knowledge of lesser value comes and goes, but the Truth lives on forever to uplift those who are receptive to it.

One

YOU ARE HAPPINESS

My first memory of life was when I was just one or two years old. I know I was very young, because my footing was not yet secure. My mother escorted me outside to the front yard on an early spring day with the sun fully abloom, shining warm on my face, and new green grass pushing up through the old of the previous year.

The gusty yet soft breezes were like invisible flying carpets jostling my hair with their feathery tassels, pushing me to and fro as I tried to catch a flight on one. I was exhilarated, brimming with joy and excitement, for this was the first spring I was to know. I toddled around as the fresh grass, blue sky, and warm sun filled up my senses and imprinted the sensations that I still remember lucidly to this day.

These memories have stayed vivid in my mind all these years because they were so powerfully pure. My joy was not encumbered by memories of the past, since I was not aware of a past, nor of the future, because that was not yet conceived. It was the here and now in its warmest, fullest embrace, and an experience of what the present moment has to offer, if only we will let it.

Each of us has our own personal path to fulfillment and will take away from this book what is needed in our own time and way. The ancient wisdom of the ages is presented here with a contemporary perspective to allow you to live a life fulfilled in the happiness that is always present within you, and that is available to enjoy in each and every moment. This wisdom is not mine. It is ours—it belongs to all of us. It's eternal and has been passed down from generation to generation from time immemorial.

We will unfold this knowledge in the following pages. Many of you will very effortlessly find fulfillment in it. It will unlock the seeds of your joy that have lain dormant for far too long. You are ready to fully experience complete happiness now, and you will quickly see that it is always available to you if you will only allow it to be so. It's present for you to take and change your life to one filled with peace in every way.

Others will more slowly take to this wisdom, which will seep in over time. There's no hurry, because you have eternity to get it. There's no rush and never has been.

Either way, all will walk away from this book with the eternal, unchanging knowledge passed down from the great masters of every age to allow humankind to choose to have great everlasting peace and happiness in life. Having this knowledge is your inalienable right, and deep fulfillment will be yours when you understand it. This is your destiny, which in time will be revealed to you. Let's hope it begins today.

INSIDE OUT: HAPPINESS, YOU ARE

Those pure early memories of childhood are moments unadulterated by the baggage heaped upon us as we grow older—the shoulds and shouldn'ts—schemas we blindly create and live by through our materialistic worldview. I, like everyone else, was conditioned by my upbringing, which set into motion some of the ways in which I act and react in the world as an adult.

Much of our personal nature is formed by what we take in and absorb as children: the grownups who influence us with their specific outlooks on life; the media's many powerful residual impressions; other children's behaviors and beliefs; and our own culture's norms and mores. There is a slow curing of the concrete of our once innocent and mutable personalities as we grow and mature. Living in a materialistic age leaves its powerful imprint on us when the "things" we see and hear are considered of greater value than the unseen "non-things."

We pay attention to noises, but silence is ignored and not thought to be of much value or importance. We notice the objects in our environment while ignoring the fullness within, the invisible subtleties we sense when quiet and still. How we're conditioned necessarily creates the basis for how we learn, grow, and perceive the world around us. All of it can be, if done crudely and without sensitivity, very binding and limiting to our awareness and the outlook we fashion in our future lives.

No one is to blame for our makeup, since in reality we are all—both parents and children alike—just trying to find our own way to that sweet spot where all our thoughts and feelings are imbued with some modicum of contentment. We all want to have lives that are abundant with the so-called good things in life. But money, success, and friends, in and of themselves, unless we first find genuine happiness inside, will never fully actualize that lasting feeling of fulfillment we are so hoping to attain.

Everyone wants to be happy, but we often put off being happy until we gain those good things in life, the material indicators that we measure our success by, because we somehow believe they will inherently bring great happiness and fulfillment to our lives. The list of accoutrements that are supposed to make us happy is very long, but even with the attainment of these imagined trappings of happiness—a big house, a lot of money, expensive cars, frequent vacations—lasting happiness still remains elusive.

Unfortunately, our ideas of how to gain fulfillment have collapsed in upon themselves, and need to literally be turned inside out to be understood properly. The good things will only be appreciated fully when you learn first to find fulfillment within. My teacher, Maharishi Mahesh Yogi, used to say, "Seek the highest first." First develop your consciousness to experience the bliss within yourself, and then all good things will come to you.

As you learn to experience true happiness inside, you will realize that you don't need a lot of luxuries to be happy. A driveway full of new cars, more money than you can responsibly spend, and an abundance of attractive companions are not required to find lasting fulfillment. In fact, excesses can conspire to spoil your peace if not understood and experienced correctly.

You certainly can have luxuries in your life and still fully enjoy yourself—if your happiness is not tied to them. And there will always be some people who have more of these luxuries than you do; this is part of the natural diversity of life. But the point is that you can be just as happy with or without them, because real happiness comes from deep within at your source in pure Being.

Each of us will have our own distinct experience of gaining fulfillment, because we are all wonderfully unique human beings. If you will follow along as this ancient wisdom of everlasting happiness is unfolded, I assure you that you will receive all you will ever need to feel abundant and full. By learning how to tap into nature's invisible intelligence, you will bypass the many obstacles that keep everything good from effortlessly flowing to you. Jesus said, "But seek ye first the Kingdom of God, and his righteousness; and all these things shall be added unto you."[1] Once you reconnect to your source in God, everything you desire will come into your life exactly as you would wish it to.

We all know how elusive happiness can be. We may have an exhilarating experience where happiness abounds one day and the next day, or sometimes even the same day, a difficult experience befalls us that causes our happiness to have a shaky foundation. Or it falls away when someone's jealousy of our good fortune causes that person to treat us poorly. When you have that first thought—"Why did he/she have to treat me that way?" or "Why did that have to happen when things were going so well?"—your experience of joy is pulled away by the gods of unhappiness. And it is likely not to be seen or heard from again until the next fleeting moment comes your way, days, weeks, months, or in some cases, even years later.

We have all experienced these ups and downs in our own day-to-day lives. I certainly have experienced them in my own life. Some days I felt like a leaf in the wind, with no control over how my day would progress. All I could hope for was that the winds of change would favor me by blowing some happiness my way, so I could experience some transient enjoyment—until the next gust comes to blow it all away. I don't mean to imply that life is all highs and lows; there certainly are "okay" moments as well. But we are all looking for something more, something tangible and lasting.

Life began to change for me as a teenager. I found myself pondering on, stressing over, wrestling with, seething about, and at times even crying over these roller-coaster experiences in my life. I would sometimes wonder how I could find even a semblance of lasting peace in my day-to-day existence in the way I had when I was younger. Although slight of build, I was a champion in several sports when I was younger, and that was enough to sustain me. Life was simple and uncomplicated. But by my sophomore year of high school, these things no longer mattered to me. I needed something more. I tried to think deeply and logically about how to regain the elusive joy of my past. I often wondered: "How do you get it?" When you find it, "How do you get it to stay?"

I kept running into a dead end in my search for greater purpose in life, which prompted me to become more of a thinker. When I was younger, I was content just focusing on the physical realm of existence. But now I was becoming increasingly cerebral. I was a jock who was turning into a philosopher of sorts. In my quest for greater understanding, I started to push the envelope of my mind to probe more deeply into what life was all about. I attempted to think my way to a more meaningful existence by pushing my intellect to try to discover how to gain greater fulfillment in life. But the complexities derived from the intellect only cloud the way if not guided by wisdom, of which I had little.

With mounting frustration I ventured off for my answers into the all too available experimental lab of youthful indiscretions. Once genuine fulfillment seems out of reach, all that's left to the unaware are the cheap thrills of novelty and experimentation. But over time it became clear that deadening the senses with the readily available poisons of the day was not going to provide the pure, unsullied joy I was seeking, and there are only so many outrageous things a teenager can do before even the excitement becomes the same-old, same-old.

I began to speak to some of my friends about deeper issues regarding the meaning of life, about subjects that I never really questioned before: "What's the real value of winning?" "Why do we expend so much energy chasing girls?" "What's the real purpose of partying?" I began to question everything, not just superficially, but on a deeper level.

Moments of happiness were becoming less and less common, and I was becoming more and more desperate to maintain the last vestiges of peace that I so cherished in my life. My lifestyle was a mess. I was getting very little sleep, because I was staying out to all hours of the night. Everything good seemed to be slipping away and I was pining for the simple enjoyments of the past. When I exhausted my own ability to find the path back to happiness, I had an experience that made me think I should be looking to those who had already found it.

I had just taken a new part-time job. I think I had only worked at a restaurant before this, which was what you did as a teen in the hospitality state of Florida. But I needed to try something new, so I took a job at a Shell station pumping gas in a small town called Terra Ceia, near the Sunshine Skyway Bridge, which traverses Tampa Bay on the west coast of Florida. This was the first Sunshine Skyway Bridge, which had some quirks. A better one with the same name was later constructed to replace it.

The location was kind of in the middle of nowhere, long before any development to speak of in that part of the state. It was between Tampa and St. Petersburg to the north and Bradenton and Sarasota to the south. There was really nothing out there but the bridge, which was about a mile north, a few houses behind the station, and some thick woods across Highway 19, which was the only road to handle the traffic exiting the bridge to the south at that time, before Interstate 275 was built.

I found the job through a friend who knew the owner. He owned several Shell stations in my fairly new hometown of Bradenton and the surrounding area. My family had moved to Florida from New Jersey just a few years earlier. But there was only one gas attendant job opening at the time, and it was in the station near the bridge, so I started there until something opened up in town.

I didn't mind, since it was only a few miles from my home and it was near the bridge, which I thought would be interesting. Many travelers would stop to get gas or oil before traveling to other destinations in Florida. Most were having a great time while on vacation in the Sunshine State, some pulling large boats with their cars or recreational vehicles. Others would just stop to rest or get some refreshments from the station store, or to buy some sunglasses from the vendors who would set up out front.

Others would stop for another reason. They had a story to tell. Some people would pull in to the station to regain their composure after crossing the bridge. They would be visibly shaken by their experience. The original Sunshine Skyway Bridge was about 5.5 miles long and probably 400 feet high at its zenith. The uppermost part had only a see-through steel grid to drive on for about a mile or so, where you could clearly see the bay waters lapping at the bridge's supports below.

A few people would pull in literally shaking after driving over the grid, particularly those on motorcycles, because there was no warning you would soon be forced to ride as if on a window 400 feet in the air. Not only that, but the motorcycle riders would say that their tires had to fight to find the best path forward on the steel grid. They said it made them feel like they were going to tip over at any moment. The situation was made worse if there was heavy rain or wind, as you could imagine. Some would pull in with white knuckles and even whiter faces to tell their harrowing stories about traversing the bridge.

We would also get some really unique characters passing through the station. Some of them, from surrounding towns, would stop at night to buy something to eat before heading out to go fishing. They seemed to be solitary sorts who didn't mind being alone in the dark, fishing for sharks and the like in the deep waters of the bay.

Some of the locals in this tiny backwater were pretty interesting as well, since they really didn't fit in with the other clientele passing through our sparkling clean service station. Their primary interest wasn't filling up with gas, but with alcohol, and they would usually arrive in any one of an assortment of stages of intoxication. It made for some interesting experiences.

After you live in Florida for a while, at least back then, you begin to realize that a small but noticeable number of people driving through Florida are not on a vacation, but are running from something up north. They were coming from hundreds or even thousands of miles away with nothing in their cars but themselves and a shady disposition. With these folks, you tried to keep your words to a minimum. But most of our customers were just happy people passing through as they headed for fun in the sun.

One evening after I was on the job a few weeks, a guy walked out of the woods a little north of us across the highway. He apparently came to buy something at the station store. This was strange, because

I never saw anyone come out of those woods before. They appeared to be a thick, swampy morass. In Florida, woods like that are home to all kinds of creepy critters: poisonous snakes, giant spiders, chiggers, fire ants by the millions, and maybe even some wild boar, Florida panthers, or alligators.

He eventually came over and spoke to me as I leaned on the wall out front waiting for a car to pull in. He looked to be in his mid-30s and was fairly clean-cut, but a bit rumpled. As soon as he started to speak, he impressed me as an erudite fellow, not just because of the words that he used, but because of his demeanor. He said, "How do you do?" He had a charm about him that elicited my respect. It begged the question, "What were you doing in those woods?" He said, "My father owns some land out there on the water and I've been camping out for a few weeks."

I knew that land had to be worth a lot of money, since it was on the bay, so I immediately asked with the directness only a youth of my age could get away with: "What does your father do?" He replied, "He's an executive for IBM." To me that was a big deal, since this was during the heyday of IBM, before the rise of Microsoft, Apple, and Hewlett Packard, etc.

He came across like an aristocratic, wise man. He seemed to be an old soul, at least to a teenager. I was intrigued, and asked, "Are you camping alone?" He said, "Yes." I asked him why. He responded, "To take in the solitude of nature. I like to be alone in nature sometimes. It's a good way to clarify my thoughts." My newly acquired philosophical frame of mind was fascinated by all this.

We bypassed the small talk and went right to the deep stuff. I asked him some more questions about why he liked being out in the middle of untamed nature by himself, and he gave me a few more profound responses, such as: "It allows me to experience the subtleties of my existence." He was clearly a man who had mastered his fears. He appeared to be at peace with himself. Looking back, I can see that this was exactly the kind of simple wisdom I was unconsciously thirsting for—something non-material and inward.

From my eagerness for answers, I sensed that he zoned in on where I was in my life, which prompted me to kind of sheepishly divulge, "I'm inclined to wonder about life myself these days." He then said in a very attentive way that I won't forget, "That's very good. You should pursue that." We talked a little more and then he bid me farewell with, "Very nice to meet you," and a nod. I thanked him for stopping in and he left. He walked back into the woods at the same place he exited and was gone just before twilight set in. I never saw him again.

He left quite an impression on me. Here was this man who strode out of what seemed an impassable thicket of woods, a bit dirty and haggard, to visit a gas station in the middle of nowhere only to dazzle me with his dignity and wisdom. I was envious of him as he walked away, because he seemed fully content, with a solid grasp on the meaning of life. He was the first adult I had divulged my new metaphysical interests to.

After my meeting with this wise stranger from the woods, a desire began to grow in me to find some profound books by those who had already mastered life, because I figured they should have the wisdom I was looking for. I knew it was not just a lot of ideas and concepts like philosophy or psychology I needed, but something deeper. I intuitively knew that only religion or spirituality could quench my new thirst for knowledge. I had never really read much on these topics before. For the most part, I only knew about these areas of life from what I had heard, and I don't think I had ever purchased a book on my own prior to this point. But inside I knew this was what I needed to do.

I went into the Walden bookstore at our local mall and quickly gravitated to the religion and spirituality section. After looking around a bit, I knew that I was getting close when I came across books that seemed to combine religion and spirituality in a way that made it more palpable to me. As I browsed, a book on developing consciousness caught my attention. I had never heard of consciousness before, but I immediately sensed that consciousness is your awareness. After reading the cover and content pages, I knew that this was where I would start.

I hurried home and read the book in just two or three sittings, feeling some small degree of clarity come to my heart and mind. It spoke about expanding your consciousness to gain greater peace. The ideas made a lot of sense to me. It prompted me to want to learn more about developing my consciousness.

As I said, before beginning my pursuit of higher knowledge, I was a very materialistic teenager for whom sports, strength, appearance, girls, and music were the primary interests in my life. But now with great gusto I was diving into a whole other untapped dimension of myself that I didn't even know existed. I was not only unlocking the mental side of myself now, but was kindling the spiritual fire within as well.

In just a few hours of reading, I began my search for spiritual knowledge in earnest. I went out and purchased a couple of other books on similar topics the next day. For the first time, I was thinking completely independently of my family and friends. I knew that others might not be as interested as me in what I was embarking on, but for the first time I didn't care. I was heading off on a spiritual journey on my own.

Even if I had to go it alone, I knew on a very deep level that this was something I had to do. I told my close friends what I was researching and they were pleasant, but seemed indifferent. I don't know what their real feelings were, and to be honest it didn't matter, because all I knew was that I needed to immerse myself in this knowledge. I read each of these three books on different aspects of spirituality thoroughly.

After some time though, I began to feel that I was only learning about spirituality on an intellectual level, because I was not having the inspiring experiences of deep contentment, peace, and happiness I was reading about. Western culture is so focused on the intellect that most of our spiritual traditions rarely address how to attain the exalted states they aspire to. This was the case with the books I was reading to some extent, too.

It was as if I was supposed to just sit around and think these wonderful thoughts about how it would feel to experience God with the hope that one day the experience would actually arrive. Although intellectual knowledge has a value, it's not enough to fully establish you in a state of union with God's divine presence. A process to culture this experience in your own awareness is also required for your spiritual development.

This is why some of the greatest spiritual traditions of the world have included the regular practice of meditation as the foundation for their teachings, and I have a hunch that some of those that don't today, once did. You gain the intellectual knowledge of the Divine aspect of life from the great ones who have experienced it firsthand, and then participate in Divine revelation yourself as you commune with God during the practice of meditation. Having an understanding of both the theory and practice of the essence of life is necessary to grow in the quickest possible manner towards spiritual enlightenment.

THE EXCEPTION PROVES THE RULE

The first book I read on spirituality included a number of profound insights about what it's like to gain higher consciousness. It even discussed meditation, and offered a technique of its own. Unfortunately, as I would soon discover, it was not real meditation. I tried it two or three times, but didn't experience anything other than gaining a better understanding of the value of closing my eyes and being quiet for a short time, which I never had done before except to go to sleep.

It kind of made me feel that meditation was of little importance to spiritual development. To be honest, I don't even believe the author thought his meditation technique was of much value, because it seemed to be just another approach to help you gain a deeper understanding of yourself, but without any details about how that would occur. Meditation is often misunderstood in this way.

There are many authors and teachers who claim to understand meditation and offer their own version of it, but some of these invented techniques do nothing more than give meditation a bad name. Even some forms of meditation from the East are swathed in misunderstanding, because the correct practice has been lost for a very long time. Any form of meditation that's difficult to perform, or causes you to strain, is only going to impede your mind's natural ability to transcend to subtler levels of thought.

Real meditation is very natural and easy to practice. It should be an enjoyable experience, where it's apparent you're doing something more than just sitting with eyes closed. Just sitting with your eyes closed is not meditation. Real meditation allows your mind to naturally settle down without strain of any kind.

As it turned out, my first attempt at meditation was only a steppingstone. It provided the preparatory information I needed to know that meditation even existed in the West. It allowed me to become familiar with the idea of meditation, because I was soon to find a real meditation technique with a whole tradition of enlightened masters behind it, and a vast body of scientific research as validation of its efficacy. I would learn from its practice how essential it is to contact absolute Being, pure consciousness, in order to gain lasting fulfillment in life.

Meditation would show me how to live my life guided from within, instead of following the overused object-oriented approach to life that can never bring the lasting happiness we all desire. Through both spiritual knowledge and deep meditation, I learned that the path to fulfillment is an illusion of sorts, because what our hearts are actually seeking is right here within us. I began to understand that real happiness comes from inside, and that the way to find it includes a *pathless path* to discovering who we really are and what we truly desire in life. A good meditation technique removes stress from the nervous system to allow for greater access to the fulfillment that resides within,[2] because that which brings the greatest peace and happiness to life is unchanging and ever present at the deepest level of our own Being.

It was not that all the previous knowledge I had gained prior to learning how to meditate was a waste. On the contrary, it was absolutely necessary for me to go through the motions of comparing and contrasting what did and did not bring happiness to my life. As a result of this, I learned how to take the next step.

Meditation is the best way to culture a deep and abiding relationship with God in your life. Although we all have our own way to progress spiritually, it's extremely rare for one to gain a lasting experience of the Divine simply by hearing an intellectual description of It. How can you know God without direct experience of Him[3] in your life? There are far too many stresses we incur in our daily lives that inhibit our ability to instantly experience God's nature in our own awareness just from being told about Him. Deep meditation allows you to remove the stresses that block your mind from going deeply into your own pure consciousness to experience His divine grace yourself.

Those few individuals who have had flashes of higher states of awareness, without first culturing their mind and physiology through the practice of meditation, likely cannot sustain these experiences, because they don't have the ability to fully integrate them into their daily life. Deep meditation allows your mind to systematically transcend the gross levels of existence to arrive at your source in pure Being, and cultures the ability to remain established in this state even in the midst of activity. Meditation is not just "another" method for you to grow spiritually. It is the ultimate method by which to experience God in your daily life.

Just learning that absolute Being is within you is not enough to allow you to live this reality. You need both the knowledge and experience of the Almighty to make real headway in your spiritual growth. Meditation provides the direct experience for you to make great progress in your personal development in order to understand all that the present moment has to offer you. Deep meditation is the component that has been missing from spiritual life for far too long; it is the ideal method by which to actually experience Divine ecstasy.

But if you choose not to practice meditation, there's still value to be found in the pages that follow. This book has been written for everyone seeking greater happiness. The value of meditation will continue to be mentioned, since it is so essential to rapid spiritual growth, but again even if you decide not to practice meditation there's still important knowledge for you in the pages ahead. All that is needed to attain great happiness and fulfillment in life can be found here.

Your pathless path is never going to be like mine or anyone else's, because no two people are exactly alike with the same conditioning, stresses, and knowledge, or lack thereof. Yours will be very personal and special to you, as mine is to me. Your approach to spiritual development will be both unique and profoundly significant to your purpose in life, but it can be much quicker and easier if you apply the wisdom of the ages to the process, which is precisely why this book was written. It's no coincidence that you are reading these pages. A time for greater fulfillment in life is upon you.

This book was not written to teach you anything new, since your DNA already contains all the wisdom that will be uncovered for you here. You have only forgotten this knowledge. I am simply going to assist in reminding you about what you already know at a very deep level. How to proceed to gain greater fulfillment in life is encoded in your physiology and already available at the subtlest level of your thoughts.

This knowledge has always been there for you, and once you know it, you can never completely forget it. Intuitively, inside, you know there is great peace and happiness available to you. You at least know this possibility exists. Otherwise, human beings would not expend so much energy striving to attain it. It's now time for you to have it. As the Truth is revealed to you, it's natural to feel that you somehow already know this knowledge, even if you think you've never heard about it before. This experience is validation that you are on the right track, that you are remembering who you really are.

A PRACTICAL SPIRITUAL PURSUIT

If you choose to come along, I promise this will not be an empty pursuit with a lot of esoteric principles that are read today but forgotten tomorrow. It will be one of the most practical endeavors of your life, because it includes powerful knowledge and techniques that can be implemented right now to bring you greater fulfillment. It includes the time-tested wisdom of the great masters to remove all that is bad from your life—boredom, stagnation, anger, sadness, depression, etc., to be replaced with all that is good—contentment, satisfaction, peace, joy, happiness, and the lasting fulfillment you were meant to experience in life.

I will not be your teacher, but your guide, for unconsciously you already know all that there is to know. This knowledge resides deep within you. All the happiness and joy you could possibly desire is already present there. You only need to remember how to access it. You are made of happiness; it's a quality of your own pure consciousness. You can never be completely without it, because it's an aspect of your very nature.

You're going to remember how to enliven the innocence and wonder of childhood in your awareness, the experience you had before your mind began to believe that frustration, sadness, and suffering are natural features of life. You will be reminded of how to live in harmony with the laws of nature, how to use nature's intelligence to guide you, and how to gain control over whether your experiences create greater ease and comfort in your life, or greater difficulties.

When you're finished reading this book, you will better understand who you are and why you are here. The best part of this process is that it's really fun and easy, which is how God meant it to be. The best way to bring greater happiness and joy into your life is also the simplest and easiest. The path of least resistance is the way forward, and how you feel in your daily life will let you know if you're on the right track.

Your true feelings are the guide that will aid you in your progress. It's simple: if you feel good, you're going in the right direction. If you feel bad, you're going in the wrong direction. Of course, there are differing degrees of good and bad, which will be revealed to you as you grow spiritually, but as a rule feeling good is always better than feeling bad.

To become happier, you have to stay in the moment, because that's how you align yourself with it. Some of you may not fully understand what staying in the moment means initially, but it probably has a familiar ring. It entails not allowing your mind to worry about that which has happened in your past or may happen in your future. You only need remain in the here and now, because this is where the endless supply of your greatest happiness is found. You need to clear away the dust from the mirror of your awareness to see that all the happiness you desire is always available in its full glory right here in this moment.

To be totally present, you need to remove the dross that has built up and covers the reality of your life. Happiness is always available to you. You just need to remember how to access it. You just have to bring yourself into alliance with it, because it's always present within you. Happiness springs eternal from within your own consciousness.

It's very helpful to understand that your soul, which is the knower of all, is one with all of physical and non-physical reality, the relative and absolute levels of life, respectively. There's no separation between you and the rest of manifest, or visible creation, and the unmanifest, or invisible creation. To think otherwise is just *maya*, or illusion, created by the stresses you've incurred that cover and hide this reality.

Your invisible essence of pure consciousness is an unbounded field which underlies everything in creation: people, trees, oceans, stars, planets, and galaxies. There is no separation or duality between you and anything else. It just appears that way because of the current limitations of your awareness. Your consciousness is bound by these limitations, because you believe in them. But it's your Divine right to know your true nature both intellectually and experientially. This is where all of our lives are headed in the natural progression of things.

Your Being is expansive and encompasses all that is. But don't worry, you will never become just some undifferentiated aspect of the larger fabric of the universe. Your individuality will always remain, but it will keep growing and expanding. Living this reality does not mean you're going to somehow meld into the infinite ocean of pure consciousness, never to be seen or heard from again.

Your unique individuality is never in jeopardy, for you are, and always will be, a very special part of creation unto yourself. Your memories will not let you forget this. They will always be uniquely your own.

But just as you can be within a crowd and still feel separate from it, you can also allow yourself to experience being one with the crowd. You can always toggle between these two realities. Your thoughts will always be distinctly your own, but again that which you consider your own will expand and grow. You will never stop creating and contributing, and your joy will only grow exponentially the more you understand and experience the subtleties of this reality.

Your soul springs forth from the same source in God as everything else, but this book is not about showing you that you're simply the same as everything else in creation, any more than it is about showing you that you are different. Rather, it is to show that you are a self-sufficient aspect of nature's Divine intelligence, with the ability to use your own powerful ideas and actions to create and achieve your greatest desires. The knowledge in the pages that follow has been written down to show you the way to everlasting happiness, which is the primary purpose of this book.

Two

SPACELESS-TIMELESS WISDOM

The quest for happiness is complicated by our conception of time. The pressure that time creates is antithetical to lasting happiness, particularly if you believe that objects must be gained and activities accomplished to have it. If you believe your life to be finite and that you have only so much of it to attain your goals, then the pressure is on. After your rational mind kicks in during your teen years, you start to believe there are actually constraints on your time. All your problems begin once you start to feel that you only have so much time to achieve your goals in life.

You have been conditioned to believe that time is limited and fleeting, which causes your rational mind to analyze what is and is not possible to accomplish, based upon how much time you have. You then use this information to arrange your thoughts, activities, and environment accordingly to try to make sure that you don't miss out on any of the big goals that you have deemed important in your life.

You intellectually examine your life to determine what you can and cannot have, based upon the illusion that you can't do it all, because there's simply not enough time. This belief system causes you to feel you need to figure out what you can do in a hurry and get going doing it before it's too late, because, as they say, "You only live once." You conjure up ideas in your head about how you have to achieve specific things to avoid being a failure. You need to make something of yourself before it's too late.

This causes you to worry over missed opportunities and time wasted, and about the very real possibility of not being able to reach your goals, which creates a lot of pressure on you. As time passes, you may even begin to resign yourself to the idea that you're not going to accomplish all that you set out to do, which can cause you to pare down your goals to something more manageable with the time you have left. Thoughts and fears about failure and inadequacy begin to set in.

Many of you think this is how life works. If you can't achieve and succeed in the time you have, you cannot be happy, particularly if you can't attain some of your bigger goals before you grow old and tired. By believing in this reality and arranging your life in this way, however, you actually make it more difficult to attain what you desire. You impede your ability to effectively focus on achieving in life, because of your belief that you don't have enough time.

Some of you take the notion of time, or the lack thereof, so seriously that you can't even enjoy yourself. You don't feel you have the time to enjoy spending an evening with friends, a weekend with your children, or a morning working in the garden, because you let your worries about time divide your attention. You may not always be aware of them, but they are always there. When you feel you have to worry or something will slip away and you won't accomplish what you want to, all of life becomes very stressful.

Before you know it, life has passed you by and you never really stopped to enjoy it. Even if you attain some of what you want, you still are never able to completely enjoy yourself, because there's always the next thing that you need to do or have before you can really be happy. It's a vicious cycle and a tremendous waste of life. This doesn't just happen to the overachievers of the world. It happens to anyone who believes they need to do or be something in particular to be happy.

By not allowing yourself to ever slow down and enjoy life, you actually inhibit your ability to have what you truly desire, which is happiness. Most of your vital energy is consumed worrying about how to get it, and not enough is used to actually experience it. You can't be happy when all your time is spent worrying about how to be happy. It all starts to become a little silly after a while when you realize what you're doing.

The belief that there are only two options—working a lot to try to achieve that which will make you happy, or giving up on happiness all together and doing nothing—doesn't leave much hope for a fulfilling life. Those who keep going can't understand why happiness is so elusive. And those who succumb often never end up doing anything constructive with their lives, but don't know why.

Some people get so tired that they give up on even that which they are really good at and should be pursuing, because they worry they're not achieving quickly enough. They say things to themselves like, "I'm not content, so I should be doing something else" or "I'm not succeeding the way I want to, so I must be doing something wrong." They say these things to themselves even if they enjoy what they're doing when not worrying about it. Unfortunately, these types of thoughts cause many people to view as a chore even what they are naturally good at.

This is how many people live their lives—or I should say, don't live their lives. They never allow themselves to be happy, because they waste their days and nights worrying about attaining something to bring them happiness. We don't let ourselves have fun because we don't think we have enough time to do so. We don't even allow ourselves to enjoy life when we're not doing anything at all. We may try to enjoy ourselves, but we never completely do, because our mind is never fully present without our worries.

I remember leaving a girlfriend once when I was in my late teens, because she wanted to have more fun than me. It wasn't that I didn't have any fun when I was young—I did, probably too much of the materialistic kind. But then at one point, I started to become overly serious about everything, because I thought I was running out of time—silly, huh? In my late teens, I actually thought that I couldn't waste any more time with anyone who was not on the same serious wavelength as me. I passed up a lot of fun by thinking there was only hard work to be done, and no more time to enjoy myself.

I never did accomplish what I left my girlfriend to pursue, because I wasn't in the right mind-set, or even in the right period for success, which I will explain in a later chapter. I made life very difficult for myself by being so serious. I literally stopped enjoying my life, thinking that it was all up to me to create my success from scratch with my own hard work. But it never happens that way. You may get some of what you want, but it's never all you thought it would be, and it never brings lasting happiness.

Even though I was very conscientious and an extremely hard worker, I didn't get what I really wanted, which was happiness and fulfillment. You can make yourself believe there's a seeming lack of time to get the big things moving in life, but this only reduces your productivity, which doesn't allow you to get any closer to what you really desire. We don't just want happiness every now and again—we want it all the time. This is what we're all striving for.

Those who are goofing off all the time are even less happy than those trying to accomplish something with their lives, because they have made themselves believe it's too burdensome to even think about being productive. They feel it won't bring them happiness. However, not only do they not ever find happiness, but they live with the guilt of not even trying to find it.

In some instances, even those with great ambition give up on pursuing their dreams, because they can't see a way of attaining them with the perceived difficulties and limited time they think they have to do so. They worry so much and apply so much pressure to themselves that they eventually just buy into the notion that they can't do it, because they cannot logically see how to turn their dreams into reality with the time they have. They end up settling for something less than what they really desire. It's a very sad scenario that so many people fall prey to.

But why is it that when you give up on your dreams, you initially feel relief? It's because when you give up, you allow yourself to accept what *is* for a brief moment and stop letting time play games with your mind. A flood of relief comes, because you have allowed yourself to stop aimlessly worrying about everything. You allow yourself to briefly be in a place where time doesn't interfere, which is how you should be living your life anyway. Unfortunately, you then begin to beat yourself up for failing, so you're right back in the same unhappy place again. The pressures we apply to ourselves and the worries we create due to our belief that time is limited are never ending, if we allow them to be.

THE SPACE-TIME MIRAGE

There is no question that time conspires against us being happy, but what if I were to say that time as we know it doesn't really exist? From the most enlightened perspective, all possibilities of past, present, and future are actually occurring simultaneously right here and now, not spilling off into the past, or overflowing into the future. They are all happening concurrently in the present moment. There is no differentiation in time and space; as scientists are just starting to realize, everything is happening in the eternal moment of now.[1]

Let me explain. We believe that when we focus our attention on a physical object and then move our attention to another, time has elapsed. This is because we have let our awareness view one object at a time in a sequence. If we are moving while viewing these two objects in sequence, for example, when we are turning our head or walking, we feel the sensation of time, but also feel that we are traversing space, hence the feeling of the existence of time and space.

But even if we stay completely unmoving in body while viewing something, our minds still flicker like a candle in the wind, because they waver as our thoughts come and go. Our thoughts also represent motion. As thoughts pass through our awareness, they give the sensation of motion. Very few people are able to remain completely still in both mind and body to witness the reality of their existence where time and space no longer exist.

Experiments have been conducted to show how we often don't see that which is right in front of us. This phenomenon is called *inattentional blindness*. There's a famous "invisible gorilla" experiment showing that even if we are looking directly at a large black gorilla, we still may not see it.[2] In the experiment, a few people pass a ball amongst themselves while some others who are watching count the number of passes. Then a person dressed in a gorilla suit walks out and stands directly in the middle of those passing the ball. Fully 50 percent of the people who participate in this experiment never see the gorilla!

More recent research has shown that even if participants expect the gorilla to appear, some still don't see it, and many participants expecting to see the gorilla often miss other obvious events that occur right in front of them. This phenomenon is becoming quite well documented. Only the spiritual adepts are able to keep their mind completely still to fully witness the reality of the infinitely eternal state of pure Being, which is devoid of all space, time, and causation.

Time and space exist for those with finite awareness who can only take in a small slice of their external environment at a time through their five senses. For example, you can only view one planet at a time through a telescope with your focused attention, but when you move the telescope to view another planet in the opposite direction, you experience a sensation of moving yourself and the telescope through space and over a period of time, which gives rise to your belief that space has been traversed and time passed.

But what if you were able to expand your awareness to become much broader than it currently is, say to infinity, so that you can take in through your newly expanded awareness all planets in the galaxy at once without the need for a telescope? With an awareness that is infinite in scope, you would be able to put your attention on every planet in the galaxy simultaneously, just as you are able to view at once a tray covered with a layer of sand granules.

This new, more all-encompassing awareness would render both time and space nonexistent, because there would be no need for motion or sequence in time to occur to view each planet in the galaxy. You would be fully aware of them all at the same time, since your new expanded awareness would encompass everything. There would be nowhere to go, because you would already be everywhere.

This would eliminate the sensation of space and time, which in fact is the ultimate reality of your existence. The here and now is all there is. Everything that we perceive to be in our past and future, or up there and back there, actually exists in the here and now. But for most of us, our awareness is not broad enough to fully comprehend this.

Let me bring this example back into time and space to make it more concrete. Let's say that you only had one small eye, which had a very narrow band of vision that limited your sight. When you looked out at the world around you, much of it would literally be out of sight, since your range of vision is reduced by having only one small point of focus from your single eye.

You would only be able to look in one direction to see a narrow slice of your environment. To see anything else, you would have to turn your head to see other equally small slices of your environment.

This limited vision, or awareness, if you will, tricks you into believing that in the process of seeing one slice of reality and then moving your head to see another, or in walking towards that which is out of sight because of distance in order to see it up close, that time has passed and that you have moved through space.

But let's say hypothetically that your entire body is covered with outward facing eyes in a panoramic view in all directions, so you can see everything simultaneously. Also, let's say all of these eyes have x-ray vision, so you can see through any obstacle, and you have infinite telescopic vision so there are no limits to how far you can see. In essence, you are able to see all of creation unobstructed.

Your newly expanded vision also has one other quality: it can see the unseen intelligence of the universe developing all of visible existence, so absolutely nothing is out of your awareness, not even the unseen field of pure intelligence. From the perspective of your new all-encompassing vision, you can now see all objects, and even non-objects, in the universe at the same time. This would immediately eliminate the perception that time and space exists, because you would be able to see and put your attention on everything in creation at once.

The expanded awareness afforded by your new, infinite vision would immediately turn time and space into an obvious mirage, because the need to move around to take in different aspects of your environment would be eliminated by the unbounded vision now available to you. You would be able to witness everything happening in the universe simultaneously, eliminating any break in your attention.

This greater capacity to see would not require any space to be traversed or any time to elapse in order to view anything in creation, in effect slowing your overall sensation of space-time down to nil. This idea of having infinite awareness allows you to better understand the reality of the eternal here and now. It's only due to our limited and bound awareness that time and space ever seemed to exist in the first place.

To now take this understanding literally to another dimension, let's include in our example of expanded awareness the ability to perceive all other non-linear dimensions that occupy the here and now concurrently with our present four dimensions, but are hidden from view. What if your conscious awareness were able to encompass not only all of our current four dimensions (up, down; left, right; forward, backward; and time), but all possible unseen dimensions as well?

This would mean that your fully expanded consciousness would be able to witness all possible realities—linear and non-linear—at once. Your awareness would span not only to infinity in a linear fashion to include our current four relative dimensions, but in a non-linear fashion as well, to include all other dimensional realities that currently cannot be perceived by us. Physicists and cosmologists alike claim this *multiverse* reality exists.[3] It must, to explain the endless number of universes they say are constantly being created and then dissolved back into the unmanifest field of pure intelligence at the subtlest level of nature's functioning. However, the multiverse is not a new concept. It was clearly described in the ancient Vedic literature of India:

> *Because You are unlimited, neither the lords of heaven nor even You yourself can ever reach the end of Your glories.* **The countless universes**, *each enveloped in its shell, are compelled by the wheel of time to wander within You, like particles of dust blowing about in the sky. The śrutis, following their method of eliminating everything separate from the Supreme, become successful by revealing You as their final conclusion.*[4]

Now let's expand our example back out into the unmanifest or non-material realm for the ultimate understanding of how your fully developed awareness would operate. Imagine if you were a field of pure unbounded awareness with no particular shape and size, but with an infinite capacity for perception. Your awareness would envelope everything that is—all of creation and beyond, which would render space and time nonexistent. That is to say, you would know anything and everything that happens or does not happen in the universe simultaneously. This would cause your past and future to cease to exist because of your omniscient awareness. Within your own consciousness, you would know all possibilities at once.

From the most enlightened perspective, this is what you are capable of achieving. Everything is completely accessible within your own unbounded consciousness. There is no inside and outside when it comes to pure consciousness, because it's all-encompassing. But most people are unable to experience this reality, because of the stress that has inhibited the full expression of their own unbounded perception.

It's not that your current finite perspective is unreal, because everything is dependent upon your perspective. Your current world-view is very real to you, and because you believe it's real, it behaves accordingly. But as you develop your consciousness to experience more and more the eternal state of pure Being, the bound perspective you know now will give way to a more unbounded view of reality. To know these greater possibilities is just a matter of expanding your consciousness to encompass and experience them for yourself.

Time and space will disappear upon your awakening to the un-bounded state of your own pure consciousness. This is why Einstein's theory of special relativity was able to show that if you travel at a high rate of speed, for example, in a space ship, time slows down for you in relation to time on earth.[5] From the space traveler's perspective, nothing seems to have changed, but from the perspective of the observer standing on earth, it appears that the space traveler is moving faster and becoming smaller.

On the other hand, if the space traveler were to compare his reality to that of the observer standing on earth, he would feel that he himself was instead expanding, because he's able to take in so much more than a person who is stationary on earth. His awareness is expanding relative to his speed, if you will. So not only does the spaceship traveling at a high rate of speed expand the awareness of the traveler inside, it also appears from his perspective to expand him in every way, which is why time begins to slow down. Your experience of time and space is completely dependent upon your perspective.

The calculations for special relativity also indicate that, in theory, if you were able to take off in a spaceship from earth to fly to the moon traveling faster than the speed of light, you would arrive at the moon before you even left earth. It takes an infinite amount of energy and mass to travel faster than the speed of light, so while you were building up the necessary energy and mass required to take off, you would expand to be both on earth and on the moon simultaneously. You would be at both your departure location and your destination location before you even left, so your departure would no longer be necessary.

Space and time are simply constructs of our awareness. Everything in creation is relative to our perspective. In the ultimate sense, every-thing is happening right here, right now. All possibilities are available to you from within the unmanifest field of your own unbounded pure consciousness. By fully developing your awareness, you can experience this reality for yourself. This is the value of spiritual development. Spirituality is not just about titillating your mind with mystical ideas. It's much more important than that—it's about expanding your knowingness in all areas of life.

LIFE IS ETERNAL

Your soul is eternal. When you let the body go at death, your soul lives on in purity. Your soul is your essence. The fully enlightened Lord Krishna, as explained in the ancient *Bhagavad-Gita*, describes the soul to the story's hero, the warrior Arjuna, in this way: "He is uncleavable; he cannot be burned; he cannot be wetted; nor yet can he be dried. He is eternal, all-pervading, stable, immovable, ever the same."[6]

The soul is comprised of intelligent energy that never perishes, it merely changes form. The First Law of Thermodynamics states that energy cannot be created or destroyed. It can only be transformed from one state to another. Water can be frozen into ice and then melted to create steam, but the energy at the basis of these different forms is always present in creation.[7] In this same way, your soul can never be destroyed; it simply changes form when the body perishes.

A soul continues to create new bodies to live and learn again. It reincarnates over and over to allow you to fulfill all your most cherished desires. Life is eternal and it's important to your peace of mind that you understand this truth. You literally have eternity to accomplish all that you want in your life. Don't believe that this mind-set will cause you to become complacent or lazy. It's impossible not to act; life cannot exist without it. You must act according to your nature, and you will continue to do so even after understanding that you have an immortal soul.

But knowing the reality of the eternal nature of your soul will remove all the unnecessary pressure about what needs to be accomplished in this lifetime. You don't need to worry that you have somehow missed your opportunity if you don't complete everything you set out to do. Most of us desire many things, and we can have every one of them throughout the duration of our soul's many lifetimes. The only thing that can stop you from fulfilling your desires is if they change. When you no longer desire something, there's no need to experience its fulfillment.

Perhaps in this lifetime you're good at business, but you really want to become a famous musician. However, you just don't have the knack for it. Continue in business, since that's what you're good at, but understand that God doesn't just choose some people to have musical skills and others have to live with an unfulfilled desire for them. You can be a musician even if you don't presently have the skills for it. All you have to do is start from where you are now to learn how to play music. You may not master it in this lifetime, but you definitely can make progress, and throughout your many subsequent incarnations you can master it.

So many of us don't even want to try, because we feel there's not enough time to master being a musician or whatever else we want to be. But you have all the time you need. In fact, you have eternity. If you have a strong desire, then pursue it and enjoy yourself as you do. You can even become a famous musician if your desire is strong enough. It's never too late to start. There's no such thing as too late.

But you don't have to be famous in every life you live in order to feel complete either. In fact, as you get to know yourself, you just might find that you really don't want recognition or fame at all. You may have had it in a previous life and it didn't appeal to you, or you have become tired of it. It may just be something you think you want, since so many others do, or a past habit that makes you gravitate unconsciously towards it in this lifetime.

You don't need fame or status to be happy, because you have many lifetimes to accomplish all that you wish. Enjoy what comes naturally to you now. Fully experience every aspect of your life without applying unnecessary pressure to yourself. Don't beat yourself up over your lack of accomplishments. You are alive, learning, and growing day by day and that's more than enough to be fulfilled about.

Every moment of your life should be celebrated. You don't need all the trappings of great success to bring serenity and peace to your heart. You don't need any particular thing to happen at any specific time, since you have forever to do and be all that you truly desire to do and be.

Why do you think some people are born with natural talents that they begin to express at a very early age? Child prodigies have developed their skills in previous incarnations, as you have developed your unique skills in the past. Prodigies are not superior to you just because they are especially good at something that you're not. You can have the experience of being a prodigy if you wish, but you won't always want this kind of success, because you eventually will desire to learn other things about life, like how to be quiet and contemplative as opposed to being out there in the world for all to see.

God is not so unfair as to give all the best talents to others, but none to you. It's not that only some people can be rich and famous and the rest of us are out of luck. This is not how life works. If your desire is strong enough, you too can be rich and famous one day. You just need to pursue your passions and they will eventually bear fruit for you. The key is to enjoy yourself. Always try to have fun with whatever you choose to do.

What about those who are born only to die as children from a fatal disease? This reality seems very cruel and unfair if you believe that you only live once. But God is never cruel. He only loves you and wants your greatest happiness. There are important lessons to be gained from every experience, including dying at an early age.

You may need to go through this process to overcome your fear of death, or because you took for granted your last life. But you will always have another chance for a long and healthy life. Those who sacrifice with a truncated life to learn important lessons gain immensely from their experiences in order to have a much longer and more fulfilling life in the future.

Life is fair 100 percent of the time. It provides you with valuable lessons for your soul's growth towards enlightenment. You always receive exactly what you need to move your soul forward. Some people get the good things in life and others the dregs for good reason: it's what they need. You always get exactly what you need for your development.

I know this may be difficult for some people to accept, but it's the reality, and understanding and accepting it is the way to everlasting peace and happiness. Be gentle with yourself, but try to learn to embrace this truth. There are only perfect reasons for all that you experience in life, and all of those lessons are exactly suited for you.

The sooner you get this, the sooner you can begin to let go of your misunderstandings about how life needs to be in order to be happy.

If you don't achieve what you want at work or at play, you have not wasted any time. Feelings of inferiority are not an accurate representation of your life. Each experience is valuable to your growth, regardless of whether you win or lose. From the most expanded perspective, you literally cannot make a mistake.

THE UNIVERSE'S PERFECT PLAN

Even when you experience great difficulties in life, you must understand that you're receiving valuable information from the universe about how to move forward. You need the contrast that is provided by nature about your mistakes to know what right behavior is. If you never felt discomfort from doing something wrong, or the repercussions of treating someone poorly, you would not know how to behave correctly in the future.

Opposites exist in creation. There is good and bad, happy and sad, fast and slow, and the list goes on. The full spectrum of outcomes is available for us to learn from. You cannot know happiness fully if you have never experienced sadness, and you cannot know calm if you have not felt nervousness. Love life for what it is—a grand educational process for you to learn and grow from.

The opposites we see in creation exist only to provide the necessary contrast for our growth. There are no mistakes on our part, or for that matter on the part of God. The universe is arranged in exactly the right way to allow you to act and react to learn your lessons and progress towards greater fulfillment in life.

We are perfect in our imperfections. This is not just a play on words. What seems like an error is actually always a lesson. It's a lesson because the way you feel tells you the way to proceed towards greater happiness. How you feel helps to provide direction to your life. If your actions make you feel uncomfortable, you should avoid performing them. If, on the other hand, your actions make you feel good in your heart, you should keep going in that direction. Contrasting outcomes in life provide us with the feedback we need to choose a better way of thinking and acting the next time.

You can actively participate in developing your awareness by using your feelings to guide you in the direction of greater happiness. So pay attention to how your actions make you feel. One of the benefits of meditation is that it allows you to purify your nervous system, so that you have the clarity of mind needed to be sure you're interpreting your feelings correctly. Too much stress in the physiology can distort reality so behaviors that are actually harmful feel good.

A short-lived pleasure isn't necessarily beneficial. For example, some of your vices may make you feel some degree of pleasure, but it doesn't mean they're good for you; in fact, they will likely do harm. But the negative effects incurred by these vices can provide important lessons for you, because you eventually see how they hurt you and disrupt your life. When I was a young man, before I learned how to meditate, I had a number of distinct preferences for music, dress, food, behavior, etc., that I thought were just fine for me. But I had no lasting happiness in my life.

I didn't realize until after I began to grow spiritually that many of my preferences were actually bad for me on many different levels. We gain most of our likes and dislikes from how we are raised, the people we associate with, and society at large. But one size doesn't fit all. Some of the things we were taught as children may well turn out to be detrimental for us in the long run, for example, how we eat, and how we behave. This doesn't mean that anyone intentionally taught us to harm ourselves. These things were probably passed on quite unknowingly.

It can sometimes take years to realize that something is not good for us, and often we don't find out until late in the game, after we've begun to experience adverse symptoms. But through the practice of meditation, you can awaken the latent intelligence within to more easily learn what is and is not good for you to live a happier, healthier life.[8] This is the value of broadening your consciousness by developing yourself spiritually. A spiritual life is not just for the whimsical; it's for anyone to live a much fuller life.

Meditation helps to reduce the stress in your mind and body, so you can become more in touch with who you are and with what makes you happy.[9] It allows you to better recognize that harsh, crude behaviors have their negative consequences, and that refined, uplifting behaviors have their positive effects. Meditation allows you to cultivate spontaneous right action in your life, action that's more in harmony with your own nature and that of your environment. This ability is tremendously important to your progress in life.

Maharishi used to say, "Knowledge is different in different states of consciousness."[10] The experience of different levels of consciousness is similar to looking through different colored glasses. In one state of consciousness everything may look as if you are wearing blue glasses, while in another everything appears as if you are wearing green glasses. As you develop your consciousness, the color of the glasses you're viewing life through will change in order to more accurately represent a reality that brings you greater fulfillment.[11]

INTELLIGENT NATURE

There is great intelligence in the universe waiting for you to tap its infinite source for your greatest benefit. This intelligence is everywhere in nature. A mango seed does not grow into a lemon tree, because the mango seed has intelligence that guides it to grow only into a mango tree. Similarly, if you watch a plant during the day you will see that it turns its leaves to follow the sun's path across the sky. The plant is expressing its intelligence by facing the sun as it moves, because it knows this is from where it derives its sustenance.

The oceans move in and out on the shore in relation to the moon's movements, because the water has intelligence that dictates how the gravitational pull of the moon guides its ebb and flow. Planets stay in their orbits around the sun because they are happy there. They don't change their path, because they enjoy the course they are on. Even the lowly rock has intelligence. When the sun shines on it, the rock knows to heat up.

These are all examples of the often overlooked intelligence of nature. They are forms of knowingness no different from our own. Their intelligence is not different in kind from our human intelligence; it's only different in degree. We obviously have more intelligence than a rock, but the rock's intelligence is similar in nature to our own. It's conscious of the sun shining on its surface. It has its manner of knowing, and we have our greater degree of knowingness.

It is important to understand that creation is filled with many levels of intelligence and that it's all very orderly. The amount of creativity expressed by anything is dependent upon its ability to accurately reflect the infinite intelligence of nature, or God. A rock reflects little of this intelligence, whereas a fully enlightened human being can reflect it in its entirety. The denser the object, the less intelligence expressed. The more refined an object's sensitivities, the greater intelligence it expresses. This is the natural order of things.

There is even intelligence that cannot be seen, because it's the unmanifest intelligence from where all of material creation springs forth. In fact, there's greater power and intelligence in what is unseen than in what is visible to the human eye. In the *Upanishads*, which is part of the Vedic literature, there's a story of a father explaining this phenomenon to his son:

> *Bring me a fruit from the banyan tree.*
> *Here it is, Father.*
> *Break it open.*
>
> *Tell me, what do you see inside?*
> *I see many seeds.*
> *Break one seed open.*
>
> *Tell me what you see.*
> *I see nothing at all.*
>
> *My son, that "nothing" is the subtle essence of all living things, which appears as nothing because you cannot perceive it. But from that nothing this great and ancient tree has grown. That infinite source of the whole universe, the Self of all that is, the ocean of pure consciousness—that is Truth. That is the unmanifest Self. Of that you are created. That thou art.*[12]

All the intelligence required to grow the large, fully developed banyan tree is contained in the emptiness of the seed. In this same way, all of nature arises out of the field of pure intelligence from the invisible gap of pure consciousness. The unseen aspect of life is where the greatest power and intelligence of nature resides.

Physics explains that dark matter, and its less manifest counterpart, dark energy, make up about 95 percent of the matter in the universe. This means that what we see in the relative universe— galaxies, planets, stars, people, etc.—comprises only about 5 percent of all matter.[13] The unseen dark matter is what ultimately manifests into that which we can see and feel. Within these subtle energy fields resides the womb of nature, which creates all physical forms. It's the invisible intelligence of God that gives rise to all of visible creation.

Max Planck, the founder of quantum physics, said:

All matter originates and exists only by virtue of a force which brings the particle of an atom to vibration and holds this most minute solar system of the atom together. We must assume behind this force the existence of a conscious and intelligent mind. This mind is the matrix of all matter.[14]

BE FULLY PRESENT

Speed your consciousness up and slow your life down by developing yourself spiritually. Begin to live in the moment by not straining so much over how things get completed, or how they will play out for you to succeed. Just do that which brings you happiness and nature will organize for your greatest success. If something is not enjoyable enough for you to find contentment spending even a little time on it each day, then you shouldn't be doing it. Just because someone else is happy doing it doesn't mean you will be.

As you become accustomed to remaining fully present, you will find you are much more successful at everything you do. This is when you really begin to live your life and accomplish great things. When you can go from one enjoyable experience to the next without burdensome thoughts of the past or future, you are living your life to the fullest extent possible, and happy all the while. This is the way to genuine fulfillment in life.

You're not expected to immediately begin to live in the eternal moment of now simply through an intellectual understanding of this state. It's not easy to keep encroaching thoughts about your past and future from getting in the way of your moment-to-moment enjoyment. Most of us were never trained to remain fully present for even a few minutes, let alone all day.

But there's no time better than the present to begin trying. Throughout your day, try to remain aware of only that which makes you happy and do that as much as possible. This may include changing to a number of different activities throughout your day, which is fine as long as you are enjoying doing each of them.

It's not that you are only going to do those things that make you feel good and the rest will be ignored. This is the beauty of remaining fully present. A dramatic shift in how you feel about everything will come when you choose to stay in the moment and do only that which is joyful, because *everything* will automatically become more joyful. You won't become less responsible about tending to your life by following your happiness. You will become more responsible, because everything will become easier and more fun to do.

Worrying about not having enough time is where our trouble begins. You are not always consciously worrying about time, but it's always in the back of your mind. We bother ourselves with negative thoughts about our activities because of it. In our minds we belabor the idea of having to perform some activities. But if you will try to believe that you have all the time you need while remaining fully present, you will begin to find that you can be quite content doing most anything.

The simple thought of doing only that which makes you happy will allow you to make this shift. If you can stay in the moment, you will find that in most cases you can enjoy what you are doing right now. For those few activities that are still not pleasing, you can focus on removing them from your life, since they're not the things that resonate with you. But you will find that most things are much more appealing by remaining fully present.

Trying to master this technique from the level of thought is very helpful, but there's a far simpler way to learn to stay in the moment. Deep meditation is the original method to train yourself to be fully present. The whole idea of staying in the moment for greater effectiveness in life came from practitioners of meditation. If thoughts come, you just let them go. Meditation naturally trains the mind to settle down to experience the peace and quiet of the here and now, so that in activity you can spontaneously flow towards that which brings you the most joy. After meditation, you naturally bring this quality out into activity to experience greater fulfillment in all areas of your life.

Meditation allows the mind to transcend all the gross levels of thought to arrive at its source in pure Being, at the least excited state of the mind. It's pleasing for the mind to experience the expanded awareness that comes from immersing itself in Being. It experiences increasing happiness as it settles down to this eternal state of life. After meditation, you then bring the stillness and deep rest that you gain out into activity, which allows you to more easily remain present and see what will bring you greater happiness.

The clarity of mind gained from meditation allows you to cut through all the superfluous thoughts and activities that get in the way of enjoying yourself. It removes all the complexity from the thinking process so you can more easily recognize that which brings greater joy to your life. There's nothing more important to rid from the mind than all the clutter that leads you to do things that are not right for you, and that can never bring you lasting happiness. Nothing does this better than meditation, which is why its practice has been lauded by the wise since the beginning of human existence.

This is the beauty of meditation. It's the ultimate mind sweeper that clears your awareness of all the unnecessary thoughts that are never going to bring you genuine satisfaction. It helps you see through activities that may bring short-term pleasure, but no long-term happiness. It expands your awareness and clarifies your thoughts to make it hard to miss what will bring the most fulfillment to life.

If you don't feel you're ready for meditation, practice staying in the moment and pursuing that which brings you the most joy. This will allow you to keep your attention on creating greater happiness for yourself. Even though it takes longer to see results this way, it is still a valuable exercise for your growth.

THE WISDOM OF THE MASTERS

Pursue the knowledge and wisdom of the great spiritual masters. Read their books and refer back to them often. I have gained tremendous knowledge reading spiritual books the first time through, only to rediscover them later and uncover even more of their valuable insights. Books with deep spiritual knowledge can be read over and over again, because their principles are timeless and always helpful to your spiritual evolution. Practicing the techniques of the masters and reading their books can be just what you need to take the next step in your growth.

The first time you read a spiritual book, you may not be ready to grasp all that's there. You may not understand everything on the first pass. But you will begin to know intuitively if there's something more to be gained from the books you read. If there's deep knowledge there, revisit those pages again and again until you absorb it. If you're a seeker of Truth, read those pages over and over to take advantage of the wisdom that's being made available to you.

New knowledge is vital for your spiritual evolution. You will find that as you consciously move towards enlightenment, the information that's required will start to appear just when you need it. This has happened to me on so many occasions that I've stopped counting. It occurs so often that it's beyond chance. I may start to read the *New Testament* just at a moment when I'm about to be treated unfairly, not knowing that it's going to provide the necessary information I need to handle ill treatment from others. Or I may receive knowledge from a discussion about patience, just before mine is tested.

If you're receptive, you will find that little messages are coming to you from everywhere about how to gain greater fulfillment in life. There are no coincidences. God is making the information you need available to you at every moment of your life. You just have to be open to it. Learning to settle the mind will enormously enhance your ability to recognize the wisdom that's being offered to you.

Remember, you have all the time you need to accomplish that which you desire, so start enjoying your life now. Every aspect of it is just as it should be. Your life experiences are not only what you need, but are what your soul desires. They include the lessons for your ultimate growth to enlightenment. Try to work through the difficulties you face without being shaken. Know that they are all for your benefit.

Your soul actually wanted many of these experiences prior to you taking on this life. You desired a life that would allow you to progress, so you chose some of the difficulties you are now experiencing. Shift your perception to accept that they are helpful and should be taken in stride. As you grow in consciousness, your suffering will begin to disappear and contentment will rise up in its place. Learn all you can in this life, so you don't have to come back again and again until you get it right.

Reincarnation is a necessary process to allow you to grow towards enlightenment from one incarnation to the next. But if you can develop your consciousness fully in this life, you won't have to come back to the earth plane again if you don't want to. You can instead choose to reside in a higher plane of existence where greater beauty and happiness abound. When you grow to enlightenment, you can come back to help others if you wish. Those who return are the great masters who come to help and guide humankind's spiritual progress. Once you reach this state, the choice is yours.

A friend once told me a story of Maharishi in the early days of his worldwide spiritual regeneration movement, when he was teaching meditation to the masses. He lectured the world over to large groups for many years. While doing so, he would often be asked questions from members of his audiences on esoteric spiritual topics, like past lives, reincarnation, and similar topics. As this particular story goes, Maharishi began to notice that some people were getting sidetracked by such fantastic subjects, and they were not asking enough questions about their practice of meditation, which is the real basis for rapid growth to enlightenment.

Maharishi always held a flower in his hand while lecturing, not only because he loved the natural beauty of a flower, but because he often used it as an analogy, with the sap representing pure consciousness, which has all the intelligence necessary to give rise to the fully blossomed flower. His description was simple yet very powerful in helping people understand that pure consciousness gives rise to all of manifest creation, just as the sap gives rise to the flower. He would say that by watering the root you are nurturing the growth of the flower, just as you nurture yourself by diving deep into the field of your own pure consciousness through the practice of meditation.

On one occasion he was holding a white carnation in his hand, when one of the members of the audience asked him about reincarnation. Maharishi held the carnation by the stem with one hand and gently tapped it on the palm of his other while saying, "One carnation is enough, one carnation is enough to gain enlightenment," and he rarely spoke about esoteric subjects again. This is how important meditation is for your personal growth to enlightenment. It's so important that any other spiritual topic is not worth discussing if it interferes with your understanding of the significance of the practice of meditation.

Maharishi was what I like to think of as a big generator behind humankind's spiritual evolution. There are literally millions of people from around the world who have learned his Transcendental Meditation. He was completely one-pointed about the value of meditation as the jetliner path to quickly develop your consciousness. All other great teachers of enlightenment have had the same message. Maharishi wanted it to be absolutely clear that meditation is the way to gain full enlightenment in this lifetime. He would say to first meditate, and then do whatever you want to, because he knew if you were meditating regularly you would increasingly do only good for yourself and others.

Maharishi was so special and so enlightened. He was at once brilliant, yet very innocent; very strong, but so gentle; authoritative, but very funny. Although he was a physically tiny man, he was a huge, fully enlightened being. When I first started to watch his lectures, I would think to myself, "This man is God-like." His awareness was so expansive, and he was such a great seer of pure knowledge. His name, Maharishi, actually means *maha*, great, and *rishi*, seer. He was an amazing seer of the reality of life. Humankind is so blessed to have had this great incarnation come to earth to clarify for us how to gain enlightenment—to let us know that it's easy and available to everyone.

The United States has such good fortune to have had several great teachers of the Vedic wisdom come to spiritually uplift the nation. Swami Vivekananda came to the United States in 1893. He toured and lectured to groups throughout the country and had many followers. He taught them to meditate for their greatest spiritual development. His organization's headquarters was located primarily in New York.

In 1920, eighteen years after Swami Vivekananda's departure from his body, Paramahansa Yogananda came and taught very large groups and raised their consciousness through the practice of meditation as well. Yogananda had followers from every strata of American society who sought him out for his great spiritual wisdom. His organization was centered in California.

In 1959, seven years after Yogananda left us, Maharishi came and in time set up much of his organization, university, and schools in the peaceful plains of Iowa. He had a huge following throughout the world, including some of the most famous personalities of our time. Students of his Transcendental Meditation program came from all levels of government; from the most successful echelons of the world of business and finance; from the brightest limelight of both the movie and music industries; as well as from every area of professional sports.

We have been so lucky as a nation to have had these great personages of India come to show us how to develop our consciousness. They have spread their teachings far and wide throughout the Western world, with each progressively having a greater influence on our spiritual development, which is all according to the Divine plan. They raised the level of spiritual development of the masses by successively building on the elevated world consciousness that was created by their predecessors. Each of these teachers was perfect for their time; one after the other, they brought out increasingly higher knowledge, even if there was no actual communication among them to do so.

Maharishi would sit in lotus position on a dais as yogis do and teach about meditation and the Vedic wisdom, while many of the greatest scientists and thinkers of the day, including Nobel laureates, would come to ask him questions about their fields of study. An enlightened being is capable of answering these questions from the deepest level of nature in a manner which is most satisfying and illuminating to the questioner, regardless of that person's area of interest or expertise.

He would explain to them how their own fields of study found their basis in the field of pure consciousness, as they sat in awe of his amazingly precise, yet expansive and enlightening answers. Only a great seer, a Maharishi, has the insight and wisdom to answer questions regarding any field in this manner, because they have access to all knowledge from the deepest level of cosmic intelligence at the basis of creation.

I became one of Maharishi's students as a young man, after his organization had become so large that it was no longer possible to see him in person unless you were a VIP, which I was not. I was just a young student, but I was blessed to have been able to use the many powerful programs he made available for humankind to develop its consciousness and grow towards enlightenment. All of these programs are still available in their entirety today, which was Maharishi's intention upon their creation.

Although I never met Maharishi in person, I haven't felt deprived in any way. He made hundreds, maybe even thousands, of video tapes discussing every topic you can imagine, and explaining how each subject area finds its source in the unbounded field of pure consciousness. I was privileged to see many hundreds of these presentations, including many live via satellite as they were being made.

It seems that technology poses no barrier between an enlightened master and his students. I can enthusiastically attest to this, because I had many profound experiences watching his videos over the years, including moments of feeling completely immersed in the transcendent while viewing some of them. They are truly a treasure that he left behind for all to learn from and enjoy.

I feel my relationship with Maharishi was very personal, as I am sure all his students do, regardless of how the knowledge was received, even if it was gained after his departure from the physical plane of existence. No void can possibly exist between an enlightened master and his student. I truly loved Maharishi, and I am thankful every day to have been able to learn about the spaceless-timeless wisdom of life from such a great sage.

Three

THE ATTENTION OF THE CREATOR

Subatomic particles have proven to be very interesting in that they act more like *waveicles* than particles. They act like a wave, because they can't be located anywhere in particular until an observer puts their attention on them. Only then do they behave like a particle and appear to be localized in space and time.

But at all other times they act like a wave, hence the name waveicle. In reality nothing in creation, not even that which exists at the grossest level of physicality, exists as a distinct entity independent of the process of observation. This understanding has tremendous import on how we know and understand our world, and how we interact with and determine our place in it.

OUR FLEXIBLE AWARENESS

The attention of living creatures is amazingly flexible, allowing us to gain and comprehend information in very unique ways. For example, there are mammals, birds, and reptiles that have eyes on the sides of their heads, which allow them to look in completely different directions at the same time. These creatures are capable of viewing one aspect of reality out of one eye, and a totally different one with the other, and can pass their attention from side to side very effortlessly to zoom in on something specific without having to move their head to view it with both eyes.

They are able to make this work because their awareness is so pliable. They're able to fill in the large void in between their eyes to create one seamless reality, which allows them to thrive in their habitat. They don't have to see everything in the blind spot between their eyes, because they are able to fuse together all the necessary information they gain from their eyes and other sensory organs to stay on top of what's happening around them.

The blue whale, which can grow to be 110 feet long and weigh as much as 400,000 pounds, has two eyes about the size of grapefruits that are yards apart from each other. Yet these leviathans are still able to exploit their environment for their greatest benefit. A blue whale could be viewing the beautiful dance of a porpoise through one eye while casing out its next massive meal of krill, the tiniest of sea creatures, through its other.

They also use another special sensing device, sonar, to know their surroundings. By making sounds that bounce off objects, they can hear what they cannot see. They have been known to do this with objects even hundreds of miles away. Whales have mastered blending their unique knowing capabilities into a single fluid reality to their greatest advantage, and this has allowed them to survive as a species for millions of years.

Let's use an exercise to see how flexible our own human awareness is. Take the palm of one of your hands and gently rub the soft, under-part of the forearm on your other arm. Focus your attention only on feeling the soft, smooth surface of the skin on your forearm as you gently rub it with the palm of your hand. It may take a moment to get your attention fully locked onto the texture and temperature of only your forearm. Close your eyes and really experience this sensation with the palm of your hand. Keep your attention focused on feeling the smooth under-part of your forearm.

After you've done this for a moment, adjust your attention while going through the same rubbing motion, but this time close your eyes and focus your attention only on feeling the more textured surface of your palm with the soft under-part of your forearm. You are just reversing your awareness from focusing on the texture of your fore-arm to the texture of your palm. Do this with eyes closed until you are locked onto feeling only the texture of your palm.

What you have witnessed is your own ability to move your aware-ness from perceiving in one way to very quickly focus it in completely the opposite way. You went from allowing your attention to only experience the feeling of your forearm, to allowing your attention to only feel your palm, by simply changing the focus of your awareness.

Our awareness is infinitely flexible in this way, and we are capable of moving and focusing it in any way we wish with just a small inten-tion. If you weren't trying to consciously focus your attention on your forearm or your palm, you would have been able to accomplish it much more easily, since you're always unconsciously moving and adjusting your awareness to better perceive yourself and your envi-ronment.

For example, when you find a mosquito bite somewhere on your body, you are able to quickly examine it with your fingers in various ways without even thinking about it. We generally don't focus our attention on any one object, since it's often just unconsciously floating from one thing to another until it receives a subtle impulse to focus in on something in particular. We have an amazing ability to send our attention out to anywhere we wish, whether it's somewhere on our body or somewhere off as far as the eye can see, and even farther. We can even learn to bring our attention inward to reflect on our inner space.

With practice, you can learn to do incredible things with your awareness, including knowing about and influencing things that are completely out of sight. Our intuition is an extension of our atten-tion, which can be developed to help us gain greater awareness of that which lies beyond our vision. Even animals have intuition. Your pets know when you're coming home even before they see, hear, or smell you. They also know when you're going out before you show any signs of doing so.[1] But our intuitive ability as humans can be honed to a much greater degree than theirs. And these skills are only going to increase in the coming years as humankind learns to push out the boundaries of our awareness more and more.

YOUR CREATIVE NATURE

The awareness we are speaking of is the real you. It's your soul's method of knowing. The flesh and the bones of your body are merely a result of your intention to interact with the manifest world around you. If your soul had never desired to interact with the material world, you would never have manifested your faculties of hearing, touch, sight, taste, and smell. These five senses facilitate your interaction with the world; your body merely houses the real you, the awareness or soul that holds the reins to your senses.

Your body is just a projection of your awareness to allow for the sensation of participating in what you believe to be the physical world. Your body is a concentration of the same mind-stuff that you are unable to see, but it has made an appearance for you in the form of your carbon-based anatomy to allow you to interact with other objects in your surroundings.

Over the eons we have all bought into this reality by agreeing that certain vibratory concentrations of consciousness are specific objects. We have unconsciously agreed that some of these energy fields will appear as physical objects: human bodies, animals, trees, etc. They appear to us not just as empty space, even though that's what they are primarily composed of, but as something tangible that we can see and feel. It's a fascinating reality we have created for ourselves.

All of us, or most of us anyway, had to buy into this objectified reality for it to work, so we could interact with one another in a uniform way. This is the illusion that we are required to take on in order to incarnate into a human body. It involves buying into the reality that our bodies are physical things and not just fluctuations of consciousness.

Prior to accepting the illusion of physicality, you were pure awareness, awake only to yourself. You had to project yourself out from this state of Oneness, to allow for a crystallized version of your awareness to participate in this increasingly impure conception of reality—the physical realm of existence. Your soul, or *jiva*, as it was called by the ancient rishis, is simply a divided aspect of pure consciousness, which you had to create through focused attention in order to give rise to the duality you experience today. You eventually had to accept to a degree the idea that you are separate from everything else in creation for the illusion to work properly.

The desire was there and hence your soul's powerful intention created every aspect of the physical you, from your DNA to the flesh and blood of your human body. In fact, all of visible creation has been created by you in this same manner. Just as a movie theater projects images onto a screen, you do the same.[2] But in your case the projector, the screen, and the images on the screen are all created from within your own consciousness through an intention of your higher Self.

Other people have been projected onto the same movie screen of pure consciousness by their soul's intention, but we are all part and parcel of the same field of awareness, hence your acceptance of their physical existence and their acceptance of yours. All aspects of the one field of consciousness are completely self-referral back to their source, such that there is infinite knowingness, infinite correlation, and infinite agreement among us about what our shared reality will look like, including the existence of human bodies, cars, clouds, oceans, mountains, etc.

There is, however, a certain degree of variation in perception from one person to the next, based upon our level of consciousness. How developed your consciousness is ultimately determines how the material world will appear to you. Most of these differences between people are not very dramatic. But the higher your consciousness, the more the physical world will appear simply as fluctuations of your own consciousness, or extensions of the Self.

Your reality is as you are. Let me explain by using two different realities: one will be the finite, small "you" perspective, and the other the unbounded, large "You" perspective. What the large You sees in the physical world is nothing more than the reflection of Its intention, which is projected onto the movie screen of Your own awareness. When the unbounded You doesn't look at these images, they literally don't exist as material objects, because they are understood and experienced as creations of Your attention.

The large You understands that Its reality is created in every moment, so when It turns away from what we perceive as physical objects, they literally don't exist. They are understood simply as fluctuations in the field of consciousness, not physical objects. When the large You turns back again to look at an object, it is created anew. A fully enlightened being, a large You reality, is always creating the world from within each time it is experienced. It's just a matter of our level of awareness that determine how we understand and perceive our surroundings.

Does this mean that one who is fully enlightened, again a large You experience, can walk right through a brick wall, since it's understood to be nothing more than pure awareness, or empty space? Yes, it can walk right through a brick wall, and sometimes does, whereas a less evolved soul, a small you experience, is bound by its finite reality with very little influence over it. The small you cannot walk through a brick wall, because its reality is that a brick wall is a hard, solid object.

Do you think at night the small you could walk right through a brick wall that is not seen? After all, it's only pure consciousness, so what the small you can't see shouldn't hurt it, since there's no awareness of the wall. Most people will rather abruptly discover that the attributes of a brick wall are so ingrained in their knowingness, far beyond their conscious awareness, that even if it wasn't seen, it would still cause a painful collision. This reality is even understood on the level of the cells in your body.

The small you is constrained by its fixed awareness. It is bound by the collective consciousness, which believes that brick walls are hard things that can hurt you. The small you is not able to create a reality independent of this understanding. Most of humanity believes specific concentrations of energy comprise brick walls, even when they are not seen. The unconscious mind has far more sway in your life than you know, to the point that if you bumped into a brick wall you didn't see, it still would be recognized on an unconscious level as a hard object that hurts.

Everything exists as you perceive it, even on an unconscious level. You accept your reality and believe in it, and through your interconnectedness in the field of pure consciousness to everyone else, a self-referral, collective knowingness is created that you are bound by. This is why most of us agree that one composition of vibrating energy is a human being and another is a brick wall, and so on and so forth.

But one who is perpetually living in a higher state of consciousness, and experiencing their unbounded, large Self reality, is forever free from the confines of physical reality; therefore, they can pass right through the finite reality that we perceive as a solid object. They have access to the full potential of natural law to create their reality with greater specificity, which can be independent and distinctly different from the reality of one who is on a much lower level of consciousness.

All of creation exists in its most subtle form as pure consciousness. The deeper your understanding of this field, the less influence the cosmic flux of the physical realm will have on you. Once your consciousness perceives physical objects as simply virtual realities, and believes this beyond a shadow of a doubt, that will be your experience. The physical guise of the world is of your own making, just as is your inability to walk through brick walls.

We have all unconsciously agreed what nearly every category of vibrating energy will look like when observed. These agreements have allowed life as we see it to take on its form. The collective consciousness, or collective psyche, of humankind is so powerful that it actually dictates what most of us are able to perceive through our senses. It has been instilled in our collective memory, *smriti*, over the ages, which has given rise to its particular vibration and structure, or *shruti*, as described in the Vedic literature.

Of course, there are exceptions to this reality. With knowledge comes the organizing power to create as your consciousness sees fit. Any number of alternative realities could just as easily be witnessed if there's agreement upon their content within the collective consciousness. The great seers, sages, and even some of you on occasion are able to peer through the facade of maya to witness a more expanded version of reality.

This becomes increasingly common as you grow in consciousness. By developing your awareness, your vision—both physical and subtle—will be enhanced to allow for perception beyond the physical realm to more refined realities currently out of sight, but nevertheless right in front of you. The magnificent beauty of the celestial realm is far beyond anything you will experience in the physical world. Many would initially be startled to see all the things currently invisible to them.

The most powerful and wondrous things are hidden from most people, and will remain that way until the collective consciousness agrees upon their existence. Science has proven that our physical eyes see only a small portion of the light spectrum, our ears hear a finite range of sound frequencies, our touch affords only limited sensation, our olfactory apparatus captures only a smattering of smells, and our tongue tastes but a limited range of flavors. You have much, much more still to experience.

A longtime meditator friend told me that someone in the audience at one of Maharishi's lectures once asked him who were the other yogis sitting on the stage with him. Maharishi asked those in the audience to raise their hand if they could see others on the stage. Only a few hands went up. Maharishi said, "When more people can see the others on stage, I will introduce them."

If you were able to view with more subtle eyes, you would see that your departed loved ones are actually right here in your presence now. As it is, they are just one slight shift in awareness out of sight. Heaven and hell are both here and now, as is every other possible reality in between these two extremes. All that ever has been, and all that ever will be, is concurrently right here.

Even now in a limited way you can influence your reality by putting your attention on that which you desire. But by developing your consciousness, you can develop an unlimited creative capacity. The degree of awareness you have of the Self determines everything about your reality—both the seen and unseen aspects of it. You can learn to create anew as you wish. Anything you desire in life can be slowly but surely brought into existence through an intention of your consciousness, in the same manner that you created your current reality.

For people who are not fully established in higher states of consciousness, their capabilities are only partially determined by themselves. They are as if slaves to the collective consciousness of humankind, because they are unable to act independently of it. In just the way that the collective consciousness determines what is and is not morally acceptable, it can also determine what is and is not physically visible. Most people believe in the current limitations of their vision, and so they are bound by it.

But if large numbers of people suddenly begin to believe that humans can see the spirits of their departed loved ones, perform miraculous feats of healing the sick with just the touch of a hand, or that we can levitate in the air above the ground, some of us would spontaneously begin to perform these feats. An agreement has to occur in the field of collective consciousness for these types of acts to be more commonly performed—when that occurs, miracles will happen. Anything is possible if it's believed without a doubt. Jesus said, "That whosoever shall say unto this mountain, Be thou removed, and be thou cast into the sea; and shall not doubt in his heart, but shall believe that those things which he saith shall come; he shall have whatever he saith."[3]

The possibilities of what you can ultimately achieve are infinite in nature. Your current reality is based upon your conditioning and the memories that have been passed down over the ages to form your worldview. But the potential of your untapped consciousness is unbounded. During the immortal existence of your soul, you will experience everything that you truly desire through your own creation. A glorious day will come when you can sit at the cosmic switchboard to effect change by manifesting all your desires here, there, and everywhere to your heart's content.

THE POWER OF ATTENTION

Maharishi has said, "What you put your attention on grows." Your awareness and attention are far more powerful even now than you know. You may have heard businesspeople say, "What gets measured gets done" or "What gets measured moves." This is because what you put your attention on is affected by you. You cannot build a large business unless a number of people all put their attention on it. Similarly, you cannot develop a new product unless you put your attention on it. This is how we use our awareness to create in life.

Learning to powerfully focus your attention on that which you want will begin to make the miraculous commonplace. You will develop the ability to send your attention out to anywhere on the immeasurable mindscape to fulfill your most expansive desires. This is what's in store for you. You should be immensely thankful for your life, because it affords you the opportunity to develop your consciousness to experience your unlimited potential. Consciously move towards a life of all possibilities.

Your consciousness is the most amazing thing, or maybe I should say that your consciousness is the most amazing non-thing, since it's invisible to most of us in its purest form. But over time you're going to learn to use it in ways that seem incomprehensible to you today.

You will be able to focus your conscious attention in such a way as to instantly create all that you want, bringing the idea of immediate gratification to a whole new level.

The idea of creating your own reality is not new. A verse from the *Bhagavad-Gita* is translated as, "Curving back on myself, I create again and again."[4] This is a concept that has existed since the beginning of human existence. By curving back within your own consciousness, you create your reality.

You ultimately want to create a reality that finds you happy and fulfilled, since that is the primary goal of life. It can be done, and it is easy when you take a broader perspective. It's not like you're trying to create a new planet or galaxy, at least not yet. You just want to experience lasting fulfillment in your life. Gaining lasting fulfillment is not a difficult task on the scale of infinite possibilities. You will have it. Just put your attention on it and you will have it sooner than you know.

Become an intentional creator by developing your consciousness, staying in the moment, and putting your attention on that which you desire. Learn to practice deep meditation to quickly develop your consciousness, so you can increase the range of your creativity in the quickest possible manner. Then, when you're not meditating, take a few minutes to ask for what you desire. By maintaining your desire and believing that you deserve it, you can manifest anything. You may not get the full expression of it right away, but if your desire doesn't waver, you will eventually attain it.

As a child, while lying in bed before drifting off to sleep, I would see many different shapes of the most vivid colors coming and going behind my closed eyes. They were of every form and hue and were three-dimensional in nature. I remember very clearly how I could manipulate them just by changing my mind about how I wanted them to appear.

They would instantly respond to my every whim as the colors would change from bright red to bright blue. I could also easily change the shapes from groupings of blocks into clusters of spheres, and any other combination, by simply having the intention. The shapes were sometimes strung together, and at other times were in clusters or arrays of different sizes. They were as if floating and tumbling in space.

There seemed to be great depth to these arrangements as they moved through my awareness. The color combinations were extremely bold—because that is what I liked as a child—and I could change them with a simple desire. I particularly enjoyed the vibrant blues and yellows, because they appeared to my mind's eye as so incredibly bright.

The shapes and colors appeared somewhat like a kaleidoscope, but much more dynamic than that, because they didn't necessarily originate from the edges of my vision. I think the closest description I can come up with is that they were like the screensavers we currently have on computers with all the various shapes morphing into one another, but with much more depth and brilliance. It was not as if they were appearing in a small space of some kind, because they seemed expansive to me. Sometimes I had the sensation of looking down on them, and other times I was peering up at them from below, or as if from right in front of them.

On other occasions, I would see colors that appeared more like some type of fractal comprised of multi-colored static, like the static you see on a TV screen when it's not tuned to a particular channel, except in bright rich colors. These visions came quite naturally and seemed perfectly normal to me.

They were simply the product of a child's ability to create and play within his own innocent awareness. They entertained me when I closed my eyes to go to sleep. I never remember trying to look much beyond these shapes moving and tumbling in my awareness to discover if there was anything more to be seen in the expanse behind them, but looking back I wish I had. There's no limit to the depth of vision available to us from the spiritual eye within.

With age and conditioning, these visions disappeared without me even noticing they were gone, replaced by the imaginings of the physical world seen through open eyes. But many years later, within a few weeks of learning to meditate, I began to see colors in the material world with the same vibrancy as I had in my inner visions as a child, particularly blues. The practice of meditation seemed to purify my sense perceptions, allowing me to perceive some blue colors in their higher vibrations as I had with eyes closed when I was younger. All of my faculties have continued to expand in this way over the years since becoming a meditator.

The experiences I have today leave me with growing excitement about what's possible within the expanse of our own awareness. Developing your awareness allows you to unfold the infinite possibilities available within yourself. The future for humankind is very bright, indeed. Don't let another day pass without participating in your own awakening by unlocking your full potential through the development of your consciousness.

In the same way that I was able to create and manipulate beautiful shapes and colors in my mind as a child, we are all able to create from within our awareness that which we desire in life. Just as you can set up computer software to allow for numerous downloads from the same file without renewing it, you have the ability to create again and again from within your own awareness without depleting the source of your creativity.

You do this all the time within your own consciousness, but with greater power and flexibility than any computer software program. Our minds don't read binary numbers to produce in a limited fashion as a computer does when it reads software. We use our own magnificent hardware—our brain—with its vast and intricate neural network to tap the software of the cosmos in an inexhaustible fashion. By reflecting back on your own awareness in this way, you create again and again.

Your attention is the most powerful thing that will ever be available to you. You can move and focus it wherever you wish. You can fold it back onto itself to conjure up brand new images and ideas; you can reflect on past memories to create through association in multiplicity; or you can do both at the same time. Your attention is at once infinitely dynamic and infinitely flexible. The product of your attention is what is unique about you.

Scientists say that we use only about 10 percent of our brain capacity. Just think of the possibilities when we are utilizing 100 percent. I should say that I think the notion that we are using 10 percent of our brain capacity to be an overstatement, because as we unlock our full potential we will not only be able to perform 10 times more than we are now, but many, many times more. By activating the full capacity of our brain to use every tendril of our nervous system to access the field of pure intelligence, I believe we will perform at an exponentially greater rate than we are now. The interaction of all the neurons in our brain will produce a synergy of a magnitude that will literally explode our creative capabilities.

Whatever you place your attention on becomes enlivened. Play with this ability. A fun experiment is to try to get someone who is at a distance to notice you by simply focusing your attention on them. I inadvertently learned that I could do this while attending sporting events in high school. Just look at the person who you want to contact and focus your attention on them. You don't want to strain—just easily focus your full awareness on having that person notice you. Often you will find that they unknowingly start to look your way, because they feel your attention upon them.

You can develop the power of your attention in this way. Use your attention to make specific changes in your life by focusing on that which you desire. For example, try putting your attention on changing your mood, bringing more money to yourself, finding a companion, or developing a new skill. Just gently put your attention on that which you desire for a few minutes each day and eventually it will manifest in your life. Be patient and enjoy yourself as you develop this ability. There are no limits to what you can do with it.

There is already a significant amount of research showing that we can affect our environment with only the power of our attention. The Princeton Engineering Anomalies Research Laboratory (PEAR) has proven this through hundreds of experiments. The PEAR research was conducted for decades under the aegis of Robert Jahn, Princeton University's Dean of the School of Engineering and Applied Science. A meta-analysis of these experiments has shown the results to defy chance by a trillion to one.[5] The research has progressed to the point where Jahn and his colleague, Brenda Dunne, have moved their ongoing research to a new organization of their own called the International Consciousness Research Laboratories.

There's tremendous potential available to us through our attention, including the ability to heal ourselves. In the same way that you used your attention to bring your body into existence, you can put your attention on making changes to it, for example, to heal an illness or to adjust your weight. By taking a few minutes each day to put your attention on these areas, eventually you will begin to see results. Always be humble and grateful for the blessings you receive, because it's literally the power of the Almighty working through you. Intentionally using it for ill will only backfire on you, which could take lifetimes to recover from.

As we collectively begin to comprehend our vast potential, these abilities will rapidly begin to unfold for humankind. There's no reason why we couldn't even make dramatic changes to our physiologies in a similar manner to those made by the cuttlefish, which has an amazing ability to instantly and accurately change its appearance to blend into its surroundings. The abilities of this fish come from the same field of pure consciousness that ours do, but it has mastered using it in a very specific way. Not that we would necessarily want to have the ability to instantly camouflage ourselves, but what about having the ability to instantly change our appearance in some way that's more pleasing to us?

You just need to put your attention on that which you desire and believe that you can have it, and it will begin to emerge in your life. Don't worry about how long it takes to master this ability. If you can remove all doubt from your thinking, it will come very quickly. Start small and learn to develop your skills. There is no hurry, so be patient and have fun with it.

WHAT EXACTLY IS CONSCIOUSNESS?

As already explained, consciousness is at the basis of all relative existence. Maharishi says that consciousness is "the source, course, and goal of all creation." It is the intelligence that underlies and encompasses everything, including what you can and cannot see. The enlightened seers say, "I am That, thou art That, all this is That, That alone is, and there is nothing else but That."[6]

Let us consider "That" for a moment to better facilitate our understanding of consciousness. Physics tells us that matter is comprised of vibrating energy. But the spiritual realm transcends objective science to fathom the subtlest of all forms of energy in the field of pure subjectivity. As you plumb the depths of physical creation, you find that underlying physical existence is a far more subtle, yet much more powerful, subjective field of existence, which is intelligently creating from within its own nature all of objective reality. The same subjective field of awareness that gives rise to your thoughts also gives rise to all of physical creation, including you.

Your brain is not the source of your thoughts, but rather it is the field of pure wakefulness at the basis of all forms and phenomena.

This field is not only what gives rise to your thoughts, but your brain and all other aspects of your human anatomy. The Vedas say, "Having created the creation, the Creator entered into it."[7] The Creator did this by manifesting physical existence within the Self, the field of pure Being, or pure consciousness.

Consciousness has three aspects in one unified whole. The whole of consciousness is the unbounded field of pure potentiality, but when it creates from within itself it becomes three: knower, known, and process of knowing—or observer, observed, and process of observation. Before time and space existed, there was only singularity, pure subjectivity, one undivided field of pure wakefulness. Pure subjectivity is all there was.

Then Oneness decided it wanted to create. It did this by perceiving an aspect of its own pure subjectivity as something other than itself, as an object. It perceived itself dividing an aspect of its own nature into something different, something separate—an object. This object didn't really become something else, but the knower perceived it as such. By creating an object in this way, necessarily an observer and a process of observation were produced as well, which gave rise to the threefold structure of the field of pure consciousness: observer, observed, and process of observation.

It was simply a change in perception from the Oneness of pure subjectivity to the three aspects of objective reality that gave rise to all of physical creation. From this simple change in perspective, all of creation came out of the field of pure consciousness. By curving back onto itself, pure subjectivity manifested the three aspects of knower, known, and process of knowing, the qualities of consciousness. All of objective reality is still nothing more than pure subjectivity, but it's perceived by most observers as separate and objective.

This process of one becoming three is the spontaneous symmetry breaking that physicists speak about when describing the Big Bang theory of the universe, where all of creation emerges from a single point. The 3-in-1 structure of pure consciousness gives rise to the ever expanding universe of space and time. It's the same process by which all of visible creation is manifested in the universe.

This is how pure consciousness creates from within itself all the diversity of relative existence. But the ultimate reality remains that it is all only pure consciousness, because nothing changes other than our perception of it. When creation comes out of itself, it is simply consciousness interacting within itself via the three aspects of knower, known, and process of knowing to create the ephemeral universe as we see it.

It's like the ocean giving rise to a wave that then looks out onto itself, but perceives something different and separate. This is the way objective creation comes into existence from the subjective field of pure consciousness. Objective reality is always comprised of the underlying subjective field, just as the wave on the ocean is comprised of nothing more than the ocean rising up from within itself.

At any point in creation the infinite potential of the entire field of pure consciousness is fully lively and always available. This is why your soul, as an aspect of the larger field of pure consciousness, always has the infinite potential of the entire field available to it. Like the unbounded field of pure consciousness, you too have the capacity for infinite creativity available within you. You are a creator by nature. It's what you were meant to do.

It's only a mistake of the intellect, the discriminating quality of nature, which causes us to believe we are separate from pure consciousness. The rishis called this mistake *pragyaparad*. When our intellect discriminates and sees three aspects within the one field, it makes a mistake, because the three are still part of the unified whole, which is the *samhita* value of consciousness. When the field of pure consciousness objectifies itself, pragyaparad occurs.

One way this objectification occurs is when our individual soul wills itself into existence to be born into what we perceive as a separate or individual human body. After we are born, in most cases, we then slowly begin to forget that we are a fully connected aspect of the field of pure consciousness. This forgetting of our true nature, and our acceptance of time-space reality, is where all of our problems and suffering begin.

When first born, you are gifted with the awareness that you are unified with all of creation. You see everything else as part of yourself. As a baby, you experience your mother as an undivided part of yourself. This can be witnessed in the way babies act and interact with their mother when they are first born; they believe themselves to still be one with most things.

After a short time, however, because of their conditioning and the stress caused by the mental and physical impurities they must now take in, babies begin to feel separate from the underlying field of pure consciousness. This allows the intellectually contrived experience of duality, or separateness, to set in. This is the process of pragyaparad, the mistake of the intellect, and it is how we forget our true nature.

When I was a child, I remember distinctly having sporadic transcending experiences of myself being unified with my surroundings. I would have very pronounced feelings of stillness in my awareness, sometimes even while engaged in playing with others, where I would stare at something in my environment and it would stretch out as if connected to me. I remember this happening on a number of occasions. The living room chair, wall, or rug would zoom in to right in front of my eyes. In retrospect, I can see that I was simply transcending in the midst of activity, which is common for children.

It felt quite normal and I was always completely aware of everything in my environment during these experiences. I could see right through whatever was expanding out to me, and make it stop in an instant if I wanted to. It was as if I would merge with other objects in the room even though they were at a distance from me. Again, I could stop the experience whenever I wanted to and often did fairly quickly, since many times I was in the midst of playing. These experiences were so natural that they didn't seem particularly miraculous to me at the time.

All of us have had these types of experiences as babies, and many of us have even had them as young children, because we were still in the habit of being unified with our surroundings. These are moments of innocent awareness before being fully conditioned to believe in our individuality. They are so natural that they are often forgotten later.

I'm sure I would have forgotten them too if I had not learned to transcend in later life during the practice of meditation, which refreshed my memory of these experiences. The practice of meditation is simply the systematization of the transcending process by which you dive to subtler and subtler levels of the mind to arrive at your unified source in pure consciousness. It's a very normal process that we are all either consciously or unconsciously familiar with, because it's a natural part of being human and participating in the thinking process.

CONNECTION TO THE SOURCE

It is important that we cultivate the consciousness of our children. They are so capable of easily maintaining broadened awareness, and avoiding the growing pains and angst that so many children have due to the onset of duality. Many children, even those who appear to have a very good upbringing, suffer in this way as their rational minds begin to develop. They start to over-intellectualize things as they grow, because they are being conditioned to discriminate between themselves and everything else in their environment.

If we can help to minimize the mistake of the intellect in our children through a good routine of meditation early in life, they can avoid many of the common difficulties associated with growing up. Children who meditate are much more capable of living a pure and simple life without getting caught up in all the complications that other children tend to deal with. Scientific research has shown that they become much more socially balanced in every way.[8] It's vital that we begin to include the experience of transcending early in their lives, so that they can very effortlessly maintain the full potential of their hearts and minds.

If we wait until they grow up to start this process, there's a lot of undoing needed to get back to the state of innocent awareness. As adults we need to remove more stress and impurities from our physiologies to gradually unlock our full potential, whereas young children are already capable of living this reality. It simply needs to be nurtured and maintained through a good routine. Research shows that children are so much happier[9] and more creative[10] when given the opportunity to continue experiencing the connection to their source through the practice of meditation.

There has also been research indicating that children who are encouraged to use their imagination are far better at understanding the world around them than those who are not. Children who regularly engage their imagination have a greater ability to grasp and comprehend things that occur out of sight or in other countries than those who don't.[11] Their awareness is expanded by using it. When children don't have their imagination nurtured in this way, they have far more difficulty comprehending with any clarity the world beyond their visible environment. By enhancing your children's awareness as they develop and grow, they will be more capable of using the full range of their mental capabilities.

Many children, even some of those labeled as "gifted," excel in only specific areas, as if powerful synapses are firing in just particular regions of their brains, while other parts of the brain are no more enlivened than anyone else's. A gifted person may even be a genius in one respect, but if they're not capable of spontaneously fulfilling their desires and finding happiness in all areas of their life, they are not gifted in the broadest sense of the word.

The worst case scenario of this type of extreme localized brain functionality can be witnessed in those who suffer from savant syndrome. Some savants can instantly multiply six-digit figures in their head, but may not be capable of caring for themselves without help from others. There also seems to be some question as to how aware they are of their unique talents and if they would opt to use them if not prompted by others. This makes some wonder if they truly enjoy their special talents.

In contrast, research has shown that the practice of meditation develops the brain globally in ways that enhance the entire personality and the full range of intelligence in the practitioner.[12] Regular practice of meditation creates children who are not only capable of enhanced intellectual capabilities,[13] but whose personalities are growing on all fronts such that they experience a greater sense of overall well-being and heightened levels of empathy. This is clearly seen through research indicating gains in the form of enhanced personal relationships, greater self-acceptance, and increased overall fulfillment in life.[14]

Adults have so much they can learn from children's example, particularly since most adults today have lost touch with the wholeness of life that many children still experience in their daily lives. The intellectual knowledge gained in adulthood is not all that's required to live a happy, successful life. There's also the importance of living a fully present life in harmony with the laws of nature.

You don't see young children worrying in advance over the final result of the sand castle they are building. Children tend to naturally stay in the moment and enjoy life without being so concerned about the results of their actions. They don't over-intellectualize things as adults do. That's why the younger participants in the Olympics often do so well, seemingly under great pressure. They don't experience pressure the way adults do with their overactive intellects. Children are much more capable of staying fully present and performing unencumbered without all the extra mental baggage that the rational mind creates in adulthood.

Wholeness and balance come naturally to children. The notion of simplicity makes perfect sense to them—not simplicity in the sense of limitations, but in the sense of going about enjoying their lives in a very simple, easy way. They haven't accumulated all the complex thought processes that adults have. Children are born with a unified perspective. They understand wholeness and unity on an intuitive level, and it can fully blossom in their awareness if not interrupted as they grow.

The natural state of joy and innocence that most children experience is very valuable to their development, and should not be interfered with by adults forcefully imposing their bounded view of reality on them. Let your children's awareness be free of duality for as long as possible—ideally forever. It's important that children be shown the difference between right and wrong by adults, of course, but the jaded worldview of adults who have closed themselves off from a unified perspective is detrimental to their children's growth. Begin to develop your own consciousness and allow your children to do the same, so they can experience harmony with nature unabated.

As parents, we are supposed to know how to best raise our children from a starting point of higher consciousness. Unfortunately, because of our own lack of spiritual development, many of us have become an impediment to our children's growth in the natural flow of life. Don't take this as advocacy that children intellectually know better than their parents about how to behave in the world. That would be a misunderstanding of my point.

Children need to learn from adults about the ways of the world and how to best perform their daily activities. "Well begun is half done": this is a truth that holds up in every circumstance, but I believe it is particularly applicable when it comes to children. Bringing them up correctly is important to their future success and happiness in life.

Children are not given to us just to become new workers for the family, as is commonly thought in some cultures. They come to learn and grow through our guidance—but they also bear important lessons for us. You are provided children to teach them how to get along in life, but also for you to learn more about yourself as you raise them. My wife and I have found that our own children allowed us to deal with a number of our own issues—issues we may not have had the opportunity to work through if it were not for them.

For example, my wife and I like to maintain an orderly environment at home. But our children, starting very early on, began to teach us that there's order even in the harmonious disorder that young children often create. We've learned from them that emotional balance in the home is more important than orderliness.

If you want your children to grow up in a harmonious environment, as parents you need to learn to maintain your balance even in the midst of disorder, and at times even chaos. Keeping the peace in a household supersedes all else, and striking a balance between your children's enjoyment and your need for order is essential when raising them. Our children taught us this.

They have also taught us the value of diplomatic communication. No one can better wake you up about the value of maintaining the feelings of others the way an adorable child can, because regardless of their transgressions, you never want to hurt them. Children don't have to be constantly chastised for their incorrect choices. It's far more effective to communicate in a manner that maintains their feelings. All parents know how hard this can be at times, but you and your family will come out of the process far better by using a gentler approach.

It's also vitally important to not only tell your children what they do wrong and where they need improvement, but what they do well and where they excel. This message is driven home by a child's tear-filled eyes and quivering chin when they only are reprimanded. For example, if your child has gone on one of their joyous rampages and destroyed something of value in your home, after you point out their wrong behavior, be sure to indicate how confident you are that they will get it right the next time, because of their intelligence and understanding of the difference between right and wrong.

A child should be told regularly that they are inherently good and given examples of how they express this quality in their daily lives. Providing positive feedback along with your reprimands helps to crystallize your lessons in your child's awareness, because this shows them that you're not only dwelling on their bad behavior, but on what's good about them as well. These are just a few of the things that my wife and I have learned from being parents.

Nothing a child does is so bad as to require inflicting excessive emotional or physical pain on them. If you tend to be strict with your children, try to balance that by also being very loving. It will go a long way towards allowing your children to grow up with a balanced perspective in life. Your spiritual development will help greatly in this regard. At times, my wife and I have even wondered if our children are causing havoc in our household just to teach us a lesson. Parents learn many things from the ongoing scenarios children initiate in their lives. You may not master these lessons immediately, but you will in time.

Don't be too hard on yourself over past treatment of your children. Remember they come into the world with their own issues to work through. Children are extremely resilient and bounce back very quickly even if you make some mistakes with them along the way, as all parents do.

If you overreact with your children, don't feel that you can't make up for it later. My wife and I have on occasion had to apologize to our children for what we thought were errors in our judgment in how we treated them. But I can tell you from experience that when you have to apologize to your children, no forgiveness will ever be as quick in coming, or as great as that which you receive from your loving children.

LEAP AHEAD IN YOUR GROWTH

All of our difficulties in life are lessened through deep meditation, because it enhances our capacity for spontaneous right action. By allowing the mind to transcend and experience its own deepest nature, you will become increasingly familiar with the unbounded field of pure consciousness, expanding your domain of influence. By regularly experiencing pure consciousness, you begin to act from a much deeper level of life, without all the confines your body-consciousness imposes on you, because your broadened awareness extends far beyond your physical existence.

As you learn to operate from this expanded level of pure consciousness, or absolute Being, you will become more aware of the infinite possibilities that are available to you. You begin to understand that you're not finite in nature, but unbounded in your ability to know and do all that you desire. This experience will enable you to grow in the quickest possible manner towards fulfillment, which is the ultimate purpose of life.

Meditation expands your consciousness and allows you to achieve greater success in life without all the struggle and strain. The transcending process is like dipping the white cloth in yellow dye. The first time you dip the cloth and remove it, the sun slowly dries it and fades the yellow away. But over time, through repeatedly dipping the cloth, it eventually becomes completely saturated with the yellow dye and will not fade, always maintaining its yellow color.[15]

In this same way, as your mind settles down during meditation to experience more subtle levels of existence in pure Being, it increasingly is able to maintain Being in the field of activity. Through repeated practice of deep meditation, the state of Being becomes stabilized in your awareness and is maintained even during activity. This allows your thoughts and actions to spontaneously become more in alliance with natural law, making them much more powerful and successful.

I practice Transcendental Meditation, which is the most researched method for self-development in the world, with more than 600 scientific studies verifying the wide-ranging benefits of this technique, conducted at 250 independent universities and medical schools in 30 countries over the past 40 years.[16] If you're going to learn to meditate, it's best that it be a time-tested technique that has the weight of both science and tradition as proof of its value.

Be willing to pay a trained teacher to learn how to practice real meditation, because the benefits you gain will be exponentially greater over your lifetime than the relatively small fee you will pay to learn. The materialistic age we live in doesn't allow most of us to feel comfortable learning such practices from a poor ascetic living on the street. A trained teacher of meditation must be paid in order to live the dignified life that you would expect from an exponent of such a valuable technique for personal development. In this day and age, you should expect nothing less.

If you don't currently have the money to learn a good meditation technique, I recommend putting your attention on gaining the resources to do so. Close your eyes, sit quietly, and try to imagine yourself having the money to learn to meditate and that you're just waiting for it to arrive. You can help to manifest it in this way. Try to do this for a few minutes twice a day. It will be good preparation for when the time comes to learn how to meditate twice a day, which will allow you to go deeply into the field of Being to fully develop your consciousness.

Also, have your attention on finding a good teacher. Go to an introductory lecture and learn about the technique you're interested in practicing. When the student is ready, the teacher will come.

I cannot emphasize enough the value of learning to transcend to develop greater happiness, success, and enlightenment in your life. As a young man, I had managed to get myself very tired and stressed by not getting enough rest and living out of harmony with the natural flow of life. Even though I was reading spiritual books, this was not enough to break through all the stress I accumulated from living less than ideally. I was gaining spiritual knowledge, but not really growing spiritually in the way I knew I should be.

My mind and body were beginning to lose the ability to perform at the level I knew they could. Even as a teenager, I felt as if I was becoming constrained. This was most obvious during my athletic activities. I just wasn't able to perform as naturally as I once did. I knew deep down that there must be a way to eliminate the obstacles to expressing my full potential. I distinctly remember thinking this even before I found a way to do it. I somehow knew that there must be a way to become more effective in both my thoughts and actions, which prompted me to keep my attention on discovering how.

Then one weekend I came across a television special on the Transcendental Meditation technique, or TM, as it is sometimes called. As I was watching the program, a light went on in my head as the scientific research of the benefits from its practice were described. I continued to watch intently as Maharishi then explained how deep meditation allows you to reduce stress to unlock your full potential. The program provided a perfect balance of scientific research with a spiritual touch in the way that only Maharishi could do.

The program also included a number of very famous celebrities and athletes who practice TM. I was surprised that I hadn't heard about it before. It seemed to be exactly what I was looking for. At the end of the program, it was announced that there would be a free introductory lecture at the Ramada Inn in Providence, Rhode Island, close to where I was studying at the time. I was absolutely certain beyond any doubt that this was something I was going to learn. I went to the lecture and sat in the middle of the first row, which is something I never do. I typically sit in a place where I can inconspicuously leave if I find midway through that a lecture doesn't live up to my expectations.

I even brought a tape recorder, just in case I missed anything. I listened intently as a couple of experienced teachers of TM explained the benefits to be gained from the practice. They were incredibly sincere and seemed to exude in their demeanor all the benefits they spoke about: reduced stress, clarity of mind, increased intelligence, improved health, and great contentment. They were the living embodiment of the benefits they described, which I found very convincing. The entire lecture was so compelling that I decided to learn to meditate straight away. It was the best choice I have ever made.

The practice of meditation is actually scientific in nature. The philosophy of science is the field of study that aims to define what science is. Experts in the field have determined that the orderly and systematic pursuit of knowledge is what makes a given discipline scientific. Scientific knowledge is attained through observation, documentation, analysis, and classification, so that the process can be repeated to determine whether the same result occurs each time it's replicated. Some feel scientific knowledge is just organized common sense.[17] Albert Einstein said, "The whole of science is nothing more than a refinement of everyday thinking."[18]

Meditation can very readily be examined via the scientific method, because it's practiced in the same manner every time and provides consistent results in line with scientifically validated knowledge. If you meditate correctly, you will receive the same benefits every time you practice. This has been proven many times through a very large body of research. Meditation has been scientifically verified to provide numerous benefits for both mind and body, because it's performed in a systematic manner and its benefits are easily replicated. Tens of millions of dollars have been granted for the study of meditation by the National Institutes of Health alone.[19]

Meditation not only easily meets the criteria for scientific inquiry, but because your awareness expands from the practice, your knowledge naturally grows in all areas of life as well, so it really is a science unto itself. As you practice meditation, you develop a greater capacity for comprehension, which increases your knowledge in a very consistent manner from one level of consciousness to the next. In many respects a meditator can be considered the greatest of all scientists, because their research is in consciousness, the most fundamental field of nature from where all other scientific knowledge and disciplines are derived.

After learning to meditate my life began to rapidly improve. I began to feel much less stressed and found far greater happiness in my life. My state of mind changed dramatically in just a couple of weeks. Those around me began to ask why I was so jovial all the time. I didn't know that I was, but after I thought about it for a moment, I realized that they were right. I had been walking around humming and singing ever since I learned to meditate. I also immediately became much more aware of the value of eating right and getting proper sleep. This understanding just spontaneously came to me after meditating for just a short time.

The changes I was experiencing all came from within—I didn't try to make any adjustments to my life. They just came. It was as if I somehow tapped into a deeper understanding about how to enjoy life. A reservoir of all good things began to open up inside of me. I was amazed by these changes; they felt very natural to me, because they were somehow exactly what I intuitively knew was possible. It was as if I was looking for a real meditation technique long before I even knew the benefits it would provide. For the first time in my life, I felt that I was quickly progressing physically, mentally, and spiritually in exactly the way I had been longing for.

I also found that what I desired in life began to come to me much more easily. All the non-productive relationships in my life began to fall away and rich new ones began to develop with the kind of people I wanted to be like. I was feeling golden and it seemed to show to everyone around me. I have been meditating for more than half my life now and I cannot say enough about what it has afforded me.

Everyone has their own unique experiences when they learn to meditate. I think I was particularly stressed when I started, since I was burning the candle at both ends by living too fast and not getting enough sleep. The benefits were very pronounced for me from the beginning. For those who are not as stressed as I was, the results may seem more subtle initially, but will nevertheless involve improvements to the whole range of your life, including greater mental and physical health.

Even if the benefits are not immediately apparent to you, they are still always occurring as you continue your practice. The great masters have all emphasized the fundamental importance of meditation. They knew the value of its practice and understood that to gain full enlightenment you need to repeatedly immerse yourself in the transcendent.

If you learn to meditate, you will find that even your sleep improves and becomes much deeper and more restful.[20] Over time, and through sustained practice, you will also increasingly gain the support of nature, which you will experience through the spontaneous right action that you begin to express in your life. You won't have to think so much about having correct behavior; it will just naturally come.

LEVELS OF KNOWINGNESS

To know anything requires there to be a knower, known, and process of knowing, the three components of consciousness. Knowledge is actually structured in consciousness.[21] Only when there is a knower, known, and process of knowing can knowledge exist. As soon as you have all three aspects together, knowingness becomes a reality. Knowledge and consciousness are one and the same, because to be conscious of something is to know it. This insight is so valuable, because it allows you to better understand that by developing your consciousness, you can have greater access to all knowledge.

The experience of higher states of consciousness comes primarily from your practice of meditation, while the intellectual knowledge needed to facilitate your understanding of these states comes from your teacher and the ancient wisdom of the Veda. This combination is needed to stabilize higher states of consciousness in your awareness as you grow to enlightenment. The descriptions of the seven states of consciousness below[22] are helpful to monitor your growth:

1. Sleeping Consciousness—no awareness of the self.
2. Dreaming Consciousness—dull or opaque awareness of the self.

3. Waking Consciousness—excited surface level awareness of the self.

4. Transcendental Consciousness—least excited state of the mind during meditation, expanded awareness of the Self.

5. Cosmic Consciousness—expanded awareness of the Self even during waking, dreaming, and sleeping, but still some perceived separation with other objects.

6. God Consciousness—still greater awareness of the Self, and the experience that the finest celestial level of other objects is part of you.

7. Unity Consciousness—unified experience of the Self, and recognition that all you see is part of you.

These descriptions of the different levels of knowingness are a guide to use as you grow toward enlightenment.

Having a good teacher is very helpful to your spiritual evolution. I know that some of you would prefer to go about your spiritual development completely on your own, but you know very well that the help of a more experienced person has always been the best way to learn new things, whether it is through the help of your parents or teachers. We learn best when guided by someone more knowledgeable than we are. The same holds true for our spiritual growth.

Knowledge changes in different states of consciousness, so one with a higher level of development can guide you in the most effective manner possible to attain enlightenment. Don't doubt the value of the student-teacher relationship. A teacher enhances your growth and can provide a *sadhana*, a spiritual program that is most suited for your personal development.

To achieve complete enlightenment, it's necessary to have a teacher who is intimately familiar with the Divine. The teacher needs to have experienced the Truth in order to impart it to others. It does not matter if you're not physically near such a teacher, or if he or she has already departed from the body. You only need be guided by the wisdom of such a realized soul to learn to commune with God.[23]

Lord Krishna said that people of wisdom who have experienced Reality will teach you their knowledge.[24] But it is important that your teacher not just expound on knowledge from their own level of consciousness. A teacher needs to speak to *your* level for you to progress spiritually. Maharishi describes the proper method to bring a student to enlightenment in this way:

> *If a man on a mountain peak, wishing to guide another who is only half-way up, keeps shouting directions about where he himself is standing, it will not help the other man to arrive at the top. The direct way of guiding him up is first to tell him where he is and describe his surroundings, thus making him aware of his own position, and then to guide him to the peak.*[25]

Do not underestimate the value of utilizing the knowledge of the great masters to find your way home. It will increase the speed of your growth towards enlightenment exponentially.

PURE KNOWLEDGE IS YOUR ESSENCE

When we forget our connection to God, we begin to lose our creative power. We lose our ability to fulfill our desires and to enjoy life. This is why we suffer so. To eliminate our suffering and bring more happiness to our lives is only a matter of bringing our awareness back to wholeness, back to Oneness with God. The state of complete happiness is ever present within you and awaits you to take full advantage of it. The best part is that it's so easy. You were born to do this, and your human physiology is perfectly suited to assist you as you do.

The human body is the only physiology on earth that is equipped to allow you to fully experience pure consciousness. Plants, insects, and animals don't have this ability, because they are much denser life forms than human beings. You are blessed to have a human body, so you can find your way back from separateness to once again experience your connection with God. The human physiology contains pure knowledge within its structure.

The ancient Vedic wisdom was written down when the possibility of it being lost arose. The Vedic tradition is actually an oral one where knowledge was passed down through word of mouth from one generation to another since the beginning of human life on our planet. Because of the passage of time, however, knowledge naturally fades. It was for this reason that the knowledge of the Veda was written down. There are many, many volumes to the Vedic literature, which are the oldest unabridged texts in existence.

The *I Ching* is old, some portions dating to 1000 BC or earlier. *The Egyptian Book of the Dead* dates to 3000 BC, but no tradition or interpretation of it is available today. The Vedic literature has more original texts than what we have available from all the world's other traditions combined. Some believe the Vedas to be at least 3500 years old, while others feel them to be still older.[26]

But the age of the volumes of the Veda does not matter, because again, they were only written down to stem the loss of knowledge. What's important is that this ancient Vedic wisdom comes from the unmanifest Veda, which is the source of pure knowledge. Pure knowledge is eternal, and the Veda, therefore, is the immortal wisdom of life. It is ageless. Originally it was gained through direct cognition by the great seers, or rishis, in their own awareness. Through deep meditation they were able to directly access this wisdom and orally share it with humankind.

This knowledge of the Veda is not created by humans. It is uncreated, *apaurusheya*, because it is *nitya*, eternal wisdom. Even the language of the Vedas, Sanskrit, was not created by humans. The ancient rishis were able to cognize or see these letters in their own awareness.

Each letter of the Sanskrit alphabet sounds as nature has given rise to it, and its shape correlates exactly to this sound. This provides the Sanskrit alphabet complete correlation between each letter's name and form. You don't have to be a Hindu to accept or believe in the value of the Vedic wisdom, for this knowledge predates religion and is available to everyone within their own consciousness. I feel myself to be a Christian, but believe the Vedic wisdom to be the foundational knowledge from which all religions arose. You cannot have a spiritual experience without enlivening your consciousness; as soon as you open yourself up to the field of pure consciousness, you enter the realm of the Veda.

I believe Jesus Christ was an enlightened being who practiced this Vedic wisdom. The years in his life from age 12 to 30 are no longer accounted for in the Bible. In the Book of Luke it becomes apparent that there's a void where nothing is known of the life of Jesus.[27] More than 100 years ago while visiting a Buddhist monastery in Ladak, India, Nicolas Notovitch was told about ancient records of the extensive travels of Jesus in India and Tibet. Those in the monastery who spoke of these documents were fully aware that they contained the story of Jesus Christ. Upon further inquiry, Notovitch was directed to an extensive volume on the legend of Jesus called *The Life of St. Issa*. He had the text translated for publication in a book titled *The Unknown Life of Christ* in 1894.[28]

One who was skeptical of Notovitch's findings was Swami Abhedananda. He was doubtful of Notovitch's account. But when he traveled to the monastery to prove him wrong, he located the same manuscript and was immediately convinced of its authenticity. He later published his account of the document in a book titled *Kashmir O Tibetti* in 1922.[29] To date six other authors have written books on the missing years of Jesus Christ in India.

Many feel that Jesus spent these unaccounted years in India perfecting himself through meditation and practice of the *sidhis*, which are advanced techniques that not only enhance one's spiritual development, but provide access to supernormal powers. The amazing feats of Jesus documented throughout the *New Testament* are what the yogis refer to as sidhis: instantly healing the sick, allowing the blind to see, walking on water, seeing the future, and much more. They involve the ability to control the laws of nature. Originally, they were not aspects of any particular religion, but can be used to uplift and enhance the religious experience.

In fact, many people who practice meditation and the sidhis, including many religious leaders, claim that they are better able to embrace their faith because of it. I have read a number of letters authored by leaders in all the major religions regarding their experiences of meditation. They all write about how meditation has enhanced their relationship with God.[30] Many, many people today, including those from all the major faiths of the world, practice meditation.

No particular belief system is required to gain the benefits of meditation. Vedic knowledge is for everyone. You don't have to worship East Indians to gain its benefits—but you might choose to if they are fully enlightened sages. We certainly owe the people of India a great debt of gratitude for being the last location on earth to maintain this highest of all knowledge. For that we should hold the nation of India dear in our hearts.

But the Vedic tradition in India faces challenges, as its people have increasingly taken on some of the less valuable qualities of Western culture, which has led many Indians to lose touch with this ancient wisdom. The rise of materialism has slowly begun to pull the people of India away from adherence to the Vedic way of life. Until recently, Vedic knowledge in its purity was nearly forgotten. But Maharishi and his predecessors came to revive this knowledge in its completeness, which has allowed for a small but growing segment of Indian society to once again live the Vedic lifestyle.

We need to ensure that this greatest of all spiritual knowledge is maintained. People from every nation should rally around efforts to ensure this knowledge continues to be taught throughout the world. Fortunately, the laws of nature are on our side in this respect, because according to the great masters, the Vedic wisdom can never be completely extinguished. It's said that nature will never allow for it to be entirely lost. But the lovers of wisdom must be vigilant in doing their part to maintain its purity for future generations. As long as there are people transcending and experiencing the Veda in their own awareness, this knowledge will continue on for many generations to come.

Maharishi recognized the significance of this knowledge to humankind. A great seer, he cognized in his own awareness the essence of the Vedas. He knew firsthand that the Vedic literature was not just words on a page, but the actual representation of the sequential unfoldment of the human physiology from the field of pure consciousness. He knew that the key to finding our way back to God was through the enlivenment of this intelligence in our own consciousness. This is why Maharishi asked the distinguished Professor Tony Nader, MD, PhD, trained at MIT and Harvard, to investigate under his guidance the connection of the different aspects of the Vedas to the human physiology.

Dr. Nader's research has uncovered in amazing detail how the intelligence used to write and organize the Vedic literature—syllables, verses, chapters, and books—is the same intelligence which gives rise to the structure of the human physiology from the field of pure consciousness.[31] His research showed an exact correspondence between every aspect of human physiology and every part of the Vedic literature. A simple example of this connection includes the foundational text of the Vedas—the *Rk Veda*—which is comprised of 192 verses, whereas the human autonomic nervous system, which is the foundation of the human body, consists of 192 nerves.

A more elaborate example includes the *Vyakaran,* which Maharishi describes as the aspect of Vedic literature that represents the expanding quality of self-referral consciousness. Dr. Nader found this expanding quality in our physiology's hypothalamus, which represents the expansion needed for the endocrine and autonomic response. *Ashtadhyayi,* the principal text of *Vyakaran,* is comprised of 8 *Adhyayas* (or chapters) of 4 *Padas* (metrical units) each, totaling 32 *Padas.*

Similarly, the hypothalamus is comprised of 8 regions—anterior, posterior, middle, and lateral, on both sides—with 4 nuclei for each region, making 32 nuclei total, corresponding to the 32 Padas of the *Ashtadhyayi.* Dr. Nader was able to make this same connection between all 40 branches of the Vedic literature and the entire human physiology, just as Maharishi had predicted. From these findings Maharishi was able to declare to the world precisely how the human physiology is the embodiment of the Veda.

This is why by meditating and then reciting the Vedic literature you can enliven the Veda, pure knowledge, in your own awareness. The experience of pure Being through meditation, complemented by the reading of the Vedic literature, is the way of the yogis to attain complete enlightenment. This discovery of the Veda in our physiology is of paramount importance for humankind, because it shows that the direct path to the full development of life is through the enlivenment of our own pure consciousness, and that our human body is the vehicle by which to do it. So put your attention on this great wisdom for enlightenment, and enlightenment will be yours.

Four

WALKING THE PATHLESS PATH

The pathless path is one that allows you to experience the field of supreme happiness within your own awareness. It's a pathless path because there is really no place you need go to have the silence within. But even after finding your way back to your source in pure consciousness, the physical "you" must still participate in the relative field of existence to perform your daily activities.

To succeed in these activities you need to understand how best to walk the pathless path in the physical world that you perceive yourself to be a part of. The most important thing is to go about your daily activities in a manner that allows you to fully enjoy every moment of every day. The outward stroke of life (activity) is just as necessary for your spiritual evolution as the inward stroke (meditation), and the ideal coordination of the two will hasten your growth to enlightenment.

MOVING TO HAPPINESS

All that you need to be happy is always available to you. To better experience this reality, try to participate in activities that come naturally and bring you the greatest joy. This is the way to walk the pathless path. This is how to use your daily activities to cultivate greater fulfillment in your life. By committing yourself to focus your attention only on happy things, a shift in your awareness will occur to help transform nearly everything you do into something that's fun and easy.

When you stay in the moment your activities no longer seem as hard, because all the negative thoughts about them are no longer entertained. It's the worrying that makes everything seem so difficult. If you break your activities down into their fundamental tasks without judging them, you will find that it is not the performance that makes them difficult. It's your thoughts that make the actions seem so hard, and this carries over into how you feel when you perform them.

As mentioned previously, a lot of what you feel to be boring or drudgery will spring to life in a way you never could have imagined before you began to live in the joyful moment. When you're worrying over the past or future, you give rise to all kinds of unnecessary thoughts that squeeze all the life out of your activities and make even the simplest things seem difficult. Just focus on the happy task at hand and you will find that most of your activities turn into joyful ones.

If the activities of your work are in line with your skills and come easily to you, but you still find yourself not looking forward to going to work each day, it's because you're saying things to yourself that make it seem unpleasant. For example, you could be saying things to yourself like, "I need to perform well at work," "I want my coworkers to like me," "I hope my boss isn't upset about me coming in late yesterday," "I can't get sick and miss any more work," "I need to get a raise soon," "I wish the project I worked on last month provided better results."

They all trouble your mind and are of no value in helping you do what you need to do right now in this moment. These thoughts about the past and future put unnecessary strain on you, and create the illusion that your work is not fun and easy. They become a heavy weight on your shoulders that makes your job seem daunting, even if it's exactly what you are good at. If you can free yourself from all the unnecessary worrying by training your mind to stay in the moment, then your day will progress much more easily.

Start consciously trying to keep your mind fully present, so you can experience the joy that's always available to you. Life will take care of itself if you remain fully present and let the thoughts of your imagined difficulties go. Have a little faith and experiment with keeping your mind steady and present so you can experience for yourself how liberating the here and now can be.

When you begin to focus your attention more and more on only what you need to do now, you will naturally start to become happier and more fulfilled. Don't allow your mind to worry that your work is not of value, and that you should be doing something else. You can't miss out on anything that's truly important to you. This will eliminate your worry by allowing the imagined baggage you attach to the performance of your daily activities to dissipate.

As you learn to focus your attention in this way you may also notice that there are a few things that you don't really enjoy doing. They may have become more tolerable, but they still are things you don't really like doing very much. This is quite natural and an indication of what you need to change in your life. For example, some people are involved in occupations that will never bring them lasting satisfaction.

People get involved in the wrong occupations for many reasons. Maybe they have friends who do the same work, or they once read that it was an excellent profession; maybe the initial appeal was that it paid well, or provided a certain degree of status. Or perhaps they just don't know what will make them happy.

By staying in the moment, you will be able to see more clearly what is and is not right for you in career, relationships, hobbies, and everything else. If it doesn't make you genuinely happy, then you need to make the necessary changes to bring greater fulfillment to your life. Those things that don't truly fulfill you will naturally begin to fall away. Nature will assist you in this process if you follow your happiness.

You will gravitate towards that which brings greater enjoyment, and that which is more enjoyable will gravitate towards you. When you stay in the moment, fun objects and activities begin to come your way. Even mundane responsibilities like balancing your checkbook, washing the dishes, and cutting the grass can change from bothersome responsibilities to enjoyable activities—when you stop wrapping negative thoughts around them. Stop entertaining negative thoughts about what you think your activities are going to be like and you will begin to experience what they are really like. This is the way to lasting happiness.

TAKE LIFE AS IT COMES

Before I started to develop myself spiritually, I tried to keep everything important that I needed to do in my head. I remember being at college trying to keep my mind literally on top of everything at once, all my class work, all my personal responsibilities, and so on. It made it very difficult to ever relax. After I learned to meditate, I noticed myself naturally letting go of some of these things from my awareness, which initially made me feel a little uncomfortable, because I thought I might miss something by not having them in my awareness at all times.

But soon I realized that my mind was only letting go of what I didn't need to be thinking about. All the important things I needed to do just spontaneously came to mind when I needed to deal with them, and this made it so much easier to take care of everything without the added creation of stress for myself. Your consciousness keeps you apprised of what's needed in your life. You don't have to think about breathing or making your heart beat. These things just happen the way they're supposed to, because you know at a very subtle level of your awareness that they need to happen.

My overly responsible nature wanted to keep everything important in my mind at all times, causing everything to seem very trying and tiresome. Letting things go until I actually needed to tend to them made life seem as if on autopilot, because I no longer had to worry about everything in advance. I still needed to plan ahead sometimes, but I didn't need to worry about these things.

All my actions were increasingly beginning to be supported by nature, as if my life was organizing itself. When I needed to deal with the next task in my day, it would just come to me and get accomplished so much more effortlessly. The excessive worrying fell by the wayside, which allowed me to take on and handle so much more in my day.

I began to just know when I needed to switch to the next project without any real prompting on my part. I also became much faster and efficient at everything I did. This happens very naturally as you develop your consciousness. You begin to take care of your activities more efficiently with each passing day. Your life becomes so much more productive. But the growth is not in just one area. You grow in all areas simultaneously. Even if you're good at one activity, but not so good at another, both of these areas will improve as you develop your consciousness.

SKILLFUL ACTION

Your activities suffer when you're attached to an expected result. This attachment doesn't allow you to perform your actions in a natural way. Your intention should be to do your work well, but while on the job, work without thinking so much about what the outcome will be. Just try to enjoy performing your activities as best you can. Maharishi used to say, "See the work, do the work, stay out of the misery." Just try to enjoy the work without worrying about the rest.

A state of non-attachment will increasingly be developed by staying in the moment and doing what you love. Try not to focus too much on the results of your work, except for the necessary preparation sometimes needed to do your work correctly. This will only divide your mind and cause undue strain. Just be easy with yourself and enjoy focusing on your work without diverting your mind.[1] This is the way to perform activity in the most efficient way possible.

It's not helpful to split your attention by listening to music or watching television while you work. This reduces the power of your actions and doesn't allow you to do your best work. Your greatest success will come from your undivided mind. So many people create incoherence in their awareness by having too many things going on at once. This only leads to inefficiency. Practice maintaining coherence in your environment to see how well you perform when not distracted.

Meditation facilitates greater orderliness in your awareness. As your mind dives deeply into the field of Being, it becomes saturated with the silence of pure consciousness. This silent level of nature's functioning is much more efficient and powerful than the grosser levels of existence. When you come out of meditation, your thoughts and actions become more focused and effective, because they have the silent, stable, intelligence of nature behind them. The more you meditate the greater your focus becomes, providing more success in all areas of your life.

In the *Bhagavad-Gita*, Lord Krishna teaches Arjuna to transcend the relative field of existence to establish his mind in pure consciousness, and then to come out and perform action.[2] Arjuna is already very intelligent and pure of heart, so his consciousness is fertile ground for Krishna to teach him how to meditate and then act in the most effective manner possible. This is the way to perform skillfully in action.

By transcending and bringing his mind into union with natural law, Arjuna is able to act with the power of nature to most effectively vanquish the wicked. In this same way, your mind should be established in transcendental consciousness to be fully present and uninhibited by distractions to perform your daily actions with the greatest skill. This is the way to gain great success in life.

Some people can have brief moments of transcending by simply participating in activities they are good at. Professional athletes often speak about being in "the zone" during their best performances. Their mind is undivided and they are acutely aware of their surroundings; this allows them to perform at a very high level with the greatest of ease. Some even say they have expanded awareness during these peak performances. Tennis players knowing where every ball on the court is, including those being held by the ball boys, and football players knowing where every man on the field is, including those behind them, are examples of such experiences.

Yogi Berra, the Hall of Fame professional baseball player and manager, was credited with inventing many funny *Yogiisms*, as they are called. A few examples include, "A nickel ain't worth a dime anymore," "It's déjà vu all over again," and the famous, "It ain't over 'til it's over."[3] Although they seem a little silly on their face, they contain a degree of truth. But some of his others contain some real wisdom.

Yogi had profound insights about the skills an athlete requires. He believed that concentration was the ability to "not" think. He said, "You can't think and hit at the same time." This statement sounds odd initially, but it includes much wisdom about the reality of life. He knew that the best way to hit a baseball was by not letting the mind get overly active. This is death to the professional athlete. He also said, "I can't concentrate when I'm thinking," which is another funny way of describing the state of innocent awareness needed to perform action most effectively.

Professional athletes have practiced their whole lives to perform their sport flawlessly. From all the practice they've done, pro baseball players have instilled the muscle memory for hitting baseballs. They don't need to think about how to hit. They simply need to automatically act. Those athletes who master this state of innocent awareness consistently perform at their best.

Yogi was implying that a baseball player needs to check their intellect at the dugout door to stay in the moment and perform with the greatest skill. This is when peak performances occur. But even for the professional athlete, these peak performances come and go. To consistently maintain this state of restful alertness, one needs to transcend. Many professional athletes have been known to practice meditation to improve their game, including a number of champions.[4]

Maybe Yogi Berra was more than just a baseball player, as his nickname implies. He was given the name "Yogi" when a fellow ball-player said he resembled a spiritual yogi sitting cross legged on the ground while waiting on deck before going to bat. Perhaps he was a real yogi putting on the guise of a baseball player to pass on tidbits of wisdom to the rest of the players. If he was, he sure could hit a baseball better than any yogi I've ever heard of!

SEEING IS BELIEVING

Visualization is another helpful practice that has been proven to work for athletes, astronauts, and spiritualists alike, and is a valuable tool in any walk of life. Visualizing yourself performing your actions perfectly before you actually partake in them is very helpful. It's a powerful aid to imagine yourself going through all the stages of an ideal performance, be it playing sports, flying to the moon, or growing towards enlightenment, to help you achieve the greatest success.

Denis Waitley is one of the most well-known experts on human performance and achievement. He has trained both Olympic athletes and NASA astronauts to visualize the activities they perform in their minds as a training technique. He found, for example, that when he had Olympic athletes run through their events in their mind, the same muscles fired in the same order that they did during the actual event. He says if you visualize yourself doing well in your event, you will do well when it comes time to physically perform it.[5]

Visualization should be added to your repertoire of techniques to improve your life. Regardless of what your activities involve, you can always practice visualizing yourself doing these activities perfectly to gain greater success when you actually perform them. Take a few minutes each day to close your eyes and visualize yourself doing well in whatever you wish to improve in your life. No matter what it is, just visualize yourself going through the motions and achieving what you desire. It's an excellent tool to bring greater success and satisfaction into your life.

But this concept of seeing what you desire is not new. It's actually ancient. The Vedas say:

vritti sarupyam itaratra
What you see you become.[6]

GAIN WITHOUT STRAIN

You don't need to strain to succeed. In fact, once you gain greater mastery over life, you won't have to work so hard anymore, because your goals will be much easier to achieve than you ever thought possible. Our whole philosophy of what it takes to succeed needs to be reevaluated. Many people are stuck on the "no pain, no gain" adage. In other words, you have to work hard to achieve what you desire in life. I don't know about you, but this has never produced results for me, because I used to work harder than anyone in my environment and it never brought me the fulfillment I craved—even when I succeeded.

Fortunately, I was born with a lot of energy, or I would have burned myself out with all the hours I put into my work. What I realized from it all was that hard work is only needed when you're doing something that's not right for you, which will never bring you lasting fulfillment anyway. This does not mean that you won't sometimes have to work long hours even if you're doing what's in line with your nature. But you won't strain or get so tired when performing actions that are right for you. As you develop your consciousness, you will automatically begin to gravitate towards that which is easy and brings you the greatest satisfaction in life.

There is a great animated children's movie called *Tinker Bell: Enter the World of Fairies*.[7] (I enjoyed watching it with my children. Some children's movies are just as good as the best adult movies.) The *Tinker Bell* series is the most beautifully animated I've seen. The illustrations and colors are stunning, not to mention a few themes that are spiritually spot on.

The first movie in the series is about how Tinker Bell, from Peter Pan fame, got her start as a fairy. The movie plays out prior to her meeting Peter Pan, and depicts her as a young aspiring fairy struggling to perform activities she thinks she wants to do, but are not at all natural for her.

By trying to do that which doesn't come easily to her, she makes a big mess out of things and gets everyone upset with her, not to mention making herself very frustrated and unhappy. But she soon discovers she has an amazing talent to "tinker" with things, to fix and create any mechanical object she wants to. As the story progresses, she slowly figures out that tinkering is her greatest calling and the activity which brings her the greatest fulfillment in life.

So many of us struggle to become something we are not, when that which we should be doing is right in front of us. Forget about the money, prestige, and imagined glory of the activities you have been applying yourself to. Go for what you love and the means to fulfill your greatest desires will be provided. The goal is to work less and accomplish more.

If you are stressing over your work, you're not going about it correctly. You should be enjoying your occupation. Never waste your life pursuing a career that doesn't bring you happiness, regardless of what you think the result may be. Just do what you love.

You will never completely excel at your work if you're not enjoying it. If you have practiced staying in the moment while participating in your work and still cannot find comfort, then you are in the wrong profession. When your occupation is right for you and you're staying fully present, you won't have to struggle to perform it well.

When you are in an occupation that resonates with your nature, it will come easily to you. If you have to excessively expend energy, then you won't have any motivation to do anything else. You should have enough time and energy in your day for work, leisure, and to develop yourself spiritually. What's the value of working hard all day if you can't find the time or energy to enjoy family, friends, and spirituality?

You are not here to keep your nose to the grindstone toiling away to achieve something that can't bring you happiness. You can have success, you can have happiness, and you can have fulfillment right here and now by doing that which you love. All you need to do to experience this reality is to be fully present in the eternal moment of now.

CLARIFY YOUR PURPOSE IN LIFE

Once you begin to clear the complexity away from your life to discover your real purpose, you will find that it has nothing to do with working hard. In fact, your real purpose in life is to have fun every minute of every day. You need to get this message. You need to understand and absorb this timeless truth. Your ultimate happiness comes from within, but performing those activities that are easy and fun will allow you to attain happiness much more easily. Work that is fun and that you're good at is a technique in itself to grow towards enlightenment.

The idea that you have to struggle to achieve success is wrong, and the idea that you are a failure if you don't have a career with status is wrong, too. It's not about having a large income or you're a failure. It's not about keeping your house clean or you're a failure. It's not about people treating you nicely or you're a failure. There are always going to be low-income people, dirty houses, and those that are unkind. True success is about being able to handle any of your experiences with balance, contentment, and happiness in your heart.

The purpose of life is not to excessively try to control your environment into something that you think will make you happy. Life is about being happy from within regardless of your circumstances. That's what real success is. You can get there most easily by performing those activities which are fun and easy for you to do. These are the activities that will bring you the greatest support of nature and are most in accord with your purpose in life. Once you reach full enlightenment, you will be able to maintain an exalted state of happiness regardless of what's going on in your life, because your bliss will supersede all other impressions upon your awareness.[8]

Behind the veil of our overly complex lives is something very simple—a single field of pure consciousness—which gives rise to all of visible creation. The most powerful activities for you to perform are the ones you don't find overly involved, but those that mirror the simplicity with which the field of pure consciousness effortlessly interacts with itself to create the entire universe. Your senses bring you out into the diversity of life and urge you to experience more and more of material creation, but this will never bring you lasting happiness. The simpler you make your life, the closer you are to God, and the happier you will be.

You can crack the facade of non-reality by allowing yourself to settle down, live in the moment, and follow your joy. The worries you create in your mind are the things that try men's souls, but they are not real. They are the false images you feel are needed to succeed in life, but unfortunately will never allow you to get there. Remember that doing what you enjoy is easy and doing what you don't like is hard, so begin now to do what's easy for you.

You need to shift your awareness away from complication and discomfort, because life is simpler and easier than this. Not that some people won't enjoy deep, profound subjects, but to them they won't seem complicated at all. Life should be fun and enjoyable in every moment. If life is not feeling this way, you need to let your worries go by consciously bringing yourself back into the moment, because not being fully present is what causes your difficulties.

It took a long time for me to learn this truth. It wasn't easy and I stumbled many times. But your experience doesn't have to be like mine. Stay in the moment, begin to meditate, follow your happiness, and the world will be your oyster. If you're tired and unhappy, you are swimming upstream. You need to have fun and go with *your* flow. Your flow will not be exactly like anyone else's, because whatever you enjoy doing is perfect for *you*.

Here is an exercise to gain some perspective. When you have some free time sit down and write your own obituary. That's right. Sit down and write your own obituary as if you are already deceased. Consider in detail how you want your family and friends to remember you. This will help to clarify what's really important to you.

Allow the emotions of having your life suddenly snatched away from you flow, and contemplate how that will affect you and your loved ones. Consider your life and ponder if it's representative of how you want to be remembered. Write about what you would most like to be remembered for when you're gone. You will find that the things you choose are far more fundamental than what your current actions seem to indicate.

This exercise will allow you to see that the most important things are simple things like love, friendship, generosity, forgiveness, and happiness. Some of these will almost surely show up on your list. Think deeply about your loved ones and how they would feel if you were suddenly gone. How would they react? Did you express to them all that you wanted to? Did you perform in life the way you wanted to be remembered? This exercise will help you put your life into perspective, and to align yourself with that which brings the most peace and contentment to your heart.

LESS REALLY IS MORE

After completing this exercise, I think you will agree that most people spend far too much time working and unhappy, and not enough time living and enjoying themselves. I have lived the life of a workaholic. I know that it's a never-ending cycle of trying to find greater and greater success, but it never comes in the form you want it to if you are struggling. I have experienced both success and failure, and before I woke up, I wasn't completely happy with either one of them. If you're honest with yourself, you will agree that our society has taken the idea of work to an extreme. There's very little time left for living anymore.

Do we really need more goods and services? Does anyone really feel we need a new flavor of soft drink? Does anyone really believe we need a new restaurant chain with a different motif? We have buried ourselves in their proliferation. Our nation was founded on the principle of the *pursuit of happiness*,[9] not the pursuit of more and more products, services, and the almighty buck. We have somehow lost our way.

No new "thing" is going to bring you the lasting fulfillment you crave. And, you will never find lasting happiness from working so long and hard that you ignore all other aspects of your life. You need to get this. You need time to experience silence and develop your consciousness. Our nation's history has always included hard work. This made the United States the most materially wealthy nation on earth, but it has long since started to be at a cost. Although the United States is at the top with regard to gross domestic product (GDP), it rates very low compared to other developed nations with regard to enjoyment of life.

A large study to determine the level of a nation's happiness gathered data from a Gallup world poll of 136,000 people in 132 countries. A review of the data shows that Americans rank 16th on a scale of overall well-being and only 26th with regard to positive feelings about our day-to-day lives. It's indicative of a nation that is materially wealthy but still cannot seem to enjoy itself. Why? Because its people are lacking in emotional contentment.[10] Although wealth can bring some degree of satisfaction, true happiness depends on deeper emotional needs being met.

Many people today are not in touch with their true nature and they have paid dearly for it with regard to the quality of their lives. The joy and happiness that our hard work and newfangled products and services promised to bring never arrived. There needs to be a change in how we live our lives to allow for a more dignified level of existence.

We have reached a saturation point of new products and services. It is now time for businesses to figure out how best to produce only new products that benefit society. Rather than just trying to discover what other products and services can be created to make more money, they need to begin focusing more on how to improve them. We don't so much need more products and services—we need better products and services.

Why create more and more things when we work so hard that we come home too late and tired to enjoy any of them? This is not living—this is dying. Our primary focus should be on developing products that make our lives easier, not more complex. It should include giving attention to products that create greater silence and calm in our lives, not more noise and agitation. This will help to provide an ideal atmosphere for our greater spiritual development. This can be our bright future, if only we will allow it to be.

We are not developing all of these technological advances just to keep us occupied; we have enough to do each day. As a society, we need to focus on developing and buying only technologies that make our lives better and easier. As we begin to unlock more of our untapped human potential, this is the direction we will go. We are going to accomplish far greater results with far less effort. This is the pure, silent, self-sufficient future we have to look forward to.

It's still a primitive civilization that requires its people to choose between their families, their spiritual development, and their work. In this day and age, employers should not be expecting such a slavish work ethic from their employees, particularly since it's a self-defeating proposition. It's obvious, the more you overwork your human resources, the less productive they become.

To reach the next level of human existence, where happiness abounds and quality and quantity of life are in balance, more time needs to be provided for our personal development. According to the International Labor Organization, U.S. workers spend more hours on the job per year than workers in any other industrialized country.[11] In 1960, only 20 percent of U.S. mothers were in the workforce. Today 70 percent of households have both parents working. In 2006, middle-income families put in an average of 11 more hours of work per week than they did in 1979.[12]

Businesses should not be making employees work harder; they should be having them work smarter. Research on meditation and other self-improvement techniques have shown tremendous results at developing higher performing people. By encouraging the use of these practices to unlock humankind's full potential, employees will be able to perform their activities better and more efficiently than ever before. It's critical at this juncture in human development that we allow people to systematically develop their consciousness. Greater time spent developing our human resources will allow us to take the next step towards becoming a truly advanced civilization.

ASK FOR GUIDANCE

If you find yourself overworked and feel you don't have enough time for your family or spiritual development, put your attention on securing a job that provides you this time. There are too many people who hang on year after year working too hard in a job they don't even like, because the fear of the unknown has too much sway over them. This is no way to live your life.

If you allow yourself to believe that you are unable to do anything more with your life, you never will. If you fear the unknown, then make it the known by doing a little research on other possibilities that are available to you. Be positive and visualize yourself doing what you love for a living, and take the necessary steps to educate yourself about how to do it. Gradually you will build the confidence to make a change to something that's more appealing.

If you are forced to make a career change, it's amazing how quickly you can do it. Perhaps you have had the experience of being forced to change your occupation without notice, either because the company you worked for went out of business, due to a layoff, or as the result of a natural disaster. These types of events happen for a number of reasons, one of which is so you can become aware of your true potential by breaking through the boundaries of your limited thinking.

Experiences like these can create difficulties in your life, but in many cases they are actually blessings in disguise, providing you lessons about how easily you can adjust. Sometimes you need to be put out on the street to be reminded of your real powers of manifestation. This is not the easiest way for you to learn a lesson, but sometimes it's the only way.

Don't waste your life in an unhappy situation if you can do something else that you find more pleasing. Living in the moment can be the catalyst that allows you to do so much more with your life. There is too much fun to be experienced to waste your life in an occupation that can't bring you fulfillment.

When you are in need, don't look to the external world for your answers—look within first. Close your eyes and ask God to help you find your way. Your spiritual eye resides in the middle of your forehead, just above the bridge of your nose. It's not an eye like your two outward-facing ones, but an eye to the Divine from which you can glean His wisdom from inside yourself. Through the practice of meditation you will increasingly learn to go within for your guidance and to see what's needed to grow and prosper in life.

Your spiritual eye provides the vision by which to know God. Jesus said, "The light of the body is the eye: therefore when thine eye is single, thy whole body also is full of light."[13] When in need, close your outer eyes and look with inner vision while asking God to show you the wisdom to attain that which you need. Don't strain, but try to look through your inner eye while at the same time opening your heart and allowing its energy to flow up and through your inner eye. Ask God to provide the insights to achieve that which you desire. In time, a light will begin to develop within to illuminate the Divine answers for your greatest progress in life.

Always ask God for help first before you do anything else. It will save you a lot of time and effort. Then go about your day. If you're not provided the answers you need immediately upon asking, know that they will come. God always answers your questions, and the answers can come in any form. God uses all means necessary to provide you the information you require, so be open and receptive.

The answers you need can come from a book or magazine; a television show or movie; or in a myriad of other ways. Know that the information you ask for has already been provided. You're just waiting to recognize it. Accept that you deserve Divine assistance and have faith that it will be provided each time you sincerely ask for it. God always provides answers: however, many of us have stressed our minds and bodies so much that we are no longer capable of perceiving them. Still, He keeps trying to reach us in ways that we can understand.

By asking for your answers within, you will experience nature organizing to bring you what you need. Initially God wants to know that you trust in Him. He wants to know that you feel deserving of His help. So ask sincerely and have faith that your answers will come.

Ask daily so you can begin to acclimate yourself to Him. Speak to Him like an old, wise friend. Don't be embarrassed. You may feel silly initially, but over time you will become comfortable speaking to Him both in your head and aloud. There are no more valuable conversations you can have than with God, so talk to Him regularly.

Eventually you will find that not only are you being heard, but that He's answering. He won't necessarily communicate in words, although that is possible too. But he will answer in such a way that you will know without a doubt that it is Him. Again, there's never a moment that God is not communicating with you. The more we pursue things that are not stressful and bring happiness to our lives, the more receptive to His wisdom we become.

When deciding which book to read next, choose the one that feels easiest and most pleasant to you in your heart. Do the same with the next movie you watch and the next radio station you listen to. The most comfortable choices are the ones that will bring you the information you need. God provides the insights you need in these ways and many more.

When you finish reading a book or watching a movie, ask yourself what message it included for you. His messages are always there. Know that when you're sad or in pain, it's only God trying to tell you to go in another direction or to take another perspective that will bring you greater happiness. By being more receptive to the messages coming your way, you will begin to develop your Divine intuition.

Do what's required to open yourself up to greater possibilities in life. Think or act in a different way. Break out of old, stale behavior patterns that no longer serve you, or think anew to become more receptive to what will lead you to greater happiness. You can climb out of any rut and overcome any obstacle by simply broadening your awareness. Be receptive to new ideas by maintaining a finger on the pulse of the Divine. Do this by always going for what feels natural and comfortable to you.

Read a different kind of book or listen to a new kind of music to open yourself up to greater possibilities. Don't allow your progress to be impeded by old ideas and emotions. If you feel caged in, break out by doing something totally different with your life. But always move towards that which is more uplifting.

Follow wherever your happiness takes you. Don't be bothered by what others think you should or should not do. Be your own person and know that fulfilling opportunities await you. Find your path of least resistance and great joy will flow into your life. Follow your *sat chit ananda*, eternal bliss consciousness, where it leads you. And transcend your troubles through deep meditation for your greatest growth.

Don't worry so much about what your family thinks of your choices. As long as you are happy and responsible, your family will know you're alright. They want you to be happy above all else, but they also want to know that you're acting responsibly. They want to find comfort in the fact that you are okay and enjoying yourself.

Deep down your family only wants the best for you, but only you know what that is. Once they see that you are truly happy, they will be comfortable with your decisions. So look within for your answers and then go about doing what brings you the greatest happiness in life. In this way, those things that are most in line with your nature will become clear to you.

You may find that you start participating in one activity that you think will bring you lasting happiness, only to find later that it's not the be all and end all that will allow for your ultimate fulfillment. Does this mean you wasted your time? Not at all. Every activity is important and builds for the next as you find your way. There are no mistakes in life, so enjoy everything that you do fully, even if that means you have to make a 180-degree turn sometimes. This is the way to a happy existence.

I know there are many people who want to stick to one thing and try to make it work no matter what comes. In most cases this is wrong thinking and will only cause undue struggle. Few people today will have only one occupation in life, one place to call home, or one companion. If you give something an honest go and it doesn't bring you lasting fulfillment, then you owe it to everyone involved to try something else.

I am not encouraging you to be overly capricious or escapist, or to jump from one thing to the next as soon as the going gets tough. You need to be responsible while walking the pathless path. But know that it doesn't matter how many adjustments you need to make in your life, or what anyone else thinks about you for doing so. You have to do what you must to find fulfillment. If that means making a lot of adjustments, then so be it.

Be conscientious and try to do everything well. It may take a number of different experiences to find what you were really meant to do. You may even be one of those who are meant to try new and different things unabated your entire life. It's okay if this is what brings you happiness. You may have a wanderer's spirit that needs many, many experiences to learn and grow from in this life. As long as it brings genuine contentment to your heart, then wander away.

But try to make all your departures good ones by attempting to create happy endings for everyone involved. You don't want to move through life in an irresponsible manner leaving a trail of bad feelings in your wake. Remember you need to be happy, but also responsible, because this combination will allow you to perpetuate your sense of well-being. The last thing you want to do is bring negative energy your way from your own bad behavior. This is a self-defeating approach that will only increase your pain and suffering in the long run.

Begin to enjoy your life now. Don't wait to get what you think will make you happy, because ultimately that which is needed to be happy is already here. Try to enjoy just being alive. If you think a change is needed to make yourself happy, then enjoy the change process as well. You need to enjoy the entire process, not just the end result. You want to feel happiness now, and you can have it now, so don't wait for anything new to happen to begin feeling better.

This approach to life will help create the awakening needed to allow you to start seeing the fun in everything you do. You just have to do now what brings you the most happiness, and all the rest will come. We all have an important role to play in life. That which you choose to do is just as important as what anyone else is doing, so train yourself to think in this manner.

Once you locate your perfect role in life, it will be deeply fulfilling to your soul, even if it includes sweeping up after others. Those who are meant to pick up the trash and sweep the streets can enjoy life just as much as anyone else if they allow themselves to. Don't ever let the thoughts of others take the joy out of what you love to do—just enjoy your life. Believe that everything in life revolves around your genuine fulfillment.

Once you own this mind-set, you just might find that you love exactly what you are doing now. You may just wake up in the moment to realize that you already have what you always wanted, but couldn't see it. If you're doing what you enjoy, you will know it when your mind is quiet and centered in the moment, because you will feel at peace with yourself.

You should make your important decisions during your silent moments when you're not contemplating the pros and cons of your choices, because this is when you will know best what is right for you. Pay attention to the innocent, unprompted thoughts that arise in your settled awareness regarding your choices. The subtle feelings associated with these thoughts, which arise before fully engaging the intellect, are your truth. More than your head, it's your heart that will show you the way.

When your mind is calm and not probing for answers, you are provided subtle impulses from nature that contain them. Be receptive to these feelings, because they give rise to the thoughts that come to your settled mind. If you have an important decision to make, know that the correct answer will come from your pure heart, not your over-active mind.

The thoughts and feelings that ever so gently arise in your aware-ness when you're not even thinking about your decision contain your answer. Your decisions should be tempered by your intellect, of course, but know that the truth is always present in your heart. Your answer may seem illogical initially, but the logic will be provided over time. As you look back, you will clearly see the logical sequence of your decisions.

If you're not doing what you love, you will know it by how you feel in the moment. If you find you are not consistently happy, then enjoy the process of finding something else that's a better fit for you. Again, don't be afraid to be different; there's no one right way for all people to live their lives.

Make the decision to stay or go based upon how you feel. Don't labor over your decision. So what if you make a mistake? Nothing is so important in life that you need to stress over it. If you make the right decision—good; if you make the wrong decision—good—because you learned a valuable lesson. Don't be rash in making your decisions, just make them and move on. You're an immortal soul who has eternity to get it right, so don't worry so much.

There's no excessively complex thinking required to find what's right for you. There is only doing what you enjoy, and that is it. If you need to change some things to more fully enjoy yourself, then put your attention on making the necessary adjustments.

You were filled with hope and anticipation when you chose this life, but you have lost much of that excitement. With a slight shift in your awareness, you can have that excitement again. You are reading these pages because you're ready for great progress. It's time now for ever-increasing happiness in your life.

ACCEPT DIVINE ASSISTANCE

Bring yourself into alliance with natural law to get the most out of life. Allow God to work on your behalf. Some of you think yourself an island. You feel that only from your own hard work and the sweat of your brow will you get what you desire. This is not an accurate description of the way life works, because real abundance comes by being in alignment with God's will. No matter how hard you work, if you are not doing so in harmony with nature, you will never find lasting fulfillment, regardless of how much stuff you acquire.

We have all had desires that, despite the effort we put forth, we could not attain. This happens when we desire what is not right for us, or when we desire that which is right for us, but not at the right time. By working with the laws of nature, you can effortlessly attain all that you need in life. In some cases that which you need will just miraculously appear, provided by a friend, loved one, or by some other means.

What we need is sometimes different from what we desire. All good people deserve to receive what they need in life. You can develop the ability to bring yourself what you need much more easily by asking for God's assistance. Ask regularly for what you need, and believe you will receive it. This process will allow you to fully attune yourself with the natural current of life to bring what is needed.

Don't just quickly ask God for what you need now and then never think of Him again. God wants to know that you are sincere when you approach Him, so be genuine and ask for what you need. You may have to prime the pump to receive His blessings, particularly if you've never spoken to Him before. Ask every day for what you need and see yourself receiving that which you desire. The belief that you can have it will assist you in attaining it.

For example, let's say that you need a better car, but don't feel you can afford to purchase one. Maybe your vehicle has problems and you're not sure how to keep it going so you can get to work and run the errands you need to each day. The way to ask for God's help is to say, "God, I desire to have a better car." Say this a few times silently. You can repeat it over and over in your mind as many times as you wish during your silent moments, but try to be conscious of what you're saying until it feels comfortable to you.

You can use any words you want to when asking, but I prefer to use the word "desire," because it has a positive connotation. After you ask, take a few more minutes to visualize exactly what this new vehicle is going to look like. Flesh out the details in your mind and really try to feel the joy of having it and driving it. You want to put yourself in the state of mind of already having it; you are just waiting for it to actually appear in your driveway.

Do whatever is needed to believe that it will come. Go to the car dealership to find the one you like and review its features. Sit in it or take it for a test drive. Do anything you need to make it seem that it's on the way. Now that you have actually seen the car and know what you want, you can visualize it that much easier. Go through the same process each day by seeing yourself driving it and having it in your driveway. Maintain a clear picture of how it looks and drives in your mind.

By following these steps, you will develop a relationship with God and learn to manifest what it is that you need in life. Try to be certain about what you desire before starting this process, but it is okay if you need to refine your desire a bit until you are certain about the details. You only need a few minutes each day to go through the asking and visualizing process. Ask for and visualize what you desire. Don't worry so much about how it's going to come to you. God will take care of the rest. Do not doubt that it will be provided.

Nature will immediately go to work on your behalf. If you don't already have the money available to buy another car, you may receive a large sum from somewhere that allows you to make the purchase, or a sale could occur that allows you to buy it with the money you already have. You could even win the car in a dealership raffle, or it could just be given to you as a gift. Just believe that it's coming and be open to all possibilities. If it's something you need, you can be confident that you deserve it. If you ask appropriately and don't doubt, God will provide.

Move in the direction that feels right to you in pursuing what it is that you need, because there may be some actions required on your part to bring your desire to fruition. Discuss with others how to purchase another car and encourage their insights, because they may know how you can do it. If you firmly believe your car is coming, then you will receive it.

I have learned that what I've needed in life, but didn't think I could afford, I actually always could. For example, there was a time many years ago when I needed a new car, because I was having problems with the one I had, but I didn't think I had the money to buy a new one. I didn't think it would be prudent to make a large purchase at the time.

But then something unexpected happened to my current vehicle. While driving it, a family member slid on a patch of ice and slightly bumped the front underside of the car on the curb. No one was hurt, but strangely the minor contact with the curb managed to push all the vital parts of the engine up in just such a way that my insurance company determined the car was totaled.

I received little insurance money for the damaged car and was forced to look for another one. This required me to speak to various car dealerships about the possibility of making a purchase. Through this process I learned how best to buy the type of car I needed. In just a couple of days of research, I realized that I could have afforded a new car all along. I just hadn't put my attention on all my options, so it never materialized for me. I wasn't whirling in all the possibilities about how to buy a car, so no real options appeared.

By convincing myself that I didn't have enough money to make the purchase, that became my reality. But God smiled on me by providing the circumstances to learn that I can always have what I need. By putting my attention on it, I was able to find a place that provided the discounts and the financing needed. That, along with budgeting my other expenses made the new car a reality. Any remaining worries I had about how I was going to make my car payments disappeared soon after the purchase when my income increased.

I needed a car and nature provided the knowledge and circumstances for me to have it, and then produced the increased income to allay any lingering concerns about how I would afford it. I learned a great deal from this experience, because I have since managed to manifest a number of other things in my life in just this same way. I have always been very responsible with money, but learned that if I was forced into purchasing something that I needed, the resources would always be made available to me. Sometimes our logical minds don't allow us to take even the first step towards having what we need. We cannot see how to do it, so we never even try.

My experience has been that each time I had to make a large purchase for something I need, I have never had any problem affording it. Nature either makes me realize how I can afford it with the money I have, or the money just comes through unforeseen means. Now I just ask for what I need and move in the direction of having it to make it a reality. It's that simple.

I learned that when you need something, you can create the reality of having it without being forced into the purchase. If you genuinely need something, God will provide the resources for you to have it if you do your part. In the beginning, it may feel that you're being a bit frivolous for even considering buying what you need, particularly if it appears you can't afford it. But you're not being irresponsible if you're only looking into the possibilities, and then find out that you can actually make the purchase.

Those who are overly serious and responsible about how they spend their money are likely to feel that the only resources available to them are their own. This is wrong thinking. God can assist in providing the resources you need if you ask properly and don't doubt that it will come. There's no harm in looking into your options, but know that it's more than that. You are actually putting the wheels in motion for nature to provide what you need each time you put your attention on having it. This is the power of your attention at work.

On the other hand, if you're just being compulsive about wanting another car, you may find that this process doesn't always work. You may not have the appropriate deserving level to manifest any whimsical desire that arises. When you don't get something you want, it is nature's way of telling you it's not right for you. If the visualization process is difficult and doesn't have a natural flow to it, you may be asking for something that you don't deserve.

You also may not be able to get what you want because you are about to discover that you don't need it. You may even find out that you didn't truly desire it, because your desire quickly changed to something more appealing. There are no mistakes in how life plays out. Over time, you will learn to determine what desires are right for you simply by the way you feel when you ask for them. But if you're a good person who is pure of heart, you can always get what you need.

So don't stress over buying what you need. It's only your attention on lack that makes it difficult for you to have it. If you need something, God wants you to have it. When you sincerely ask for what you need, it's already been given. You just need to claim it. You have to believe that you deserve it and move your energy and attention towards having it. That overly responsible approach to finances only limits your ability to manifest what you need.

The paradoxical part about this is that those who are extremely cautious with their money are often conscientious people who want to do everything right. But in their shortsightedness they diminish their ability to use the laws of nature to bring the abundance they deserve. Unfortunately, this is a common occurrence for people who don't believe in, or don't consciously attempt to have a relationship with God. Ask for what you need, and put it out there. Jesus said, "Ask, and it shall be given you; seek, and ye shall find; knock, and it shall be opened unto you."[14]

You may not be able to get what you want if you don't deserve it. But after you get acquainted with God and have some practice asking and receiving, try asking for some things you desire just because you want to enjoy them. Start small and build up over time to determine your deserving level. This is fun and will allow you to begin to create the life you desire. Be creative and have faith. At some point you must receive all that you wish for. Those desires have to eventually be satiated, so experiment by trying to manifest them in your life.

I used to be the type of person who felt the need to refuse large gifts, or I would feel guilty if I accepted them, because I felt I needed to earn such things on my own. But when a gift is genuinely offered, it's because you deserve it on some level. Freely accept any legitimate gift, because it would not have come to you unless you deserved it. Allow yourself to enjoy what life has to offer. I say "legitimate gift," because people give gifts for all kinds of reasons, including ones that are not always in your best interest. Sometimes people give gifts to benefit themselves, without very much thought about what you want or need.

Don't waste your opportunity for greater abundance by feeling that you alone through your own intelligence and hard work must earn what it is that you desire. Again, you may feel that it's illogical to wish for more than you can afford, but it's this wishing and dreaming that prepares the way for the fulfillment of your desires.

By believing you can only play by the rules of the material world, you're limiting what is available to you. Yes, you can get some of what you desire by working hard for it, but you can have so much more by harnessing the power of nature to unlock your good fortune. If you ask the universe for assistance, you can open the gates to your full bounty. Life can be frustrating when you limit yourself to having only those things that you can attain through your own efforts. You need to believe that what you desire can often come by simply putting your attention on having it. This will allow you to manifest the level of prosperity you deserve.

Maharishi's teacher was called Guru Dev. He was a magnificent incarnation of enlightenment. He was pursued by the spiritual community of India for years to become the *Shankaracharya* (spiritual leader) of the whole northern region of India, headquartered in the Himalayas at Jyotirmath. This important position had been vacant for 165 years for lack of a suitable replacement. Guru Dev hesitated to accept this very public responsibility, because he was a quiet man who loved living his life secluded in the forests and mountains. But, he eventually gave in to the desire of the people that he take on the Shankaracharya role and impart his spiritual wisdom to the masses.

When Guru Dev became Shankaracharya, he would not accept donations, which was highly unusual, particularly since at the time the buildings of the headquarters, including temples of worship, had to be completely renovated and reestablished. Many people were amazed by his ability to miraculously come up with hundreds of thousands of rupees to reconstruct the institution of the Shankaracharya, when he seemingly had no money.

On one occasion he caused a stir by managing to come up with 100,000 rupees in one evening to make the purchase of a building the next morning. When he was asked where the money came from, he said, "No human being was involved in this." However, upon further prodding he said, "When God gives, He gives all that is required: the whole thing, the real thing." Guru Dev was the first Shankaracharya to have the words "Infinitely Bestowed" added to his title by his followers.[15]

Learn to transcend to commune with God and raise your deservingness. Even if there's a desire that you're not yet worthy of, if you keep your attention on it without wavering, it eventually will be yours—if not in this lifetime, then in one still to come. Why not start today?

ENJOY IT WITHOUT POSSESSING IT

You don't necessarily need to own a thing to enjoy it. I have found that I sometimes can enjoy something that someone else has more than if it were my own. On various occasions in my life I have experienced this with other people's homes, cars, music, food, etc. I remember when I was in high school I would enjoy riding around in my friend's car listening to music more than I did in my own. How could I fully enjoy the music-ride combination when I was preoccupied with driving?

I have also had occasions where I would go out and purchase something appealing that someone else had, just to find that I didn't enjoy it as much when I owned it. When you own something, all kinds of attachments can occur that cause you to overlook its essence, which dilutes the innocent awareness that made it charming to you in the first place. Your mind no longer sees it or experiences it in the same way when you possess it yourself.

The great masters don't own anything, but still enjoy a truly comfortable life. They may have a large following with much money being spent to dispense knowledge to their followers, but they don't consider the money their own. Yet they are able to enjoy the best things in life through their devotees. Wealthy followers often invite them to spend time in their beautiful homes and to ride in their luxurious conveyances. They can enjoy luxuries if they choose to, but without the worries of ownership.

Try imagining the object of your attraction and feeling the joy it brings you, or go and look it over in person without invading anyone's privacy, but nevertheless enjoying every minute of it. By being fully present in the moment, you can gain fulfillment from many more things than you do now, but without the obsession and heart palpitations of possessing them or trying to own them yourself.

When you are sincere about wanting to spiritually develop yourself, nature will embrace you. God is patiently awaiting your acknowledgement that He exists. So begin to talk to Him as if He's right here with you now, because He surely is. Ask for what you need. Learn to believe in the unseen. Learn to become comfortable asking That which you cannot see for what your heart desires. Just make this adjustment in your awareness and you are on your way to attaining greater good fortune in life. This is the Divine way to walk the pathless path.

Five

BALANCE WITH THE COSMOS

As you learn to calibrate yourself to consistently stay in the moment, you still will have days that are more difficult than others. This is quite natural and normal. But just remember that these are the days you're getting your clearest lessons about what you should *not* be doing.

Try to understand your difficulties by first assessing them fully. Be introspective and try to discover what you are thinking or doing that may be causing your troubles. If you can't pinpoint anything in particular, just accept that in this life or another you put into motion that which has made things hard for you now.

PERSPECTIVE IS EVERYTHING

Try to understand that the emotional pain that comes with your difficulties is not real. Yes, you can feel it, and at times it can be excruciating. But your pain is an illusion that you are perpetuating inside of yourself by feeling that you are in some way missing something: objects, respect, happiness, love, etc. In reality, however, you are not lacking anything you need to be at peace, and you can choose this reality whenever you wish.

You could be in a fight, in the midst of losing your job, feeling ill, out of money, and you can still choose to be in a state of peace if you wish to be. You can choose respectively to:

- Realize that you don't need to defend yourself, because you are always perfect and complete.
- Delight in the fact that you get to look for a new, more fulfilling job.
- See that illness is an indication of an unhealthy lifestyle, which you are now more conscious of and can begin to change.
- Accept that losing your money is an opportunity to use your creative power to rebuild your finances anew, the way you wish to.

How you feel is a matter of perspective, as is all of life.

I know this adjustment may seem daunting or maybe even impossible initially. But you will arrive at this level of understanding at some point during your soul's existence, because this is the stuff real happiness is made of. It's inevitable that you one day realize the power you possess to create your own reality.

You also need to understand that there's no need to exact revenge on anyone else for your difficulties. You can free yourself from this burden, because the laws of nature will always make sure that justice is appropriately served. If you've been treated poorly by another, the intelligence in nature will necessarily provide the lessons that person needs to better understand their wrongdoing. No one is ever overlooked in this regard.

You just need to learn to take life in stride. Gently move yourself in the direction of this understanding, and know there are going to be days that seem harder than others as you acclimate yourself to feeling good all the time. That which makes you sad is an indication that you need to take another approach to find happiness.

In time, as you work on being more positive and accepting, you will learn to master the tough days and move through them with peace and contentment in your heart. There is always a balance in life. It's hard to see with the untrained eye, but when you feel you're being treated unfairly or unjustly, from a cosmic perspective you really are not. You always get exactly what you deserve—nothing more, nothing less.

KARMA IS ACTION

Isaac Newton's third law of motion inadvertently proved that the law of karma exists by demonstrating that every action has an equal and opposite reaction. In other words, any force exerted by an object upon another object has an opposite force exerted back upon the first object.[1] Unbeknownst to Newton, he verified the axiom that as you sow, so shall you reap. He did not set out to prove that karma exists, and may never have realized he did, but he did it all the same.

Karma simply means action. You can have good karma and bad karma in your life, good actions and bad actions. You have performed both good and bad actions in the past, which have given rise to your karma in this lifetime. This is a very complex cause and effect relationship, as you can imagine. Even the enlightened cannot fathom all the actions that have set into motion the spaghetti of karma that's unique to our lives.

But nothing happens by chance; you always get exactly what you have earned, but thankfully also what is needed for your growth. The lottery winners who defy all odds to take home the jackpot more than once are examples of this reality. They win against all odds because they deserve to win. Your difficult lessons in life will continue to be painful until you accept them for what they are—learning opportunities. You need your difficulties, because the pain they cause allows you to learn how to act more appropriately in the future. At some point you have to accept responsibility for everything you experience in life, because your past actions provide the impetus for your current experiences, both good and bad.

Somewhere during your soul's existence, you performed the actions that set into motion the vibrations that radiated outward and bounced off of other material objects—people, planets, stars, and the rest of creation—to come back to you as a happy or unhappy event.[2] You could even experience what seems like your body's untimely termination, but know that it will have resulted from your own actions in this lifetime or a previous one.

You don't have to understand exactly why your karma unfolds the way it does to gain value from it. But just as sure as a calf finds its mother in a crowded pasture, your karma will find you. You cannot escape it in the material field of existence without putting into motion actions to mitigate or eliminate its impact.

You planted the seeds for all your experiences. Taking responsibility for this will allow you to heal much more quickly from even the most traumatic events in your life. Many people spend their entire lives suffering due to their belief that they've been victimized by others, never accepting that they themselves had everything to do with their circumstances. Most people have never been taught any other reality than to blame the people who bring them their difficulties, so it should be no surprise that this is the most common response.

But this is a very one-sided way of looking at life, because you blame all your difficulties on your external environment. No responsibility is taken by you for your circumstances. This type of thinking only perpetuates your suffering and never allows you to fully heal from the difficulties you experience in life.

You need to be more inward by recognizing that your reality has been created entirely by you. If you don't begin to analyze your life honestly in this way with broadened awareness, you will never comprehend the reality of your circumstances. You need to know that by acting negatively, you bring negativity upon yourself. By acting positively, you bring positivity to yourself. There is a very real relationship between what you do and what you get in return.

Our culture of blame has caused many to avoid accepting responsibility for their life at any cost. But this only blocks your growth, which dooms you to make the same mistakes again and again. Acceptance opens an avenue for healing—without acceptance, it's so difficult to get over your pain.

God does not randomly choose to inflict pain upon you. The last thing He wants is for you to suffer. He created the laws of cause and effect for your growth. How you choose to act determines what your experience will be. It's your doing, not His, that causes your pain. Begin to take responsibility for your circumstances, so that you can move towards a healthier and more fulfilling way of life. This may be hard at first, particularly if you have been really hurt through what appears to be no fault of your own.

Accepting responsibility doesn't mean that those who brought you your difficult karma are innocent of bad behavior. If their actions were wrong, they will most certainly suffer repercussions from them. Many people intentionally hurt us, but exacting revenge or punishment on them is not your primary concern. Certainly you will protect yourself against physical attack, that is natural, but you shouldn't do so with vengeance in your heart.

The laws of nature mete out justice at the exact time and to the exact degree needed to maintain perfect balance in the cosmos. No one is ever allowed to transgress natural law without a cosmic response. The pain and suffering that we experience are lessons to teach us to always act righteously in order to increase our good karma, so begin to take responsibility for your life.

Ponder for a moment what taking responsibility will look like. But be easy with yourself. If it's too difficult for you to do this all at once, then begin by trying to take responsibility for some small portion of it, so you can begin to experience the healing power provided.

If you can begin to take responsibility for even some of your problems, regardless of who did what to you, a great release will be created, particularly if you have a number of difficulties currently playing out in your life. By accepting your circumstances and looking for the lessons in them, you will find that your life becomes much lighter.

It becomes much easier to let go of your pain, because you start to understand that it all comes from you. It is as if swinging a hammer wildly, you accidentally hit yourself on the head—but in this case the hammer is invisible. That's really all it is when another brings us difficult circumstances, because they are an aspect of the same field of pure consciousness as we are. It's really only us causing pain to ourselves.

There are some life experiences that are so traumatic that once they happen there is no undoing their painful consequences unless you accept responsibility for them. You can punish others for your loss, because punishment may be required, but it will not undo your pain. Only by accepting responsibility for what happens to you can you take control of your life and begin to heal. Don't allow your life to be destroyed by someone else's ignorant behavior. Accept responsibility, heal yourself, and move on.

The cycle of non-acceptance and avoidance can only go on for so long. You cannot continue to incessantly inflict undue pain and suffering upon yourself by refusing to take responsibility. It only stunts your growth and compounds your pain by pushing responsibility out onto others. This type of behavior will only continue until you build up so much pain that you're forced to take responsibility in order to feel some relief. Some experiences are so agonizing that not accepting responsibility for your immense pain and suffering will literally destroy you.

Each time you deny your participation in your difficult experiences, you create an unhealed place in your awareness. As these wounds continue to grow, you become more out of balance because your avoidance blocks the healing process from occurring. Eventually your pain and suffering grows to the point that you cannot live with it any longer. You either let it destroy you, or you pierce the shroud of your unreality to accept and allow the healing power of nature to rush in.

When your pain is acute, for example when a loved one's life has been taken by another, it can be very difficult to overcome the hurt and anger that follows. But if you allow yourself to believe in the Divine order of things and understand that everything happens for a reason, you can make it through these difficult circumstances more easily. The lessons may not always be clear to you, but know that everyone involved needed to experience this event in order to learn and grow. Take responsibility for your pain and anger, because if you don't learn to release it now, it will continue to haunt you for years to come.

In time you will find your footing again and move on from your loss. Also know that you will most certainly see your loved one again in the afterlife. Or, as was mentioned earlier, you may see your departed loved ones even while still residing here on earth. They can come to you in your sleep, or even while you are awake in broad daylight.

These experiences are real and should not be doubted. With a slight shift of your awareness, you can gain the subtle vision to view that which others cannot. Your deceased loved ones may not be with you in person, but they most definitely are in spirit. Speak to them freely; they will hear you.

Many young people in particular feel that one bad event in their short time on earth is going to wreck their lives forever. They have barely learned to live, and one painful event, like breaking up with a boyfriend or girlfriend, makes them feel like giving up on life altogether. In the worst cases, they become suicidal over such events—the Romeo and Juliet syndrome.

They may entertain such thoughts the first time they experience severe emotional pain. This is because they haven't been taught the reality of life, that they are eternal souls who will have many more opportunities in this lifetime and future ones to experience the love and friendship they desire. Such experiences should not be taken so seriously. Some young people have not been taught that their pain will pass and that they will have ample opportunities to feel love again in exactly the way they desire it.

Unfortunately, it has not been explained that their life is not a limited period of time, but a series of lifetimes throughout eternity to do and experience all that they could possibly wish for. For this reason, they can't comprehend that their present pain will be short lived. They have not been provided the opportunity to develop their consciousness to allow them to more easily put in perspective these transient episodes in their lives.

Some become so overwhelmed by their illusion of pain that it's hard for them to find even a moment's relief. The worst thing to do in these cases is to try to eliminate your pain by debasing yourself with alcohol or drugs. Nothing is worse for you than trying to escape your problems through the deadening effects of these toxins. They will only prolong your pain by not allowing you to maintain the expanded awareness necessary to understand and accept your circumstances.

If you're suffering from grief, guilt, sadness, or any other strong emotion, and don't yet have a solid spiritual foundation to help you find relief, then bolster yourself by trying to distract your mind with something good. Spending time with friends and loved ones will always help to ease your pain. Uplifting movies and books can also help to keep your mind occupied with thoughts of the better things in life until your anguish becomes more manageable.

When I was young and had recently moved far from home to attend college, I broke up with a longtime girlfriend. There was no one to help me through this difficult period. But I managed to find a benign distraction that made it easier for me. Some may find it silly, but the playoffs leading up to the World Series were on television, so I began to use these games to distract my attention.

I wasn't even particularly interested in sports at the time, but I just began to watch the games because I remembered how they would capture my attention when I was younger. Naturally my mind began to gravitate towards favoring one team over the other. As I began to cheer for one of the teams, I automatically became caught up in the details of the games and all the hoopla that surrounds the major league baseball pennant races.

I continued to watch the games day after day and began to lose myself in rooting for the teams I wanted to win. It allowed me to stop thinking about the pain I was experiencing. I watched these games for many days all by myself. Whenever possible, I was glued to the television set cheering on the teams I ultimately wanted to go to the World Series.

It helped me forget about my troubles and the suffering I otherwise would have had to endure, until I was better able to process the split with my girlfriend. It sometimes takes a distraction to get over intense pain until you can find better ways of overcoming your suffering. The key is that whatever distraction you choose, it should not be something bad for you, because that will only prolong your difficulties.

Divine wisdom begins to unfold in your life as you develop yourself spiritually. As Divinity grows in your awareness, you cannot help but more easily move through any experience you have, however painful. As you approach full enlightenment, no healing will even be required, because you will never be hurt. You will become impervious to being hurt, because enlightenment has established you in evenness of life.

The life of Jesus Christ was a great example of the power of enlightenment. Many people feel he suffered during his crucifixion, but he didn't. He was an invincible being whose eternal contentment was so deep that it could not be extinguished even during the violent dissolution of his body. On the cross he said, "My God, my God, why hast thou forsaken me?"[3] He was not saying this because he didn't want to die. He was saying this because he couldn't wait to die and then resurrect himself. He was simply wondering aloud before God about the reason for the delay in departing from his ephemeral body.

Jesus had the power to vanquish all his persecutors with a mere glance, but did not do so because he wanted to fulfill the prophecy of his resurrection. He wanted to teach both his persecutors and disciples that death is an illusion because the soul has eternal life. Rising again gave his tormentors pause regarding their sinful actions and bolstered his followers to stand up for the Truth even under the threat of imminent death. Fortunately, today such sacrifices generally don't have to be made to seek the Truth.

AFFIRM YOUR HAPPINESS

Once you have recovered from the pain you're experiencing, you can begin to do more spiritual work that will help you finish healing and establish a solid foundation for dealing with such experiences in the future. As you implement more subtle and spiritual methods for your personal development, you will find that you naturally have more resilience in overcoming your difficulties.

Even while still in the throes of your pain, you can start to use affirmations to uplift your mood. Affirmations are uplifting words or phrases that you repeat to yourself to change your thinking and become more positive. They are a further expansion on using the power of your attention, which is so important to gaining greater fulfillment in life. In the same way that you can affirm your desire for a new car, you can affirm that you become happier by using positive thoughts. You can do this by repeating these words silently in your head, speaking them aloud, or writing them down.[4]

You can practice affirmations whenever your mind is not occupied, but they are particularly helpful when you're alone, which is typically the time that you will most focus on what is bothering you. By focusing on your affirmations without dividing your mind, you can get the most out of them.

Affirmations don't have to be witty or well written. In fact, you don't have to write them down at all. Just say something to yourself like "I am happy" over and over again until it begins to penetrate your awareness. Or you can say, "I have a bright future ahead of me." Anything that comes to mind that fits how you want to feel is fine. I assure you that if you say, "I am happy" again and again and try to visualize yourself being happy, you will begin to feel some relief. You can say affirmations aloud, but I feel they're most effective when said to yourself in silence. They penetrate your awareness at a much subtler level this way.

Train your mind to regularly think positive thoughts and visualize what feeling better will be like for you. You should also make yourself smile. Yogananda, who was a great proponent of affirmations, also used to advocate smiling often. He said in order to be happier you should smile, even if you have to grab the sides of your mouth with your fingers to form a smile for a little while each day.[5] The idea of forcing a smile and trying to think positive thoughts may seem unusual initially, but this combination will actually help you feel better.

Repeat your affirmations during silent moments throughout the day as you wish, and smile whenever possible. Positive energy is what's required, and this energy will come most abundantly if you can imagine yourself feeling the way you would like to. If you can create an image and a feeling of yourself being happy, you can pull yourself out of any malignant mood, no matter how long you've been experiencing it.

It is important when practicing affirmations that you use affirmative language. Don't use phrases like "I am not sad," because it will only focus your attention on your sadness. Use positive language that actually describes how you want to feel. If you want to feel happy, say "I am happy," and say it in the present tense as if it has already occurred. This is how hypnosis works. The person being hypnotized to quit smoking, for example, feels so strongly that they have already done so that they actually find stopping quite easy, without all the hard work of quitting still ahead.

You can train yourself to have this power of suggestion on your own mind. Learn to speak to yourself about what you want in life, and eventually you will begin to believe it. Don't doubt that you have this power. Jesus said, "What things soever ye desire, when ye pray, believe that ye receive them, and ye shall have them."[6] You can do anything with your mind if you truly believe it can be done.

Broadcast out to the universe that you are already happy. Repeat your positive, uplifting thoughts over and over again in your mind until you believe them. If you want to feel strong and confident, say "I am strong and confident," and continue to repeat these words throughout the day whenever you're able to do so without dividing the mind. You are the creator of your life. What you think and feel creates to a large extent what you experience, so take control by thinking and feeling how you desire your life to be.

When you are able to turn your affirmative thoughts into feelings, you have started to take control of your life. We are accustomed to focusing on what we don't have, which only perpetuates that reality in our lives. You need to learn to talk more positively to yourself to create more positivity in your life.

Practicing meditation makes your thought force much stronger, which will add power to your affirmations to create the reality you desire. Once you are completely finished with your meditation, recite your affirmations for a few minutes to allow for their greater manifestation. Your mind is much more powerful at this time, because it has just tapped the deeper forces of nature during meditation.

THE STARS AS YOUR GUIDE

A good way to bring your life into greater alliance with the cosmos is to have an astrological reading done. I'm not kidding. Find a reputable astrologer to do a life reading to help guide you on your way. A good astrologer should be able to help you better understand both your strong and weak qualities, and tell you when they will most fully express themselves in your life.

I use Vedic astrology to review the patterns in my own life. Vedic astrology is the mother of all forms of astrology. It's commonly referred to as *Jyotish* (pronounced *jo-tish*), which literally means "light of God." With Jyotish you can shed God's light on your life to gain greater understanding of what you're experiencing on a day-to-day basis, and to help you determine your natural purpose in life.

The horoscopes that you read in the newspapers are not the kind of astrology I'm talking about. You may have noticed that these astrological tidbits are not advice to live by, since their insights rarely relate to your real-life experiences. Astrology is much more involved than just looking at the placement of the sun to determine how your life is going to progress each day.

The placements of all seven planets (*grahas*) and the nodes of the moon (*rahu* and *ketu*), the planetary period that is currently operating in your life (*dasha*), and the planetary transits (*gochara*) on the date you're predicting for all have to be taken into consideration when examining a horoscope. Where the sun resides on a given day does not provide enough information to make decisions about your life, which is why many people who have read the horoscopes in the newspaper have concluded that there's no validity to the practice of astrology. But a real astrological reading can be very helpful in determining the karma you were born with in this life, and how to use it for your greatest success.

You can ask a good astrologer any questions you wish, but it's always helpful to ask what periods are going to be the most beneficial for you, and which are going to be the most difficult, as well as what your strong qualities and weak qualities are. These are always good questions to ask an astrologer, because the answers you receive will help you lay out a plan for your life so you know when to expect your best and worst experiences. A good astrologer can even recommend remedies to aid with the bad periods and provide insights to enhance the good ones.

I have watched people get themselves into financial trouble by not asking for the timeline of good financial periods in their life. They may ask an astrologer if they will earn a good income, and the astrologer may say, "Yes, you will." But they rarely ask specifically when it will occur. Then they go out and begin to spend freely, because they were told they would make good money. They get themselves into financial trouble months or even years before they can expect their good earning period to arrive. Astrology is a discipline of the relative world and, therefore, timing is everything in its practice. Jyotish is excellent at predicting when you will have your ups and downs in life, so be sure to ask when they will occur.

There is so much to be seen in an astrological birth chart that you cannot expect an astrologer to automatically see all that you want to know without direction from you. It's not as if everything about you is completely obvious from just glancing at the chart. There are many subtleties involved in providing a good astrological reading. Astrology is a very deep science—it's as deep as life itself. An astrologer has to put attention specifically on what you are interested in knowing in order to provide the information you need. So, it's your job to focus their attention on the areas of life you want to know about.

You have the free will to pursue what you wish to in life, but much of what you receive is dependent upon what the planets indicate at the time of your birth. Those karmas that are the most strongly indicated are very, very difficult to change. But you won't want to change a fixed karma if it's something good. If it's something bad, the only way to change it is by devoting your entire life to fully developing your consciousness in an attempt to transcend its grip.

There are three levels of karma that we bring into life at birth: *Dridha* karmas, which in most cases are fixed and cannot be changed in this lifetime; *Dridha-Adridha* karmas that can be changed over time with a good spiritual routine and serious effort on our part; and finally, *Adridha* karmas that can be changed fairly easily without much difficulty, through the force of our will.[7]

Depending on your level of consciousness and the remedial measures used, you can change much of your karma. But only the fully enlightened have any hope of significantly affecting the more steadfast Dridha karmas in this lifetime. However, through a good spiritual routine and will power you can change the lesser Dridha-Adridha and Adridha karmas to greatly improve your circumstances in life.

Paramahansa Yogananda did not want to believe in astrology when he was young, because an astrologer mentioned some difficulties indicated in his birth chart. There were signs of problems with health, and possibly even with some of his relationships. But in later life his guru, Swami Sri Yukteswar, taught him the importance of astrology and how to use it to overcome his difficult karma.

Yogananda said that Sri Yukteswar explained that the greater the enlightenment of the man, the more his spiritual nature influences the cosmos and the less he himself is influenced by the forces of nature. Yogananda said that during his worst planetary periods he did have tremendous difficulties, but he was still able to succeed because of his spiritual development and the strength of his will.[8]

A great master like Yogananda is able to overcome difficult circumstances regardless of his astrological map, and to gain the necessary support of nature to succeed in life in a way that only the most enlightened are able to achieve. There certainly is hope of transcending the planetary influences in life where the snapshot of your karma at birth indicates problems, but you need to raise your deserving level through spiritual practices to do so.

I suspect, however, there are some karmas that even Yogananda could not overcome, including that of becoming a great yogi and spiritual teacher. I doubt he could have withstood the draw of spiritual life to have chosen to go in another direction, and why would he have wanted to? Some karmas, both good and bad, are so fundamental to your purpose and the lessons needed in life that they cannot be completely transcended in a single incarnation. But the good news is that you have many lives to improve yourself, so have an astrological reading completed and discover your natural proclivities and tendencies.

It will help you better understand the general experiences that are going to play out in your lifetime.

But I should provide a caveat: do not immediately buy into all that you hear from your first astrological reading, because a few of the astrologer's predictions may not be completely on target. Astrology as a science is being revived in our age, so you have to accept that your astrologer may not get everything exactly right the first time through. But if you consult a good astrologer, a lot of what they predict will be exactly in line with your life experiences.

It is also recommended that you not start making huge changes in your life just because you're told one thing or another about your life from an astrologer. Test the predictions against your life experiences. For example, ask yourself if you like the activities that they predict you have an inclination for.

An astrologer reviewing a birth chart cannot see all aspects of your life as if viewing it on a videotape. If it's predicted that you will make money in business, and you're not presently in business, then experiment to see if it brings you joy and happiness. If you begin to have some success at it, then you have some actual proof that the prediction is accurate.

Test their predictions in a responsible manner so as not to get yourself into a bind. If you're not comfortable with all that was said in your first astrological reading, then triangle up by having a total of three astrologers perform separate readings for you; keep the information that lines up and makes sense. Put the rest in the back of your mind until you can verify its validity through your life experiences. Even a reading that misses a few things is valuable, because you will gain a better understanding about yourself and how your life is going to unfold.

There are a few things you should do first to make sure you receive the very best astrology reading possible. Your reading will only be as accurate as the birth time, date, and location you provide the astrologer. Little differences in these details can sometimes make a big difference in what the horoscope foretells, so try to provide as accurate information as possible.

If you can't find birth records to indicate your exact birth time, but have a rough idea from your parents of when it occurred, you can consult an astrologer who practices birth time rectifications to determine the time. Based upon the dates of major events in your life, a rectification can be completed to fine-tune your birth time so that the planetary placements in your chart match the events from your past. You can even have a rectification completed to verify that the birth time on your birth certificate is correct.

It's very common for a birth time to inadvertently be recorded incorrectly by the nurse or doctor when you were born. It may not even be that person's error, since they may have been very conscientious about recording the time accurately as it appeared on the clock. But if the clock was not set correctly, your birth time will likely be off by a few minutes. This slight difference can have an effect on some readings.

Before I received my first astrology reading, I went through all the necessary steps to obtain my correct time of birth. I contacted the department of vital statistics in the state where I was born and paid the small fee to have a birth certificate that included the time of day I was born sent to me. However, the time seemed to be wrong. I remembered my mother saying that I was born in the PM, but my birth certificate indicated that I was born in the AM, although at the same hour she had said.

I then contacted the hospital where I was born to have the actual paperwork for the details of my birth sent to me. Most hospitals in the United States keep this information, or they contract with a data company to store it digitally for them elsewhere. I paid another small fee to have a print-out of the original paperwork sent to me by the company that maintained the hospital's records.

When the paperwork arrived, it had a very strange format where my birth time was typed in. Upon closer examination of the document, it was absolutely clear without a doubt that the time recorded at my birth was actually PM as my mother had indicated. The formatting of the document was so odd that the birth time was easily misread as AM if not examined closely, which is why my birth certificate was printed with this error.

After feeling confident I had the most accurate time I could attain from my birth records, I had two birth time rectifications completed by two independent astrologers. Based upon the dates and times of the major events from my past that I provided, they were both able to rectify my birth time to six minutes earlier than the hospital records indicated. Both astrologers rectified my birth time to the exact same minute. It's important to put a little effort in to get your correct birth time. It's quite easy to do and can make a difference in the accuracy of your astrological reading.

The practice of astrology has been around since the beginning of human life, but like all knowledge it comes and goes. Due to the recent interest in all areas of Vedic knowledge, Jyotish is rapidly being revived by many excellent Jyotishis from around the world. This upsurge in interest has helped to re-enliven some of its techniques, and hopefully will continue to inspire the wise to put their attention on a complete revival.

All knowledge about you is in your horoscope, but our capacity as humans to fully comprehend it is still being developed. As humankind's consciousness grows, the practice of Jyotish will increasingly develop in the astrologer what is called *jyotish mati pragya*, all-knowing consciousness, which the great sage Jyotishis of the past embodied. But even while some aspects of astrology are still being revived, the basics are completely intact today, so you can feel confident that you will gain valuable insights about your life from a good astrologer.

Astrology helps to provide direction in your life, particularly in the major areas of career, finances, health, and relationships. As I said, there are many fine astrologers today, including quite a number of westerners who have become excellent Vedic astrologers. An astrologer who has completed many readings of those born in your country will be the best to consult, since they are more informed about how different planetary configurations will play out for one born there, not to mention their greater facility with the native tongue.

Astrology is particularly valuable when you're struggling, because your struggles are an indication that you're doing something wrong. Either you're trying to do something you shouldn't be, or you need to change your perspective about life until your difficult period passes. For example, if you're hoping to earn a good living but are struggling financially, you may be told by the astrologer that you need to wait until a better period begins in order to earn more money.

You can use this advice to culture patience in your awareness while you deal as best you can with your financial difficulties. You have free will to participate in the activities you want to in life, but that does't mean you will be successful. Many people today pursue career paths that are not right for them, which of course causes them to be unhappy when they can't make it work. Having an astrological reading will steer you in the right direction by helping locate a career path that's more suited for you.

The first time I had a Vedic astrology reading, I was amazed that the Jyotishi could see so much from the planets. He first said a few things about my character that seemed to be accurate, and then looked at me and said you must have studied politics. I had just finished a degree in government, which he had no knowledge of. He also mentioned some worldly things that I definitely had interest in, but I ultimately decided not to pursue. So in some areas he was exactly on target and in others he was able to see my tendencies, but not whether I would actually pursue them in life.

What I ignored initially from the reading was his emphasis that I would continue to become more and more spiritual throughout life, because I was still fairly worldly and wanted to do something more mainstream with my life at the time. But all these years later, I can safely say that he was exactly right on this point. With the passage of time, I have become increasingly committed to spirituality to the point that I now plan my entire life around my spiritual practices.

After my initial astrology reading, I immediately began to study Jyotish myself to better understand my own birth chart. It has brought me great enjoyment over the years. The most appealing part of astrology is that you can never exhaust the knowledge available to you from this holy science, because it will take you as deeply as you want to go. You may even find that *you* have an affinity for learning to read the stars. Who knows, maybe you can even become a predictor of great incarnations like the three wise men, astrologer priests, who foresaw the coming of Jesus Christ.

UNDOING YOUR PAST

There are ways to reduce or avoid reaping some of the bad karma you have set into motion by raising your consciousness through right action and sustained practice of meditation. With right thinking, speaking, and acting you are able to gradually reduce your future karma, but by contacting your source through regular practice of meditation, you can dramatically reduce your negative karma.

If there are miracles in life, this is surely one of them. The idea that you can reduce the bad things you have set in motion from coming to you is one of the more fantastic aspects of the laws of nature. For some it's difficult to even accept the reality that bad karma exists. But once you believe that it's real, it's even more difficult to accept that you can mitigate or eliminate these difficult experiences before they arrive.

Many believe that life includes negative experiences and we just have to live with them. But the sooner you accept that you're not just a poor pawn in the hands of fate, the sooner you will move towards greater happiness. This gives you the ability to create better experiences in your life and to be happy whenever you wish. Even if you're not able to completely eliminate your more difficult karma, you can certainly change your perspective about it to experience happiness in the midst of your difficulties.

The nature of life is to grow. You progress from one lifetime to the next whether you intend to or not, but if you are consciously developing yourself, your growth will occur much faster. Astrology helps you to do this. For example, you could have very strong karma to work in the financial industry and to earn your living through making financial deals. This is something you have to experience in this life, because it's strongly indicated in your birth chart.

But you may also have some lesser karma that brings you a spiritual inclination, causing you to sometimes feel you want to spend your days in deep meditation with little participation in worldly affairs. The more pronounced of these two tendencies requires your life to revolve around finance and worldly interactions, which you would have great difficulty changing in this lifetime. So your greatest comfort will come from a career in this area, but you can also balance your existence through greater expression of your spiritual inclinations at the same time.

Even people with karma for worldly affairs can develop themselves spiritually. I know of many people who live this type of lifestyle and are quite happy with it, even some who are highly successful in the world of finance. By developing themselves spiritually while participating in worldly pursuits in this life, they may well develop the karma to completely immerse themselves in spirituality in subsequent incarnations. This is how life develops from one lifetime to the next. Life is set up for you to progress from one incarnation to the next, so you can eventually experience the fulfillment of all your desires.

Some of us have greater flexibility with our choice of careers than others. For example, some people have a strong indication in their birth chart for a period of working in the world and earning money, and then a later period where a more spiritual lifestyle is predicted. There are an infinite number of combinations for karma to play out in human life.

You probably know of people with multifaceted lives like this too, some who even have more than one way of earning money at a time. Some people may spend part of their day developing real estate and another part creating art. Many people participate in more than one career at a time in this way today. They split their days among their career passions and earn from both. This is fairly common and it will show up in their birth chart.

Each of us is born with an allotted duty, or *dharma*, to perform in life. Your dharma is your purpose. On a very deep level you know what actions are right for you. If you develop your consciousness and follow what feels most comfortable, you can better attune yourself to your dharma.[9] You always have free will available to you, but you will not find complete support for your actions unless you are operating in those areas most in alignment with your dharma. Some people are able to determine their dharma intuitively. But for others it's not so clear. For clarification of your dharma, or if you have no idea what yours is, a good astrologer can provide assistance.

Not everyone wants the same things, which is normal and allows for the natural diversity of life. We each want that which resonates with our soul, because we are unique beings and yearn for activities that are in harmony with our life purpose. Yes, many of us want some of the same things in life—more money, a nice home, and loving relationships—but on a more granular level we want to experience different things throughout the span of our lifetimes.

Life is arranged in this way because we all have performed different actions in the past, which gives rise to our specific karma and, in turn, dharma in this lifetime. By performing unique actions in the past, you have set into motion some unique tasks you must perform in this life. Remember, karma is just action—whether good or bad. From your past actions you have created unique good and unique bad responses to play out over your lifetime. You have free will too, but some experiences you simply must have this time around in order for you to develop and grow. Your past actions have honed your skills in specific areas, which have given rise to your particular dharma or purpose in life this time.

But just as your past actions determine some of the activities you must undertake in this life, they can also determine what you cannot do in this life. If you treated money poorly in past lives, for example, you may have to struggle with making money in this one. If you took your good relationships for granted in the past, you may have to work very hard at them this time, or you could have trouble even finding a loving relationship in this life. You get the idea.

On the other hand, you may have practiced and performed music so selflessly for the upliftment of all in a past life that you were born a virtuoso this time. It's true that many of your lesser karmas can be changed through your efforts and will power. But again some are so deeply ingrained in your nature that they, for better or worse, will be virtually impossible to completely overcome without attaining full enlightenment to escape their influence.

If you are meant to be a musical prodigy, it's unlikely that you will be able to change that in one life. Many would ask why you would want to. But if you are meant to suffer from ill health most of your life, it's likely you would want to lessen the impact of this karma, and you can certainly do so.

By performing right action, you can lessen the impact of your bad karma. For example, the performance of good deeds will help mitigate the results of your previous bad actions, and reduce or eliminate some of the negative karma that you've not yet experienced. By performing good deeds in this way, you are sending vibrations out into your environment that will come back to you to help balance out the effects of your previous bad actions. These types of actions can sometimes be prescribed by a Jyotishi.

There are also other remedial recommendations you can receive from an astrologer to propitiate the planets to lessen or eliminate bad karma that has not yet arrived. If difficulties are indicated in your birth chart, a Jyotishi can make very specific recommendations for this.

The most common of these is called a *yagya*. A yagya involves chanting in such a way that the laws of nature ruling a particular planet or planets can be enlivened to reduce the affliction that existed at the time of your birth. This includes a fire ceremony where oblations are offered by one versed in the Vedic rites to help reduce or eliminate your negative karma.

Yagyas help correct the imbalance created by being born under the influence of a planet or planets that were afflicted at the time of your birth. A good astrologer can look at your birth chart to see how the planets are arranged and prescribe various types of yagyas to be performed to mitigate your particular difficulties. These specific types of yagyas can be very helpful, but the greatest yagya of all is the regular practice of meditation, which gradually reduces all your difficult karma simultaneously.[10]

Astrology is not just about a fortune teller describing your destiny. It's about shining the Divine light of pure consciousness on both the good and bad aspects of your life, and then providing remedial measures to lessen your difficulties. A good astrologer will also give you sound advice to take advantage of the good aspects of your life in order to grow towards greater happiness. Seek out a skilled astrologer and learn what you can about how to enhance your life.

Never despair about an astrological reading that indicates difficulties. Your life can always be improved regardless of your circumstances, and your soul has an eternity to allow you to do so with each new incarnation. Although you may have problems at times, you will experience all that your heart desires over your many incarnations in a body. So be patient.

Don't strain trying to undo that which cannot be changed. Your spiritual development will help to reduce your troubles many times more than trying to struggle against them. Just do what comes naturally and start enjoying yourself now. You can find increasing happiness regardless of what's playing out in your life, because it comes from within. To open the floodgates to greater happiness, just begin to develop yourself spiritually. This is the way to everlasting freedom in life.

Some will quickly find complete fulfillment by using the various facets of this Divine wisdom in their life, while others will first need to purify themselves of excessive stress before gaining the full benefits of this knowledge. But increasing happiness will immediately come to all who set out to implement this wisdom in their lives. The only difference between those who wake up quickly and those who wake up gradually is their capacity to fully comprehend and utilize this knowledge.

Arjuna, the great archer of the *Bhagavad-Gita*, was able to quickly become enlightened on the battlefield as the Pandhava and Kaurava armies prepared for battle. Growing to enlightenment does not have to take long. When your heart is pure, enlightenment can come very quickly. Start to move in this direction and all your desires will be fulfilled in the quickest possible fashion.

FINDING YOUR WAY

The steps to attain greater happiness in life are unique for each of us. You may desire a spiritual pursuit that includes immersing yourself in deep meditation and learning about yourself through astrology. Another may choose to perform only positive thinking and visualization to remove negativity from their life. Still another may be prompted to go more deeply into the teachings of their religion. All of these approaches are fine.

Your way is completely valid as long as it allows you to move towards greater happiness. Religious teachings are ideal for some people. They serve an important purpose in their lives that allows them to grow towards greater fulfillment. You certainly can develop yourself by delving into your religion and looking for the deeper meaning in the words and beliefs of your faith. By pursuing that which brings you the most comfort, you cannot miss growing in life.

The direction you head to attain greater fulfillment is customized by you. You can create an approach that is completely new, or you can assist in developing and bringing to fruition an already existing approach. There is no wrong way to grow. There are people progressing from every walk of life, but to attain ultimate fulfillment your pursuit must eventually include a way to systematically experience pure consciousness. This will happen for each of us in our own time.

There are criminals who suddenly wake up to the futility of their actions to become unwavering in their pursuit of higher consciousness, as there are religious zealots who in a flash of clarity realize that with a slight change in approach they can bring greater fulfillment to themselves and others. Who are you to judge which approach is best for a person in any given lifetime? The way to enlightenment includes many variations—some quick and some slow—but in the end they all eventually bring us into greater balance with the cosmos.

Six

CLEANING THE LENS

You can make great progress towards happiness by purifying your body. Physical purification raises your consciousness, because your body in its essence is consciousness. Similarly, and from the opposite perspective, raising your consciousness purifies your body. You cannot do one without the other, because purifying your body and raising your consciousness necessarily occur simultaneously. So embrace the idea of doing them at the same time for your greatest spiritual development.

Your physiology is the lens through which you perceive higher states of consciousness—keeping it pure and functioning properly is vitally important to your spiritual growth. Most of us have forgotten how to live a pure life through right behavior and proper care of the body, which slowly but surely has caused our physiologies to begin to malfunction. By correctly purifying your mind and body, you can improve your health, enhance your consciousness, and bring greater happiness to your life.

REMEMBERING HOW TO BE HEALTHY

When you don't have a clear connection to your source in pure consciousness, it causes your actions to become out of sync with the natural flow of life. As time goes by, your body begins to forget how to function properly and, in turn, forgets how to maintain ideal health. Diseases like cancer and AIDS are not outside invaders that take over your body, but are created by the loss of intelligence in your physiology.

When your body forgets how to operate properly, it gives rise to disorderly cells that can create cancerous tumors. Likewise, when your body forgets how to maintain its immunity, it can give rise to AIDS and other diseases, which then open you up to all kinds of lethal invaders. But the initiator of these diseases is the loss of intelligence in your physiology, not a germ or virus. Your healthy physiology has in place natural defense mechanisms to guard against such things.

We know that cancer is not a disease that needs to continue in human life. It was not so prevalent in humans in the past, and we know of other forms of life that are not prone to cancer now. For example, sharks are far less susceptible to cancer than other species. The Mote Marine Laboratory in Sarasota, Florida has been studying sharks' resistance to cancer for nearly three decades. Its research is funded by the National Institutes of Health.[1] The reason for a shark's low incidence of cancer must be in part because it is living a life more in accord with the laws that govern its physiology than other species.

By not causing undue strain on themselves through proper behavior and diet, they have for the most part managed to avoid cancer. The field of pure consciousness that gives rise to the shark is the same one that gives rise to human life, so there's no reason to think that we cannot tap into nature's intelligence to rid ourselves of this most dreaded of diseases, too. We can just as easily live a life free of cancer by not allowing stress to block the intelligence controlling the natural healing mechanisms in our bodies.

What's more, the medical community is aware of many cases of people living with cancer cells in their bodies today who have never contracted the disease.[2] There are also people who have been living with the HIV virus for years, but have no symptoms of the illness.[3] They have managed to maintain their body's natural ability to stem the growth of these diseases. Through the proper balance of mind and body, human beings are capable of overcoming any illness.

But due to improper eating and behavior, the intelligence in our body begins to break down and this gives rise to an ever-increasing variety of illnesses. I am not a medical doctor, but feel comfortable saying that cancer and AIDS are never going to be completely eradicated by vaccines and allopathic medicines alone, because they are diseases caused by our cells forgetting how to function properly. Memory loss in the physiology on such a grand scale cannot be fully remedied through the intake of medicines. It can only be regained in its entirety by enlivening the dormant intelligence of the body, which will eliminate our susceptibility to disease.

Your body is nothing more than a concentration of energy, comprised at its subtlest level of pure consciousness. Making a correction on the level of consciousness will automatically give rise to a corresponding correction on the cellular level of the body. All physical maladies can be prevented or eliminated by simply tapping the field of greater intelligence at the level of your own pure consciousness.

There is no need to look outside yourself to prevent illness. You only need purify your mind and body to take instruction directly from nature to know what is good for you and what will inhibit the flow of intelligence in your body. The best way to prevent disease is to reduce stress. By removing the stress that interferes with the natural expression of your body's intelligence, you can quickly move towards ideal health and a greater sense of well-being.[4]

There's a new nomenclature that has arisen describing some human behaviors as "cancerous" to life. We have all experienced people with toxic personalities who create blockages in the flow of energy in their environments, similar to that which occurs with cancer cells in the body. This new language is an accurate description of what can occur from the practice of intense negative emotions like jealousy, anger, hatred, and any other incoherent emotion that causes undue stress in the environment. When you participate in such behaviors, it's because you have forgotten how to act in accord with natural law, which necessarily creates disharmony in the environment.

By acting in an exceedingly discordant manner you are not only creating cancerous symptoms in your environment, but are actually training the cells in your body to become misguided and forget their proper life-supporting functionality. Your cells then become the seeds to the manifestation of *dis-order* and *dis-ease* in your physiology. If these stressful behaviors are not remedied through pure thoughts and actions, they will eventually result in your cells forgetting their natural rhythms, disrupting the web of intelligence in the body.

LIFE-SUPPORTING ACTIVITY

To create a lifestyle that's more life-supporting and allows for greater peace and happiness, you need to develop a healthy daily routine —and weekends should not be an exception. Your daily program needs to allow for good sleep, naturally healthy food, and a good spiritual routine. This will bring greater ease and comfort to your physiology. Once you have established a program of eating and sleeping well, practicing meditation, and thinking positive thoughts, you won't want to break your routine on the weekends, because you will feel so much better while on it.

The right program for you is never boring and only good for your overall health. Over time you will find that you're so much happier when you have a good routine and will feel bad if something prevents you from staying on it. If you change your schedule frequently, you will find yourself constantly trying to regain your balance in life.

This type of inconsistency is disruptive to the expansion of your awareness towards higher states of consciousness. Keep your life as consistent as possible without straining, and you will find that you have greater success and satisfaction in all you do. You never want to strain to stay on your program. Be gentle with yourself and aim for staying with it each week. If you fall off, then just gently move your-self back onto it again. In time you will notice how much better you feel; the benefits gained will be enough to keep you going.

After I learned to meditate, I decided to go back to college full time. During this time I created an excellent routine of rising early to practice yoga and meditation. I would then participate in my daily activities in a manner that allowed me to avoid excessive stress, so I felt rested and refreshed all day long. I ate healthy food and slowly moved myself to a completely vegetarian diet. My routine was so complete and fulfilling that I didn't want to alter it.

I took long walks after meditating in the morning and evenings. During these walks, I would often experience waves of concentrated happiness coursing through my body, bliss literally bubbling up from the field of pure consciousness into my physiology. It was a magnificent feeling. All of creation seemed to be alive and breathing in the rhythms of nature around me. The flowers and trees glowed and pulsated with pure consciousness. My years in college provided tremendous growth mentally, physically, and spiritually. Even now after so many years out in the working world, I still make time to keep my daily program as steady as possible in order to maintain good health and to further develop my consciousness.

THE REST REQUIREMENT

Unfortunately, much of life today seems to be working against us maintaining a good routine. Many of our recent technological inventions that were supposed to bring greater ease to our day have instead become increasingly taxing to our lives. It's not technology's fault. It's ours. As the proliferation of new gadgets grows, so does the time many of us spend with them, which can increasingly consume our day if we let it.

Today there are many more things vying for our attention than anyone could have imagined twenty years ago. As a consumer, you're made to feel you need a computer, email account, cell phone, iPod, Facebook account, Wii, etc. Each of these items in and of themselves is a good product. Each has value. It's the overuse of them that causes problems. When you use them incessantly without taking breaks, they begin to occupy all of your free moments and can begin to drain your vital energies.

Much of our technology was created to save time, but with too much of it in the mix, you end up wasting so much of your life that you don't have any left over for yourself. Due to the captivating nature of these technologies, many people can't help being distracted by them. We all know of people who think they can't live without the latest and greatest gadgets. This has become an addiction for many, and long ago stopped being something that helps them, but rather something that actually hinders their life.

I know this is hard to take for many, particularly those born after the advent of these technologies. It has always been there for you, and you've had it drummed into your head that technology is good and that it represents our future. You've been told both by your parents and teachers that you need to stay on top of the latest technology or you'll somehow fall behind.

Unfortunately, no one has told you that the excessive use of these technologies is going to have detrimental effects on the health of a whole generation of people.[5] You have to choose wisely about what you're going to let consume your energy. You need to take time away from all the buzz of your high-tech lifestyle to just *be* every once in a while. It's critical to your health and well-being.

It's essential to feel the contrast between the din of technology and peace and quiet from time to time. Being alone and silent on occasion is necessary for good health, not to mention that it's the only way to rapidly grow towards higher states of consciousness. You're not going to grow to enlightenment when all your waking hours are spent immersed in the titillation of technology. Technology is valuable to the development of human life, but silence is also required to get the rest you need for your greatest personal development.

Deep rest is essential for the refinement of your nervous system. You cannot fully establish yourself in pure consciousness without it. If you sit down to practice meditation without being fully rested, your meditation will do exactly what it's supposed to do, which is to provide you the necessary rest you need, including prompting you to fall asleep if you have incurred too much fatigue.

But if you're sleeping, you are not meditating. You need to be well rested to get the most out of meditation. By falling asleep, you're defeating the very purpose of meditation, because you're not allowing yourself to experience the subtleties that your research in consciousness is trying to provide you.

Falling asleep is okay when you first become a meditator, because you need to rid yourself of any excess fatigue you built up in your nervous system. For two or three weeks after learning, I had to set my alarm clock when I sat down to meditate, because I kept falling asleep. I needed this sleep, because my physiology hadn't received enough for a very long time, and meditation predictably provided what was required—deep, profound sleep to provide the necessary rest my body needed.

But the goal is not to fall asleep when you sit down to meditate, because there are so many more glorious experiences to aim for— like cognizing the Veda. The goal of meditation is to have increasingly refined experiences of pure consciousness, and to grow towards enlightenment. It's far better to stay well rested, so that you can more fully experience the transcendent within. If you're always tired and only catch up on your sleep during meditation, you will miss out on all the benefits to be gained for both your mind and body through the practice.

The deep rest you gain from experiencing the silence of meditation will heal your nervous system to the point where you're able to perform activity for longer periods with clarity and focus.[6] It allows your physiology to always remain deeply rested.[7] But even if you're not a meditator, there is no substitute for staying well rested. It's a requirement of living a happy and healthy life.

A growing body of research shows the benefits of getting rest, and the downside of not getting enough. In fact, there's now research showing that not getting enough sleep, and then trying to catch up on the weekend, doesn't work. Once you miss sleep, it's gone and the damage incurred. You can't get that rest back by trying to take additional sleep later.[8] It's critical that you allow yourself to regularly get good rest, because you may not be able to undo the harm by getting it later.

I cannot overemphasize how valuable proper sleep is to your total well-being. Without it your awareness becomes cloudy and dull, which causes you to make mistakes and become irritable and unhappy. Instead of feeling buoyant and energetic, you feel sluggish and agitated, and underperform in all you do. Put simply, missing sleep is not conducive to a fulfilling life.

There's a vicious cycle you can get into that you might be familiar with. It goes something like this: on Monday night you skip some sleep to work late or enjoy yourself a little more in the evening. On Tuesday morning you hear the alarm clock go off, but don't want to get up because you're not fully rested. You pull yourself out of bed and go to work a bit tired and less effectual than you should be. You make a few mistakes during the day and possibly even do a little damage to your relationships at the office because of your irritability.

This may cause you to become nervous and insecure, since that's a common experience from lack of sleep. By the end of the day, you're a little weaker emotionally, and maybe even feeling a bit guilty about your behavior. This creates the need to be with friends or loved ones, so to bolster your spirits you stay up late again, which causes you to get to bed late Tuesday night.

You then wake up to the alarm going off Wednesday morning, but this time it's been blaring for a minute without you noticing it, because you're so tired. You once again begin your day on the wrong foot, or at least on a sleepy foot, and bumble through your day to increasingly poor results. Many of you know this cycle, because you've experienced it at some point in your life.

Some people do this to themselves day after day. By the time you finish work on hump day, Wednesday, you figure you're on the down-hill side of the week, so what's it matter if you pass on a little sleep by going out again after work. Thursday arrives with an even easier excuse to miss some sleep, since the weekend is almost here. Friday comes and it's just a given that you're not going to bed early.

On Saturday you do the same thing, because after all it's the week-end, right? You can sleep in all day Sunday if needed. So you sleep late both Saturday and Sunday mornings and think you're catching up on your rest, but you're really not. Once that sleep is gone it's gone for good, or rather for bad. The damage has already been done to your physiology. Many people then start this cycle all over again on Monday.

Additional research indicates the other detrimental effects caused from sleep deprivation. Your nervous system becomes seriously damaged by all the missed sleep: you have less ability to focus, make more mistakes,[9] and are at greater risk of obesity.[10] You are also prone to any number of other physiological and mental ailments like diabetes and depression.[11] You seriously short circuit your entire physiology by not getting enough sleep.

There's even been research that shows that intelligence is stunted by four years at a university where young people typically stay up late at night partying and cramming for tests. It's a very sad testament to college life today. Students at a university with a more balanced life-style of rest and activity, including the practice of meditation, were able to increase their IQs by four points over two years and nine points over four years.[12] They also showed significant improvements in char-acter development, while the control students at the other universities showed declines.[13]

The place you sleep is always nearby when you're at home. Use it no matter what time of day it is to get the rest you need. It will only provide you with benefits. Take a nap during the day if needed, so that you're fresh and productive all day long. The best part about adding meditation to the mix is that the more you practice, the more you find that you really don't need as much sleep, because it helps you remain well rested throughout the day.[14]

I still try to get seven to eight hours of sleep a night, but I don't always need to. After many years of meditating, I am able to work with little sleep for a period of time without a noticeable effect on how I feel or my productivity. I try to avoid doing this, however, because I always want to remain well rested. To live a happy, healthy life, you need to get your priorities in order. There's nothing so important that you can't put it off to make sure you're well rested. Rest is the basis of effective activity. Remember, you have eternity to experience all that you desire, so there's no need to try to fit it all into one day.

DETOXIFY EARLY AND OFTEN

Some young people today are so tired and stressed that they have grown accustomed to never feeling real fulfillment in their lives. Some have even given up on the idea of fulfillment altogether. An increasing number of them are losing hope in their future. They have become so hopeless that they've just given up on some level. You can see this in the lack of interest some of them have for their most basic personal hygiene. You also see it in the increasing trend toward self-destructive behaviors like the excessive use of drugs, alcohol, and other activities that impact both their minds and bodies, which is an indication of their lack of foresight and concern for the future.

This trend towards fatalistic behavior is the expression of a generation not able to fathom a happy future ahead. I don't blame young people for their decisions, because I made similar errors in judgment myself when I was their age. Decisions like these are not so much made out of ignorance as they are out of defiance and hopelessness.

I don't write these words to belittle young people, but rather out of concern for them. When I was young, I made some very foolish decisions of my own stemming from my lack of contentment in life. Society has let our young people down. But they need to know there's hope for a happy and fulfilling future ahead. Although some have hardened themselves to their circumstances, they nevertheless are longing deep inside for some genuine happiness in their lives. Everyone seeks happiness, and defiant young people are no exception. Every action a person takes is with the hope of finding greater happiness in life.

Many of them don't even know how to have good, healthy fun anymore. They have become so stressed that only overstimulation excites them. Many are so tired that they can only really feel when they're literally jarred out of their boredom with excessive exhilaration, which unfortunately often expresses itself in the form of being destructive to property, others, or to themselves. I remember some of the wanton destruction that I participated in as a youth. It's a product of our educational system failing to teach young people how to find happiness in their lives.

They are not being taught how to gain lasting fulfillment, because the teachers instructing them often don't even know how to find it in their own lives. We need to better educate society as a whole about the supremely fulfilling process of developing our consciousness. It seems society is so at a loss about how to help our troubled young people that in many cases it has just given up and accepted that this is the way they are. It's a very pitiful situation.

But there are solutions available right now to unlock the tremendous potential that our young people have within them. The following are just a few:

- Teach them how to develop their full potential by learning to meditate to expand their consciousness.
- Provide them the knowledge of how to live in the moment so they can experience greater happiness in their lives.
- Educate them to see that the more positive they are, the more productive and fulfilling their lives will be.
- Teach them the value of becoming confident, independent thinkers who are strong enough to abstain from the harmful indiscretions of youth, and to stay in harmony with nature.
- Help them understand that by avoiding destructive behaviors they will be far more valuable to themselves, their families, their friends, and society.

- Explain to them the importance of regularly detoxifying their mind and body of harmful substances to improve their health and well-being.
- Show them how to say no to many of the distractions of consumer society in order to live a simpler, silent, more balanced lifestyle.

Many young people need to detoxify not only from drugs and alcohol, but from the excessive consumption of materialism. They need to expand their awareness to once again see the simple pleasures that life has to offer.

SOLD ON SOLITUDE

The times we live in occasionally require independent thinking. Don't go along to get along, because you can just as easily get along without going along, if you do it properly. You don't have to do what everyone else is doing to be successful. You have to be alone sometimes to make the greatest progress. Be strong in your desire to seclude yourself a little while each day to develop your awareness.

Yogananda used to say that great humans are formed in seclusion.[15] Just like the yogis and yoginis, it's valuable to take time alone to be silent, think higher thoughts, and meditate. You don't have to live the life of a recluse, but you do need to take some time each day to be silent and think without distractions. Too much socializing is not good for you. Many things are being acted out in the mainstream today that are not healthy or productive for you or for anyone else, so you should try to avoid them.

There are times in your life when you cannot just follow along like the lemmings that jump off a cliff just because those in front of them have already done so. Take time alone to learn about yourself. "Know thyself," because "the unexamined life is not worth living," as the great Socrates used to say. You cannot unlock your full potential by only frequenting social gatherings and theaters, because spiritual progress is made in silence. Spend a little time alone each day to improve yourself. This will allow you to make great strides in your life.

There is no better way to walk the straight path with the narrow gate[16] than to be alone sometimes without distractions. As you grow spiritually, you will find being alone comforting. You don't have to be alone all the time, but it's helpful sometimes. Spending time alone is not an austerity for the truly spiritual, because as your consciousness expands you will find immense pleasure in the peace and quiet that comes from solitude. If you're growing spiritually, you won't have to force yourself to be alone, because it will come naturally to you. Silence brings far greater enjoyment than the transient pleasures most people today waste their time on.

Those who don't understand the value of silence believe it involves going without, but this thinking is not correct. It is a misunderstanding. You can accomplish great things by bringing more silence to your life. The adepts achieve their spiritual gifts through silence, and they continue to seek it whenever they can. As your consciousness grows, you begin to understand that great fulfillment is gained from the silence within. By taking some time away from everything to go within, your joy will no longer be finite—but infinitely abundant in nature.

A highly spiritual person does not find a life lived with less noise to be a reclusive measure at all. You can still have fun and live in the world while taking a little silence each day. Having the contrast of some silence in your life will increase the enjoyment you experience while participating in your worldly activities, because you will bring that steady, silent awareness to all you do.

You can develop yourself in a very comfortable, natural way without straining or abstaining from life. When you meditate, for example, uplifting and life-supporting activities will just come to you. Since becoming a meditator, I have never needed to force myself to implement the simple, healthy behaviors that I perform in my daily life. They just came without any strain on my part. I didn't have to force myself into a more serene lifestyle before I was ready. I just meditated regularly and all that was good for me just flowed into my awareness, which I then implemented in my daily life.

Maharishi used to say, "Expansion of happiness is the purpose of life."[17] If you are developing yourself spiritually and begin to desire more silence, it's not because silence is boring and no fun. This would make no sense. You gravitate towards greater silence because it has become more appealing and brings you greater happiness. Just think of what you could accomplish if you didn't socialize as much and used that free time to develop your potential so you can achieve all that you wish to in life. You would be much more productive and self-sufficient, because you would have all the time and energy you need to accomplish great things.

Don't worry, you are not going to become a monk after you begin your spiritual practices in earnest. It's possible, but it's not required, nor is it likely. The naturally quiet person who has the desire to be alone may choose more of a cloistered lifestyle, because it's natural and easy for them. But this will not occur for most, because there are far more worldly people out there than those who desire complete seclusion. Spirituality only brings greater happiness to your life, without any feelings of loss. Spiritual life is just as much for the dynamic householder as it is for the renunciate.

Most who try to go off to reside in the Himalayas to live the life of a spiritual renunciate very quickly realize they can't be happy with this lifestyle, because of the karma that compels them to worldly activity. Many who think they want to, soon realize they are not equipped for such an existence. But you certainly have the free will to try.

The majority of us have karma to be householders, which means we are inclined to live active lives in the world with family. It's very easy to live a spiritual life even as a householder. There's no contradiction in these concepts. Many people around the world participate in this very lifestyle every day. You would be surprised at how many people are diligently working on developing their consciousness while living and working in the city centers of the world. Spiritual awakenings come to people from all walks of life and from all parts of the world.

Maharishi has said that you want to live 200 percent of life: 100 percent of the absolute field of existence, and 100 percent of the relative field of life. *Purnam adah purnam idam*, the absolute is full and the relative field of existence is full.[18] Believe me when I say that you're not going to miss out on anything by living a spiritual lifestyle. Life only becomes exponentially more gratifying.

Spirituality is a requirement if you wish to attain lasting fulfillment. You will never find complete satisfaction from a solely outward-facing existence. You must go within to experience contentment, which requires taking a little silence each day. Jesus said, "The Kingdom of God is within you."[19] You can experience this reality right here on earth by developing your consciousness with a little silence each day.

Good things come to those who know the value of silence. You may even want to try dedicating an entire day to remaining silent. Many great spiritualists have recognized the value of this practice. Mahatma Gandhi took a day of silence regularly even with his busy schedule.[20] He would write notes if he needed to communicate with others on the days that he was in silence. But you should keep this to a minimum to gain the full benefit of your quietude. Taking silence for a full day is quite refreshing for both your mind and body, because we expend so much energy talking. Maintaining silence in this way will invigorate you, particularly if you are used to a busy life.

Choose a day when you don't have to work and tell your family and friends that you would like their assistance to avoid talking that day. They will probably find this interesting enough to help you just to see if you can do it. Retreat for the day, so that you're not engaged in a lot of worldly activities and just rest your vocal cords and physiology. Being silent will allow you to reduce the outward flow of your energy to sustain it within. It's a good way to get some extra rest.

PURITY IN, PURITY OUT

The most direct way to purify and energize your body is to monitor what you eat. Your body in large measure is a product of what you metabolize. Like getting sleep, eating is something we do every day, so it's often taken for granted and the importance of what we eat is overlooked. But what you take internally is so essential for your good health.

The foods you eat are the building blocks of your physiology and directly affect the lucidity with which you perceive the world. Your physiology is the lens through which you know the world, so you need to keep it clean to experience it in its full glory. Take the time to learn how best to keep your body pure, so there are no obstacles to your spiritual development.

You need to put healthy, wholesome food into your body if you want it to work well for you. And healthy food doesn't necessarily mean products that happen to say "healthy" on their label, because many of these items are not healthy for you at all. A good measure of the wholesomeness of food is how *close to nature* it is. The closer to nature your food, the more life-giving energies it will have to nourish your body.

Many foods are so processed that by the time you eat them, they've lost most of their nutritional value, and may have even become detrimental to your health. You can take very healthy, natural food and process it excessively with machines and refine all the life-giving qualities right out of it. Then there are all the preservatives and additives included in processed food to keep it from decaying in transit to you and while sitting on the grocery store shelf. Many of these preservatives and additives are very bad for your health. The Center for Science in the Public Interest online has a long list of commonly used ingredients you should reduce or avoid, like sodium nitrite, saccharin, aspartame, acesulfame-k, olestra, potassium bromate, and many others.[21]

Some of us have become so accustomed to eating processed foods that we have forgotten what many of the fresh plant-based foods even taste like anymore. I've heard about grade school science projects showing that children cannot identify many of the common fruits and vegetables through taste and smell alone. They are not familiar with fresh fruits and vegetables anymore, which is likely caused by the trend towards processed foods today.

The excessive handling, shaking, grinding, pureeing, mixing, etc., that take place during the processing of food in production plants can kill what was once a very fresh, healthy product. The lively energy in the food is lost. This is why overly processed foods are commonly referred to as *dead food*, because all the life has literally been processed out of them, which you experience in their flat, lifeless taste.

Just as disconcerting is that fruits and vegetables today are being grown in depleted soil with synthetic fertilizers that inhibit the creation of vitamins and minerals. Fruits and vegetables no longer have the same nutrients they once did, according to U.S. Department of Agriculture food composition data.[22] For example, broccoli grown in the United States today has 63 percent less calcium than it did in 1950. Six essential nutrients have been reduced since 1950—protein, calcium, phosphorous, iron, riboflavin, and vitamin C—some of them significantly. Good soil is alive with an abundance of naturally occurring minerals necessary to grow health-nurturing fruits and vegetables. But the industrialization of agriculture has caused much of our soil to become overworked and depleted.

You may have noticed, for example, that some types of apples you've eaten since childhood do not have the same flavor they once did. This is particularly true for those of us who have been around a while, since we have witnessed the change in taste over a number of years. The soil many of these apples are grown in no longer has the nutrients that give rise to healthy, delicious tasting apples. And synthetic fertilizers cannot replace the naturally occurring vitamins and minerals provided by Mother Earth.

Although there's far more food in greater variety available in the United States than in most other countries, much of what you find in supermarkets today is so far removed from nature that it has lost much of its taste and nutritional value. When my family and I travel to developing countries in Central America, for example, we always notice that the food there is much tastier and easier to digest than the same products we find here in the United States.

My guess is that this is because the foods there are produced closer to home and are not so processed. You can even taste it in the baked goods, which are full of taste and vibrancy compared to what we get in the United States today, probably because it's handmade with local ingredients. Comparatively speaking, baked goods here have become flat and tasteless.

In developing countries, much of the food comes from local markets, with minimal processing, and therefore is still fairly close to nature. When you begin to eat fresh foods that are produced nearby from small farms, you'll notice they are healthier and tastier compared to processed foods transported long distances to your grocery store.[23] That's why you should always try to buy food as close to home as possible.

The main difference between foods grown locally and those produced in other states or other parts of the world is the huge amount of handling and transportation they are exposed to. Even fruits and vegetables that appear to be freshly harvested have often been seriously processed. Most of them have been picked unripe so that they last until arriving in the grocery store. But some of these fruits and vegetables don't continue to ripen after they are picked, which greatly reduces their flavor and nutritional value.

Fruits and vegetables are also often washed and coated to make them appear more ripe and appetizing than they actually are. And as was already mentioned, many are transported from around the globe to your grocery store. All the time in transit, and the movement and vibration they're exposed to during transportation, cause them to lose their life-nourishing energies. This is why it's always best to eat food that's grown and developed by the local laws of nature close to where you live.

Organic foods are the healthiest available, since in many cases they are grown domestically or near the market that they are sold in, and are not exposed to the unhealthy chemicals that are used to grow non-organic food. What's more, the nutrient content in organic food is very similar to that of the 1950s,[24] and the taste is at least comparable to, if not better than, non-organic food.[25] Try to buy organic food from the farmer's market or natural food store, since it's harvested ripe nearby and involves very little processing. You will find the close-to-nature gauge very helpful in determining what foods are the most nourishing for you and your family to consume.

FEEDING YOUR BODY TYPE

But even if you consume food that is close to nature, it still doesn't mean it's specifically good for you. So after you've determined how best to procure healthy, wholesome food, you need to understand that not all food is good for everyone. Foods that are good for another person may not necessarily be good for you. You need to feed your body type, because each of us has a different physiology. Unfortunately, the restaurant industry is completely unaware of this fact, which means that many of us have to suffer the negative side effects of eating food that is unsuited for our body's needs when we eat out.

Most of the foods you find in restaurants are very spicy, not necessarily excessively hot, but nonetheless filled with heat-producing ingredients. Restaurant food almost always has a lot of salt, pepper, garlic, onions, and tomatoes, which are all heat producing to your body. Although abundant quantities of these spices make for robust-tasting food, it's not good for everyone's body type. In excess they increase the heat element in the body, which is not healthy for some people.

Some of us have physiologies that are already prone to heat. If you mix heat-producing food with an already fiery physiology, you get an uncomfortable person who, over time, will become susceptible to illness and disease. It's very important to know your body type, so you can eat in a way that enhances your health.

Let me tell you a little about my eating habits as I was growing up. My mother is an excellent cook who can make any dish taste good. She intuitively knows how to prepare food so that it blends for a synergistic effect such that the final taste is greater than the sum of the individual ingredients she used in it. Many people add good spices to their food, but few know how to blend them to create one delicious, unified flavor. My mother knows how to do this every time she prepares a meal.

She made a number of delicious dishes for our family when I was growing up, but used many of the mildly heat-producing ingredients mentioned above. She didn't cook with hot peppers and cayenne or anything like that, but nevertheless her recipes included the heating spices so commonly used today. My family never suffered for a lack of good-tasting food, but after I learned about feeding my body type, I began to realize that many of these ingredients were not particularly good for me.

It wasn't my mother's fault, because who knew? But meals with even subtly heat-producing spices caused problems for my naturally fiery physiology. I loved this type of food, and I ate it liberally as I was growing up. But it slowly but surely caused some health issues for me, as did most of the other food readily available to me at the time.

I would periodically come down with various heat-related ailments —heartburn, excessive heat in the body, irritability, etc.—but I initially didn't attribute them to what I was eating, since I really didn't know the cause of these symptoms. There was nothing out of the ordinary with the food I was eating. For dinner I would often eat some type of pasta with marinara sauce, or one of the common cuts of meat with the normal vegetable side dishes and maybe some dinner rolls.

At lunch I ate a lot of sandwiches with all sorts of tasty breads, meats, and cheeses. I would then add to these sandwiches olives, mustard and mayo, onions, pickles and tomatoes, salt and pepper, and anything else that was available for creating a sandwich. I usually included salted chips of some kind. I would also almost always have an ice-cold drink, usually soda or juice. Sometimes we would also have homemade soups that were well spiced for the greatest flavor.

For snacks it would not be unusual for me to eat some type of cake or cookies. I have always loved sweets and still do. I ate all types of baked goods, especially ones that included chocolate. In the morning I would typically eat eggs or cereal with cold milk, and follow that with orange juice. Many of these items are common foods for most families.

The problem is that even though they may taste great, and you may be able to get them very close to nature, they can harm the health of people with certain body types. I didn't know this when growing up, and no one else did either. Most people don't even know this now. But depending on your body type, certain foods can be bad for you, and some are actually bad for everyone. This is not just a problem in the United States, but throughout the world, since people everywhere are regularly eating foods that are not good for their particular constitution.

Let me explain a little about body types and how you can easily determine yours based on the ancient and time-tested principles of *Ayurveda*. Ayurveda is translated as the science of life, and it has its origins in the ancient wisdom of the Veda, which is the oldest continuous body of knowledge known to humanity. Ayurveda was revived in its entirety and brought to the West by Maharishi more than 30 years ago.

Ayurveda describes three primary body types. You may remember when we spoke about the three components of consciousness being the knower, known, and process of knowing, or *rishi, chhandas,* and *devata,* as they are respectively known using Vedic terminology. These three components are also present in the human physiology as *vata, kapha,* and *pitta.*

Their physical properties in the body are equated to air, earth, and fire, and comprise your physical constitution or *prakriti*. Everyone's mind and body include some combination of these three prakriti elements, or *doshas,* often with one or two of them being predominant. For example, you may have a vata-pitta prakriti where vata is the primary dosha and pitta secondary. Or you may have a kapha-pitta prakriti, or body type, where kapha dosha is primary and pitta secondary.

The vata aspect of the physiology is comprised of the air quality. People who are predominantly airy *vata types* tend to have a thin build, quick minds, and poor memories. They are dry, gassy, and prone to worry and nervousness when out of balance.

The fiery *pitta types* tend to have a moderate build, sharp mind, ruddy complexion, moles on their skin, and a propensity for irritability and anger when out of balance. The *kapha type* has a heavy build, slow metabolism, good memory, and has a tendency to be methodical in nature. They are prone to mucus buildup in their body, and can be lazy and slow when out of balance.

Most of us have a body type that's a combination in varying degrees of these three doshas. But some of us are predominantly just one of them, like a pure pitta type, for example, with very little vata and kapha present. There are even some people who are tri-dosha, with all three doshas—vata, pitta, and kapha—present to the same degree in their physiology.

Each of these body types thrive on specific kinds of food, and don't do well with others. You need to know your body type and feed it appropriately in order to remain happy and healthy. If the fiery pitta type eats too many heat-producing foods, it will throw their mind and body out of balance and cause discomfort and potentially even illness over time.

Let me give you an example. I have a pitta-vata prakriti, with pitta, or the fire quality, being my predominant dosha. When I eat anything that's spicy or hot, it's not good for me, sometimes resulting in acid build-up in the body and increased irritability. Think about it this way: when a fiery person eats fiery food, it agitates this quality in their mind and body, causing additional heat and anger to arise in them. It's kind of like adding fuel to a fire.

I have included a simple test below for you to quickly get an idea of what doshas need to be tended to in your own body.[26] Although the test below is helpful, it's always best to have the results verified by an Ayurvedic physician, or *vaidya*, as they are referred to in Sanskrit.

Do You Need To Balance Vata?

Vata dosha governs flow and motion in the body. Answer these questions to see if you need to balance vata:

1. Is your skin dry, rough, thin?
2. Are you underweight?
3. Is your mind constantly active?

4. Do you worry incessantly?
5. Are you constantly restless or agitated?
6. Do you experience constipation?
7. Do you suffer from insomnia?
8. If female, do you suffer from vaginal dryness?
9. Do you have spells of forgetfulness?
10. Do you experience discomfort in the joints?
11. Are you easily fatigued?

*Total "yes" answers:*_____

If you answered yes to most of these questions, you need to balance vata.

Do You Need To Balance Pitta?

Pitta dosha governs metabolism and transformation in the body. Answer these questions to see if you need to balance pitta:

1. Do you tend to be demanding or critical?
2. Are you often frustrated, angry, or intense?
3. Is your skin ruddy and prone to rashes and eruptions?
4. Are you often irritable or impatient?
5. Is your hair prematurely gray or thinning?
6. Do you wake up in the early hours and find it difficult to fall asleep again?
7. Do you feel discomfort in hot weather?
8. Are you a perfectionist?
9. If female, do you experience hot flashes?
10. Do you have excess stomach acid?
11. Do you experience loose bowel movements?

*Total "yes" answers:*_____

If you answered yes to most of these questions, you need to balance pitta.

Do You Need To Balance Kapha?

Kapha dosha governs structure and fluid balance in the body. Answer these questions to see if you need to balance kapha:

1. Do you tend to be overweight?
2. Are you often over-settled and lethargic?
3. Do you experience sinus problems?
4. Do you sleep long hours yet wake up unrefreshed?
5. Are your skin and hair oily?
6. Do you find that you are possessive and over-attached?
7. Do you feel discomfort in cold, damp weather?
8. Do you tend to feel lazy, complacent?
9. Do you experience bloating, water retention?
10. Do you feel stiff and heavy, especially in the morning?
11. Do you experience congestion?

*Total "yes" answers:*_____

If you answered yes to most of these questions, you need to balance kapha.

You can determine your primary dosha by the one that had the most "yes" answers above. The dosha that had the second-most will be your secondary area of imbalance. So if most of your "yes" answers were for vata and your second-most "yes" answers were for pitta, than you're a vata-pitta type.

The predominantly vata body type needs to avoid, or eat in moderation, certain foods so as not to vitiate their airy constitution. This includes any cold food and drinks; dry foods like chips and crackers; leafy green items; and unripe fruit.

The pitta type needs to avoid all heat-producing foods to stay in balance. You may be surprised to learn that some of these foods include the following: tomatoes, corn, carrots, nuts, pickles, vinegar, yogurt, yeasted breads, carbonated drinks, coffee, and alcohol. All of these should be avoided or consumed in moderation by pitta types.

The kapha body type needs to avoid, or eat in moderation, rich foods and dairy products: cheeses, milk, pasta, oily foods, and overly sweet, sugary foods. A more complete list of foods to favor and avoid for each dosha can be found below. Eating for your body type will make it so much easier for you to remain pure and in balance, which will provide a solid foundation for you to gain greater health and happiness in life. The information on diet and behavior below will provide insights about how to balance your doshas.[27]

Balanced Vata Results in Quality Sleep, Supple Skin, and Proper Elimination

Vata governs all movement in the mind and body. It controls blood flow, elimination of wastes, breathing, and the movement of thoughts through the mind.

Since pitta and kapha cannot move without it, vata is considered the leader of the three doshas in the body. Therefore, it's very important to keep vata in balance.

Tips for Balancing Vata

1. Warm temperatures.
2. Warm, cooked foods (less raw foods).
3. Early bedtime, lots of rest.
4. Favor warm, oily, heavy foods, and sweet, sour, and salty tastes.
5. Reduce light, dry, cold foods, and pungent, bitter, and astringent tastes.
6. Regular daily routine.
7. Avoid stimulants.
8. Regular, daily elimination.
9. Stay warm in cold, windy weather.

Vata-Pacifying Diet

1. Eat larger quantities of food, but not more than you can digest easily.
2. Dairy: all dairy products pacify vata. But always boil milk before you drink it, and drink it warm. Don't drink milk with a full meal.
3. Sweeteners: all sweeteners are good (in moderation) for pacifying vata.

4. Grains: rice and wheat are very good. Reduce the intake of barley, corn, millet, buckwheat, rye, and oats.

5. Fruits: favor sweet, sour, or heavy fruits, such as oranges, bananas, avocados, grapes, cherries, peaches, melons, berries, plums, pineapples, mangos, and papayas. Reduce dry or light fruits such as apples, pears, pomegranates, cranberries, and dried fruits.

6. Vegetables: beets, cucumbers, carrots, asparagus, and sweet potatoes are good. They should be eaten cooked, not raw. The following vegetables are acceptable in moderate quantities if they are cooked, especially with ghee (clarified butter) or oil, and vata-reducing spices: peas, green leafy vegetables, broccoli, cauliflower, celery, zucchini, and potatoes. It's better to avoid sprouts and cabbage.

7. Spices: cardamom, cumin, ginger, cinnamon, salt, cloves, mustard seed, and small quantities of black pepper are acceptable.

8. All nuts are good.

9. Beans: reduce all beans, except for tofu and mung dahl.

10. Oils: all oils reduce vata.

Balanced Pitta Results in Even Temper, Healthy Hair, and Decreased Acid

Pitta governs all heat, metabolism, and transformation in the mind and body. It controls how we digest foods, how we metabolize our sensory perceptions, and how we discriminate between right and wrong. Pitta governs the important digestive *agni* or fire in the body.

Tips for Balancing Pitta

1. Keep cool. Avoid hot temperatures and food.
2. Favor cool, heavy, dry foods, and sweet, bitter, and astringent tastes.
3. Reduce pungent, sour, salty tastes, and warm, oily, and light foods.
4. Moderation: don't overwork.

5. Allow for leisure time.

6. Regular mealtimes, especially lunch at noon.

Pitta-Pacifying Diet

1. Dairy: milk, butter, and ghee are good for pacifying pitta. Reduce yogurt, cheese, sour cream, and cultured buttermilk (their sour tastes aggravate pitta).

2. Sweeteners: all sweeteners are good except honey and molasses.

3. Oils: olive, sunflower, and coconut oils are best. Reduce sesame, almond, and corn oil, all of which increase pitta.

4. Fruits: favor sweet fruits, such as grapes, cherries, melons, avocados, coconuts, pomegranates, mangos, and sweet, fully ripened oranges, pineapples, and plums. Reduce sour fruits such as grapefruits, olives, papayas, unripe pineapples, and plums.

5. Vegetables: favor asparagus, cucumbers, potatoes, sweet potatoes, green leafy vegetables, pumpkins, broccoli, cauliflower, celery, okra, lettuce, green beans, and zucchini. Reduce hot peppers, tomatoes, carrots, corn, beets, onions, garlic, radishes, and spinach.

6. Spices: cinnamon, coriander, cardamom, and fennel are okay. But the following spices strongly increase pitta and should be taken only in small amounts: ginger, cumin, black pepper, fenugreek, clove, celery seed, salt, and mustard seed. Chili peppers and cayenne should be avoided.

7. Nuts: all nuts should be eaten in moderation as they increase pitta.

8. Opt for unyeasted breads, because yeast aggravates pitta dosha.

Balanced Kapha Results in Corrected Weight, Increased Energy, and Decreased Congestion

Kapha governs all structure and lubrication in the mind and body. It controls weight, growth, lubrication for the joints and lungs, and formation of all the seven tissues—nutritive fluids, blood, fat, muscles, bones, marrow, and reproductive tissues.

Tips for Balancing Kapha

1. Vigorous regular exercise, a little each day.
2. Warm temperatures.
3. Fresh fruits, vegetables, and legumes.
4. Favor pungent, bitter, astringent tastes, and light, dry, and warm foods.
5. Reduce heavy, oily, cold foods, and sweet, sour, and salty tastes.
6. Seek out variety and new experiences.
7. Stay warm in cold, damp weather.
8. Early to bed, early to rise.

Kapha-Pacifying Diet

1. Dairy: low-fat milk is better. Always boil milk before you drink it—which makes it easier to digest—and take it warm. Do not take milk with a full meal or with sour or salty food. You might add one or two pinches of turmeric or ginger to whole milk before boiling it to help reduce any kapha-increasing qualities in the milk.
2. Fruit: lighter fruits, such as apples and pears, are better. Reduce heavy or sour fruits, such as oranges, bananas, pine-apples, figs, dates, avocados, coconuts, and melons, as these fruits increase kapha.
3. Sweeteners: honey is excellent for reducing kapha. Limit sugar products, as these increase kapha.
4. All beans are fine, except tofu, which is made from soybeans.
5. Reduce all nuts.
6. Grains: most grains are fine, especially barley and millet. Do not take too much wheat or rice, as they increase kapha.
7. Spices: all are fine, except for salt. It increases kapha.
8. Vegetables: all are fine, except tomatoes, cucumbers, sweet potatoes, and zucchini. They all increase kapha.

As mentioned earlier, most restaurants serve foods that are heavy on the heat-producing ingredients, which aggravate the fiery pitta dosha. They are prepared with a lot of salt, pepper, garlic, onions, peppers, vinegar, tomatoes, frying oils, and cheese. For this reason, the pitta types need to pay special attention to their diet when dining out, because they will suffer the most from consuming these types of ingredients.

There are pitta-pacifying products that I use regularly to neutralize heat-producing ingredients in my food, since it's sometimes difficult to escape this property while away from home. I drink a cup of whole leaf organic aloe juice daily to help reduce the heat in my physiology. I usually drink it with a meal, particularly if the meal includes heating ingredients, but otherwise I drink it before bedtime.

I also regularly consume dandelion leaves, which are very easy to procure. Anything bitter helps to reduce the pitta quality in your body, and dandelion leaves are very bitter. If you live near an untreated grassy field you can pick your own in the spring and summer. Sometimes I will even drink a cup of aloe juice and eat some dandelion leaves together when I've eaten hotter food than I should have. If eaten right before or during your meal, this combination will help to extinguish the heat in your body caused by pungent foods. There are also *rasayanas*, Ayurvedic herbal remedies, which can be taken to aid in the balancing of any of the three doshas.[28]

Most kapha types can tolerate eating out much more than pitta types, since their constitution absorbs heat-producing foods quite well. In fact, on occasion a little heat is good for the digestion of a kapha body type. They just need to watch out for the richer, oily foods and dairy products that are also fairly common on some restaurant menus. If a kapha type is feeling overly congested they should eat a slice of fresh ginger root or drink some hot ginger tea to help clear out any excess mucus and to kick start their sluggish physiology.

The vata types need to avoid the dry chips and crackers that are so prevalent as appetizers or as a side with sandwiches, and they should also be careful not to consume the ice-cold drinks that are in over-abundance in restaurants. Actually, no dosha type should consume ice-cold drinks, not even the fiery pitta types, because ice-cold drinks extinguish the digestive fire, or agni, which is so vital to good assimilation.

But the vata types in particular need to really watch out for ice-cold drinks, because anything cold can make them very uncomfortable and nervous, which is a clear sign of a vitiated vata dosha. Of course, most of us are a combination of these three doshas, so we have to adjust our diets accordingly. As you begin to practice feeding your body type, you will learn how to regulate your diet appropriately.

If a vata person feels overly cold or dry, they should drink some warm milk or warm decaffeinated tea, and add some additional vegetable oil or ghee to meals to reduce the dryness in their physiology. They can also sip hot water when eating. Drinking hot water is very good for vata types while eating a meal, particularly if their digestion is sluggish. Hot water is really good for any body type, particularly in the winter, unless you're pure pitta and hot all the time. It's always best to bring your water to a boil briefly to refine its properties before you serve it.

I know that many people today think they are too busy to prepare fresh food for themselves, let alone cook for their body type. But after you get used to what you should be eating, you will find it's no more difficult to prepare this type of food for yourself than any other type of cooked food. If you can manage to eat for your body type even a few times a week, it will make a dramatic difference in the way you feel, and greatly improve your health.

Eating appropriately may take a little extra time and attention, but the illusion of time is what you make of it. If overwhelmed, repeat to yourself for a few days, "I have all the time I need," and it will become available to you. Start to think and feel that you have the time to prepare fresh, healthy food that is in alignment with your body type and the laws of nature will arrange for it to happen. It's very important that you eat well, so put your attention on it.

If you can, try to reduce the amount of meat you have in your diet. I know this can be difficult for some people, because many of us were raised eating meat daily. A physiologist once told me that humans were never meant to eat meat. He said, in the animal kingdom, those that are carnivorous like lions have very short intestines, whereas herbivores like cows have very long intestines.

Humans also have very long intestines and should try to eat a vegetarian diet to maintain ideal health. If you have interest, start slowly and gradually, without forcing yourself. Begin to eat more bean products to compensate for the protein you lose from not eating meat. The less meat you eat the better, because meats are very heavy and produce toxins in your body that can throw your physiology out of balance. Try your best in this regard without straining and you will see that you feel much lighter and more energetic over time.

It's very important to eat only pure food that doesn't create toxins in the body. As was mentioned, the purity of your physiology is vital to your state of mind and the development of your consciousness. If you want to feel good, you need to keep the toxins out of your body. Eating pure food brings pure thoughts.

DIGEST WELL TO LIVE WELL

When you sit down at the table to eat, you should not be distracted. Don't do other things while eating. As with working, it's best not to distract your mind while eating. You want to eat in a peaceful, quiet space with family and friends, or by yourself. You should not watch television or listen to music while eating. You should just eat slowly in a very calm state of mind. This aids in digestion and proper assimilation. You can have pleasant conversation with your family and friends, of course, but don't talk about emotionally charged topics or about things that make you upset. It's not good for your digestion.

Many people don't realize how important good digestion is to their health and well-being. The digestive tract allows you to extract nourishment from your food to sustain your body. To maintain good health and the purity of your physiology, it is extremely important that this process not be impeded.

More people put a higher priority on servicing the engine in their car than on making sure their digestive system is functioning properly. In the same way you keep clean oil in your car to ensure impurities don't damage your engine, your digestive system has to be nourished with pure food and regular cleansing so that toxins and impurities don't build up and damage your physiology. Residual toxins, or *ama*, as it is called in Ayurveda, can very quickly develop in your body when you eat food that's not right for your body type, eat food that's impure, or eat when your digestion is not functioning properly.

One easy way to eliminate toxins from your body is to eat only all-natural fruit and fruit juices one day a week. By performing a fruit fast in this manner, you can quickly eliminate some of the excess toxins from your physiology. This may take some getting used to, since many of us are accustomed to eating solid foods every day. But you can train yourself to get used to a lighter diet of only fruit one day a week if you put your attention on it.

Fruits are very good for you, because they include essential vitamins and minerals, require virtually no energy for your body to process, and help to purify your digestive system. When you eat fruit it doesn't even stop in your stomach, because it has no need to be digested. It just goes straight through to your intestines with very little expenditure of energy.

When you're ready to begin your first fruit fast, have a decent quantity on hand, since you will feel hungry much sooner than with heavier types of food. Some heavier fruits—like bananas, avocados, or oranges—will go a long way towards providing the weight your stomach expects from eating. You can choose any number of other fruits to include with some of these heavier types. You will find that you can fast for a day quite comfortably with three bananas, three apples, and some other small amounts of fruit like grapes or berries of some kind. Follow the pacifying diet from above that's appropriate for you to determine which fruits to choose for your body type. You may also want to drink some real fruit juice throughout the day.

You will figure out exactly how much fruit you need to last the entire day from your first fast. Performing a fruit fast regularly will help keep your system clean. If you start to feel hungry during your fast, eat some more fruit, but you should try to go hungry for a little while each time you fast, so your body can burn off any extra residue that may be present in your stomach and digestive system.

Your psychology is important in this respect. Many people are so used to having their stomachs full that they believe they need to feel full in order to feel good. You're not going to die if you go without solid food for awhile. Most of us can live for days without food. But again, if you feel really hungry while fasting, just keep eating fruit, as much as you need to maintain your comfort level. As you get used to fasting in this way, you will also become more comfortable going with less food on non-fasting days.

If you don't have a ravenous appetite, you might even want to try a day of fasting on just natural fruit juice or even without food of any kind. You should consult your physician first, however, to make sure you're healthy enough for such a fast. If so, you will find it very beneficial to your health, because it will purge a lot of impurities from your physiology.

I also opt for an all-fruit diet if I feel like I am getting sick. It allows all the energy in my body to go towards fighting off the illness, while also purifying myself of excess toxins that may be contributing to my illness. In most instances the illness will never fully develop if I start early enough. As you purify your mind and body, you will naturally become more capable of recognizing even the slightest indication of the onset of illness. I have fended off sickness many times by going to an all-fruit diet in this way over the years.

It's okay to feel hunger pangs on occasion. When most people start to feel even the slightest sensation of hunger, they immediately start eating. But it's good even when not fasting to sometimes allow your digestive fire to burn for a little while before putting more food in your stomach. You can get used to this by abstaining from food every now and again when you're a little hungry. It will train your mind to know that you don't need food every time you feel a little hunger.

You never want to struggle or strain to resist eating, but it's good to stop your food intake for a while before eating again. Allow your body to fully digest your food first. If you eat before fully digesting, you will cause the food that's already in your stomach to solidify like when adding uncooked rice to a pot of nearly cooked rice on the stove. When this happens in your stomach, the food becomes very difficult to digest. This is why grazing all day is extremely bad for your health, and over time causes ama to accumulate in your body and illness to set in.

Also, try to become more conscious of your digestion. Many people don't even think about their food after they eat it, as if the food's gone and there's nothing more to consider after swallowing it. It's helpful when eating to imagine you have a little window on the outside of your stomach allowing you to peer inside to see how the digestive process is going.

Imagine your stomach with its digestive acids heating up to allow you to properly burn the nutrients out of your food. Then picture different types of food being dropped into your stomach and how your digestive system handles them. A first consideration is that an appropriate amount of chewing is needed to make your food more digestible. You don't want to just inhale your food, because when it's not properly broken down it's hard to digest.

As already mentioned, well-ripened fruit doesn't even need to be digested in your stomach, since it's very soft and easy on the system.

Cooked vegetables can also go through your system quite easily. But what about cheese? Cheese is actually very hard to digest, because it's very gooey and rubbery once heated up in your stomach.

Some kapha body types can't digest cheese. It just sits in their stomach as their digestion tries to work through it, causing excessive mucus to build up in the body. But cheese is not so easily digested by vata or pitta types either—not to mention that many cheeses are also fermented, which heats up your body and creates a lot of toxins.

Do you think meat is easy to digest? Think about looking through the little imaginary window in your stomach to determine how it will handle meat. Cooked meat is a heavy and tough substance that is difficult to digest. Meat also causes a lot of toxins to remain in your digestive tract, and it goes without saying that everyone should be concerned about what an animal is fed before it becomes your food. Whatever they eat, you eat. Most people never think about what they eat in this way.

You also need to pay closer attention to what food combinations you are consuming. Let's consider how different types of food mix in your stomach after eating them. What do you think will happen if you mix orange juice and milk? Try adding a teaspoon of whole milk to a glass with about a quarter inch of fresh squeezed orange juice in it. Let stand for about fifteen minutes. You will soon see that the milk curdles. You should try to avoid eating dairy products and fruit together, particularly citrus fruits. They are not good for you when eaten at the same time and will cause ama to be created by the body.

What about mixing orange juice and chocolate cookies? It's probably not a good idea to visualize what this mess will look like, since it's sure to be disgusting. Clearly this kind of mixture is going to create havoc in your stomach and is certain to cause excessive ama in the body.

If you are conscious about how different foods will mix in your stomach, you will quickly learn to eat in a way that doesn't cause undue difficulties. There are some Ayurvedic techniques for cleansing your physiology every few months in order to eliminate ama. For example, you can use the Ayurvedic procedures called *virechana* with ghee, and/or *panchakarma*, which is a much more elaborate form of cleansing involving various oils and massages.[29] These techniques allow you to purify your entire physiology of toxins in a very gentle, natural way.

Many of the new cleansing techniques that you may have heard about over the past few years were prompted by the popularity of the Ayurvedic cleanses, which were brought to the West by Maharishi. Whenever something good is introduced into the free market system there are always new products created to compete with them. Unfortunately, many of these new cleanses are not particularly good for you, and some are so harsh on the system that you should avoid them altogether. Use your own judgment and experiences to help you make the right choices about what to do with your body. Don't just assume because a product is available in the marketplace that it's going to be good for you.

Another consideration about food is how much you consume. Many people eat far too much food at one time. You should actually only eat as much as you can fit into your two hands when they are placed side by side with palms up in the shape of a bowl. This is the ideal amount of food to eat during a meal. This small amount may seem very difficult to comprehend for some people, but it's something to be aware of and aim for over time.

The supersized portions some restaurants serve today have contributed to a very dangerous trend of overeating. We don't like to leave food on our plates, because it seems like such a waste. Well, get used to it, because eating everything on your plate with the portion sizes of today is very, very bad for your health. These large portions have caused many people to become accustomed to eating huge amounts of food and drink, far more than is healthy for anyone to consume, which in part is responsible for the obesity epidemic we are facing today.

According to a recent comprehensive study by the Trust for America's Health and the Robert Wood Johnson Foundation, there are no less than 40 U.S. states with obesity rates at or above 25 percent, with 8 of those states above 30 percent. Less than 20 years ago no state had an obesity rate above 20 percent.[30] It's far better to waste some extra food than to suffer the devastating health consequences of diabetes and hypertension that have so often been linked to overeating. Again, you don't want to strain to make these changes in your life, but put your attention on them and over time they will become a reality.

MOVE AND BEND YOUR BODY

You also need to exercise your body to maintain a happy, healthy lifestyle. You may have heard some people call the human body a temple. They say this because the body houses the most holy of things —your soul. For this reason you want to keep it in excellent working order. This helps make sure all of your cells and organs are working and firing correctly, so that you can keep illness out and good health in.

When I say that you need to exercise your body to stay in good health, I'm not implying that you need to perform strenuous exercises or build big muscles to do so, since this could actually be antithetical to living a happy, stress-free life. Too much strain is not good for you, and can inhibit the development of your consciousness. If you are young, or in really good physical condition, some of this type of exercise is okay, but too much strain is not good for anyone.

Take a few minutes each day to perform some low-impact exercises. Don't push yourself, because you want your body to feel good, not tired. There's no need to run when walking works just fine. Walking is so underrated. If you can walk for a few minutes each day you will feel much better, because it gently activates your cardiovascular system and gets your juices flowing. It's a very simple and effortless way to get your blood circulating and muscles moving. You don't even have to walk fast.

Just take some time to walk for a few minutes a day at a medium pace and in a couple of weeks you will notice that your endurance has improved. Starting to exercise in an easy manner like this, or even continuing on in this way indefinitely, is so good for your health. After your stamina has increased, you can choose to exercise more vigorously if you wish for a few minutes each day. There has been research to show that exercising for just 10 minutes continues to provide benefits to your body for up to an hour afterwards.[31]

People always think they have to start exercising in such a big way, when just taking some simple steps towards improving your health is all that's needed. Make up your mind that you're going to exercise without straining for just a few minutes a day and you will find that you are able to stick to your regime much more readily. All the strain and seriousness that people put into exercising is the reason why most end up quitting. You want to feel good. You don't need another thing in your life that requires work.

The best form of exercise is *Hatha Yoga*. *Ha* means sun, and *tha* means moon. The word *yoga* is translated as union, so Hatha Yoga means union of the energies of sun and moon. Yoga, as it is commonly referred to in the West, improves your cardiovascular health by using low-impact stretching postures (*asanas*) to build flexibility and strength, while actually preparing the mind and body to settle down. You don't want to overexert when performing yoga, which unfortunately has become fairly common today. The correct practice of yoga settles your nervous system in a way that's conducive to practicing quiet meditation.

Practicing a cycle or two of the basic asanas every day without overstretching or straining is very good for you. It will keep your body fit and will fully prepare you for the transcending experience if you are a meditator. What's more, yoga is the only exercise I know of that actually helps to reduce your appetite. There is a growing body of research validating this fact.[32]

The first time I practiced yoga, it was shortly before breakfast. Afterwards when I went to eat a breakfast cereal that was only mildly sweet, I found I couldn't finish the whole bowl, which was unusual. I wasn't very hungry and it just seemed too sweet. This had never happened before.

Yoga works on many different levels of mind and body to improve your health. A lot of research on yoga is currently being conducted by the National Institutes of Health's National Center for Complimentary and Alternative Medicine (NCCAM) in the treatment of high blood pressure, chronic low-back pain, insomnia, diabetes, depression, and multiple sclerosis.[33] It's definitely worth adding to your exercise routine. In fact, it can function as a stand-alone exercise routine all by itself.

BEHAVIOR IN HARMONY WITH NATURE

It's important to always strive for what brings the greatest joy to your life. But you need to do so in harmony with your environment. What I mean by this is that you want to express your happiness, but you don't want to make anyone else unhappy by doing so. Until your awareness is broad enough to intuitively know not only what will bring greater happiness to you, but to your environment as well, some of your actions may not always resonate with those around you.

For example, you may have witnessed someone playing a radio so loud that it irritates you. If you ask them why they play it so loud, they will likely say that it makes them feel good. Knowledge is different in different states of consciousness, so what makes you happy might not make another person happy, and vice versa. Your goal should be to develop your consciousness to the level where your behavior pleases not only you, but your whole environment.

A good indication of whether you're really making your higher Self happy is if you're making those around you happy. Right action is right for everything in creation, not just for you. Do your best to exercise proper decorum while expressing yourself. As you learn to live more consciously, ideal behavior will naturally increase in your life. If you are making those around you unhappy, then there are likely things you are doing that will make you unhappy in the long run as well. Let this be the litmus test for your actions.

Similarly, if you are making those around you happy, it is probable that your actions in the long run will also make you happier. This does not always hold true if you're around people on a much different level of consciousness than you are, because they may interpret your behavior differently than you do. But all things being equal, those in your environment will be pleased by your good behavior and bothered by your bad behavior.

You don't have to do what everyone else is doing to make them happy. It's enough just not to make them unhappy. Some actions are not even noticed by others, because they're so in harmony with nature that denser beings may not even notice them. The subtlety of these actions are often overlooked.

The most spiritually evolved among us tread very lightly. Be your own person, but maintain the thought in your awareness that your actions should always please your environment. Putting your attention on this will assist in dissolving your ego, the false you, so you can quickly move towards higher consciousness.

KEEP PURE COMPANY

You also need to keep good company. This is very important to your spiritual development. If you want to be a doctor, you associate with doctors. If you want to become an engineer, you need to associate with engineers. If you desire to purify your consciousness to enhance your spiritual development, then keep company with those who have already done so.

Likewise, if you want to be happy, you need to spend time with happy people. You will find that truly happy people are not just people who participate in silly activities and laugh a lot, because these types of people tend to have considerable ups and downs in how they feel from one moment to the next. Genuinely happy people tend to be well-balanced, spiritual people who are always poised and even in temperament.

Try to associate with the most pure and spiritually evolved people you can find and you will begin to absorb their wisdom and even their mannerisms. Their example will be very helpful to your growth. You cannot grow spiritually if you only associate with materialistic sorts. You want to spend time with those who have developed their consciousness and are on a good spiritual program.

Start from the level you're at. If you're just beginning on the spiritual path, and not yet acclimated to the purity of more evolved souls, you may feel uncomfortable around them initially. Find someone who is on a good spiritual program that you can relate to and spend time with them. As you grow, you will find greater comfort with spiritual personalities and learn to appreciate their purity.

This is how my life progressed. Initially those who were highly evolved spiritually seemed too refined for my taste. I didn't feel comfortable associating with them at first, because I felt like a bull in a china shop. Their vibration was so different from my own. But I was easily able to locate spiritual people who were more at my level that I could relate to. It was easier to associate with them at first, because I was able to more freely discuss my spiritual experiences.

But as you progress, you will gain more wisdom and become more refined yourself due to the development of your consciousness. And over time, you will naturally feel more comfortable with even highly evolved souls. You will find that being around them actually calms and settles you down, and that you can gain higher knowledge from them. Just associate with those people who bring you the greatest happiness and everything else will unfold very naturally for you.

Many people don't know how blessed they are to have come this far, to have incarnated not just in a body, but a human body. There were many lessons you needed to learn to get to this point. It's time now to wake up to your good fortune and begin to consciously move towards higher consciousness. This is the way to great peace in life.

This knowledge is always available for the taking as God's gift to you. As certain as the sun rises, this knowledge will be there when you're ready for it. When the time is right, you will realize you've been trapped in a bad dream of your own making, while right inside of you is all you ever needed to be completely happy. Your ultimate purpose is to enjoy yourself, so clean the lens of your awareness and everything will naturally fall into place for your greatest fulfillment.

Seven

THE SWIFT-FLOWING RIVER

Life is like a river. It's always moving and changing, and try as you may, you can never step in the same place twice. To fully understand the nature of spiritual growth, it's important to understand that change is necessary in the relative field of existence. To know the Truth requires the acceptance of everything in your life, not just those things that you are comfortable with, and this sometimes requires changing your attitudes, beliefs, and behavior. Today, many more people in the world are beginning to seek the Truth, so the river of life is flowing swiftly now, and with it the pace of change.

Real wisdom is not readily available from most institutions of higher learning; so in order to find it, you sometimes need to turn over a few stones. Practically speaking, this includes embracing change in your life to gain greater access to Divine wisdom. Some people are not interested in discovering the Truth, so they feel no need to look beyond their current circumstances. Those who *do* seek the meaning of life, however, must necessarily go through a process of great discovery—a process of change.

THE FULLY EXPERIENCED LIFE

When your spirituality is evolving quickly, you need more experiences to facilitate this rapid growth. When I began to grow spiritually, my life started to be filled with so many different and varied experiences; each of them proved necessary to bring me to the next level. Greater clarity dawned from each of these changes to show me how to bring more peace and happiness into my life. Those who are not experimenting and changing are either not growing or are already there.

As discussed briefly in Chapter Four, you sometimes need to explore in order to make spiritual progress. To really advance spiritually, you need to be growing in consciousness, which requires you to make some changes to your life. You don't want to strain or make your life erratic, but when you feel yourself stagnating, don't be afraid to make a change. Working for 30 years at the same company or living in the same town your entire life is not very common anymore, because the pace of growth is too great in the world today for someone to stay in any one place for very long.

This is not meant to demean those who have worked at the same job or lived in the same town for many years. If you can find sufficient variety to keep growing and learning, you can do whatever you want to. Change can come in a big way or small way, but it will inevitably come to your life.

When enlightenment predominates in the world, these changes will no longer be required, because people will be in greater alignment with nature. But when society is just beginning to pull itself out of darkness to experience the light, many changes are needed to allow the light to express itself. People today need to experience much more than past generations, because it provides greater opportunity for discovery and growth.

There is no mystery about why even the most responsible young people don't stay with any one thing for very long these days. They want fulfillment and are not going to slow down until they have it, hence their incessant moving and changing. They are trying to find fulfillment, but are not sure how to do it, so they restlessly move from one thing to the next to try to find the peace and contentment they desire.

But if you're immersed in the Truth, you have already found peace and happiness, so there's no need for so much change. After you find fulfillment, the pace of change will tend to slow down, at least from your perspective. But for those who are still seeking, new experiences are required to find what it is they are searching for.

Over the years I have had jobs that I was very good at, but because I wasn't satisfied, I moved on. I learned what I needed to learn and was on my way. There was nothing more for me there, and I was never one to stick around just because of a title or the prestige I might gain from additional advancement. All I ever wanted out of life was greater happiness. If that wasn't forthcoming, I moved on. If your spiritual pursuit is genuine, nature will help make all your changes positive ones. You will always land on your feet.

I would surprise those around me by walking away while I was on top, or when I was doing really well at something. But if you desire to know the Truth above all else, titles, promotions, and accolades mean very little to you. I always desired to have experiences that would bring greater growth and understanding to my life, so I was never afraid to make a change. It has never scared me to walk away and start over again, because it was essential for my growth.

Do what you have to and go where you need to in order to find the Truth. Greater happiness has always been my primary concern, and it has determined what I've chosen to do with my life. On several occasions I left what appeared to be desirable circumstances only to pursue greater understanding elsewhere. For example, the first time I attended college, I walked away and withdrew from all my classes even though I was a good student and on my way to receiving "A's" in some of my classes. I simply wasn't content with my life at the time, so I withdrew and waited until the urge to really learn came calling.

I am not implying that you need to quit whatever you're doing if you're not happy. After you learn to stay in the moment, you may well find you can be completely happy right where you are. But, don't be afraid to make a change if you can't find fulfillment. You will always be supported in your pursuit to find greater happiness in life.

It's okay to look for a different job or lifestyle that's more in line with your personality and proclivities. Enjoy your life and discover who you are. Ideally, you'll practice being fully present before you make any rash decisions about moving on, however. The way you feel will tell you if you're moving in the right direction. It's best to develop your consciousness, and then to choose where to go and what to do with eyes wide open. This is the surest method to find your way in life.

You cannot judge another's life from the outside looking in. Someone who appears to be leading an unproductive or nonsensical existence may well already be self-realized, like Chance the gardener in the comedy-drama *Being There*.[1] Chance is a very simple gardener who is apparently completely fulfilled. His silence, childlike innocence, and simplistic wisdom make him an odd but endearing figure to all who meet him, even the power brokers in Washington, DC.

As his renown grows, his quiet reserve is seen as great strength and his knowledge of gardening as profound wisdom to live by, even for the president of the United States. Chance the gardener is suddenly catapulted into his new persona as Chauncey Gardner by simply staying in the moment and following his happiness. *Being There* is a humorous movie that creates a caricature of what it's like to be enlightened, and how it might be greeted by others.

If you are not growing in your job, and just hanging on because you're too scared to take the first step to find something else, you are stunting your own growth. If you need to get out, then make the necessary arrangements and take the leap. Life will go on. Perhaps you'll need to become more frugal and save money before you make the change. That's being responsible. Maybe you'll lose that spouse who thinks you're nuts for trying to find greater happiness in life. To think that you deserve happiness—what a radical idea! But it's probably best that this spouse leaves anyway.

You may think you're losing by making a change, but you're only gaining when you make a change for more happiness. The transition could be tricky and you may be frightened, but these are all valuable feelings for your growth. Again, I'm not suggesting you make a precipitous change in your life to get out of a bad mood. Don't just start packing your bags or clearing off your desk preparing to leave your current situation behind without any thought of what comes next, unless of course that's something you need to do. But do what you have to in order to find greater fulfillment in life, and don't look back.

Again, if you're certain you can't find happiness in your present arrangement even after practicing staying in the moment, then by all means start thinking about what it will take to begin to live and grow again. You need to find your place in life. If your first change doesn't complete you, then make another until you're living a fully conscious life.

As you know, you must learn not just what will make you happy, but how to be happy while finding it. This is the key. You don't just need to enjoy attaining what you want, but the process of attaining it, too. It's not only the new opportunity or new surroundings that are important, but the transition from what you have to the manifestation of what you desire that's also important. When you can honestly say that you are enjoying every minute of every day, you have arrived.

There's nothing so important in life that you should lose your balance over it. You may need a change, but you can remain even and balanced while you do. As you develop your consciousness you will become more comfortable in all circumstances. This is the goal. If you've been laid off from your job, don't allow yourself to constantly worry until you find a new one. Stop and smell the roses from time to time. Enjoy yourself during the free time you've been given.

If you need a job, don't spend all your time sulking over your unfortunate luck. This will only block you from seeing the possibilities available to you. You don't want your worrying to get in the way of the subtle impulses that will guide you to your next opportunity. Have some fun while looking for a job.

It's the turmoil in your awareness from worrying so much that causes you to stress over not having a job. You may actually be getting signals to slow down and take some rest. Nature will provide what you need. Believe in yourself and in God's plan for you. If you can't find work right away, then accept that you're not supposed to be working at the moment. Keep looking, but also try to enjoy yourself.

Maybe your perspective is all wrong. Perhaps losing your job was not bad luck at all, but supreme good luck. Maybe you have been provided an opportunity to rediscover or reinvent yourself. Try to live in the moment and understand that you can be happy regardless of what's going on in your life. When you follow your joy, new opportunities will often just fall in your lap.

Don't be afraid to pursue what you love. You don't have to initially see how you're going to make money from an appealing opportunity in order to investigate it. Just follow your joy in a responsible manner by putting yourself in touch with people and circumstances that will allow you to do what you want to. This is how to test if a legitimate opportunity can come from something that's new and appealing, but you're not quite sure if it can work. Move in the appropriate circles and talk to the right people to see if something comes of it.

When you're settled and enjoying yourself, opportunities will come from places where there appeared to be none. You don't have to see the logical progression of events to take the next step. Just have faith and follow your happiness. This is where God is nudging you to go. If you allow yourself to enjoy life, it will begin to bloom before your eyes. Everything will become fresher and brighter, and new opportunities will appear out of nowhere.

The only difference between those who are doing what they love and those who aren't is that those who are doing what they love decided to allow themselves this courtesy. They decided that they deserved it. They decided they were worthy of being happy and made the internal shift necessary to either realize they love what they are already doing, or to find something new to do that they love.

Losing your job has financial ramifications, of course. But did you ever think that maybe you need to go bankrupt? I'm not joking. You may need to go bankrupt or have your home foreclosed on to wake up and find your real purpose in life. These types of events don't just happen to make you depressed and dejected, or to destroy you. They happen to show you that you are going in the wrong direction. Every difficult circumstance is God trying to wake you up to that which will bring greater fulfillment to your life. Bankruptcy and foreclosure are inconsequential in comparison to finding your true purpose in life.

I assure you that most people who were forced to go through bankruptcy or a foreclosure, if they are honest, will say they were greatly relieved because of it. Those who live in countries that have these safety devices to alleviate their debt are lucky to be able to move on to enjoy another day. These instruments may not always be there, so we are blessed to have them today. In many countries, people are never forgiven their debt. They have to suffer the burden of it their entire lives with no assistance from the government to help them recover, which is one of the reasons why the suicide rate is so high in many of these places.

Enjoy yourself while looking for what life has in store for you. By being fully in the moment and happy, you can get some rest while looking for something new to do with your life. Maybe nature arranged for you to be out of work for a time to enjoy some of the things you couldn't while you were working. Perhaps you were headed for a nervous breakdown or a heart attack if you stayed on at your job. Now that you have time on your hands, use it responsibly to look for your next opportunity, but enjoy yourself as you do. You don't have to wait until you find work to begin to enjoy your life, because your mind can always conjure up another reason why you have to wait to be happy. Choose to be happy now.

Be diligent about finding work, but know that it rarely takes the whole day to search for a job. Be careful with your money, but you don't have to just sit at home. There are lots of fun things you can do that cost little or no money. Go to the bookstore or library and read some interesting books or magazines. Go down to the mall for a while and look around. Take a ride out in the country. Play with your children or have some fun with your spouse and friends. Enjoy the moment.

By allowing yourself to have fun, new and unexpected opportunities will come your way. It could even include a job that allows you to enjoy yourself while making more money than you ever have before. You're starting anew, so many possibilities exist for you now. But remember, money is not the goal, happiness is. And if you're enjoying yourself, you will be more open to what nature is trying to bring you, which will make finding work much easier.

Sometimes looking for a new job requires you to search in places you never would have considered before, because you had blinders on. The safe route is not always the best route. Maybe you've always played it safe before, but were you ever happy with it? Perhaps you would be happier in an occupation making less money. Don't rule anything out; just follow your happiness.

By only pursuing that which is safe, you may wind up with the same thing you didn't like the last time. Try to look at your situation differently by pursuing things that you have the skills for, but that may be different from what you've done in the past. Look for something new. It might be a bit out of your comfort zone, but it gives you greater exposure to other opportunities. It just may allow you to find a type of job you never knew existed, and that's more fulfilling than what you've done in the past.

Try this exercise: write down with as much specificity as possible your predictions about how tomorrow will play out. Try to predict how your day will go. You will quickly find that you really don't know much about the details of how tomorrow will unfold, even with the aid of a good astrologer, since they would be hard pressed in this day and age to predict about all the minutiae in our daily lives. You may be able to predict that you will eat, participate in certain activities, and go to bed, but most everything else will just spontaneously unfold.

Even if you know exactly what you're going to do tomorrow, you don't know what the results of your actions will be: Will you win or lose? Will the car start or won't it? Will you have a good day or bad day? Many of the events in our lives, even when we have a good day, are unpredictable, often leading us in directions we couldn't have foreseen.

You may think you know what life is going to bring tomorrow, which instills some confidence about moving forward in your current circumstances. So why risk a change? But what if you're unhappy? The truth is, no one really knows exactly what life has in store for them, even in good times.

A well-thought-out change is not much more risky than what you are currently doing. If you feel that something else will make you happier, but don't think you can make the change, put your attention on examining it a little more closely. Sometimes just putting your awareness on what you desire is all that's needed to bring it to you.

Much of life is an unknown, so what's to lose by looking into something else that's also an unknown? It may just turn out to be everything you ever wanted. Be responsible, but put yourself out there to see what life has to offer you. By putting yourself in the mix, you're giving credibility to your hopes and dreams. You're helping to create the future you desire. You are giving the life you want the necessary energy to make it a reality.

Experiment with this in a risk-free way to see for yourself how it goes. Put your attention on what you want and believe you can have it. Take a few minutes each day to talk positively to yourself about what you want and to visualize it happening. Then spend some time pursuing it in a responsible fashion. Use the rest of your time to enjoy yourself without a thought about it.

By pursuing what you love, you may even find a job at a company that didn't even know it had one available. For example, you might visit a company that has a job you would like to ask if you can take a tour as an interested member of the community. Companies like to show people what they do and often provide tours. But be easy with yourself and unattached to getting a job. Don't conspire about how you might secure one. Just enjoy the tour and ask questions.

The person conducting the tour might notice how fascinated you are with the business and say they could use someone like you. Or if an appropriate opportunity arises, you can ask if they're hiring or suggest how your skills could work for the company. Maybe the firm didn't think about hiring anyone, but decided you would be a good fit after getting to know you. These types of things happen when you are enjoying yourself, but not if you're worrying and straining to make something happen.

Before you contact the company, try to make yourself feel as if you're already employed, because you don't want them to pick up on your stress about not having a job. Take the tour as if you're excited about knowing more about the company, but not feeling like you're in need of a job. This will help take the edge off. You will be surprised at what can come out of having some fun and asking a few enthusiastic questions.

But be open to the possibility that after the tour nothing may come of it, or that you may decide you don't want to work there after all. This is okay, and no time has been wasted, because you just narrowed down your options for your next job opportunity. Now you can happily move onto investigating other interesting opportunities. This is how to enjoy yourself while looking for what you would like to do, and it can be done just as easily in other areas of your life as well.

WITH CHANGE COMES GROWTH

Always anticipate change. The more things change the more they really do stay the same. You need to understand this on a very deep level, because change will always come. Just when you're comfortable with things, they will transform into something else. This is the nature of life. Even if it seems that they are the same, they are still changing in very subtle ways.

You may say, "But I really like the way things are going, and don't want them to change." Life will always change, but this doesn't mean that it will all be disagreeable to you. It may include change that's easy to embrace. But even difficult change is ultimately for your own good, because you need to have these experiences to learn and grow. It's required to keep humankind moving forward.

In the past, change was slower and more gradual, but today everything is moving very quickly. Much more growth is occurring now than in the past. Some of you may think that many of the changes happening in the world are making life worse. I know, because I had to struggle with this perception myself.

On one level this may be true, but on a deeper level, life is actually improving, because consciousness is growing in the world. Humankind's awareness is expanding. The greatest spiritual growth may still only be occurring in a small portion of society, but there are more people developing their consciousness today than in many thousands of years. Sometimes it's not so easy to see the good changes happening in the world, because they're hidden from view. But they are there if you look for them.

Try to be happy and don't worry so much about how life plays out in the world. God is aware of all that happens on our planet. It's all part of His plan. Ask to see the good things that are occurring and you will gravitate towards them, and they will begin to gravitate towards you. Even if many aspects of the material world appear not to be progressing, life as a whole is moving forward according to God's perfect plan.

God allows for changes in the world not so that we suffer, but because they are exactly what each and every one of us needs to move towards greater fulfillment in life. These changes are tailor-made for you, arising from all that you have done in the past. To deny this fact is to deny the existence of an all-powerful and all-loving God.

To deny that God is providing what's needed for your greatest progress in life will only hinder your growth, and prolong your suffering. If you can just accept that God never forgets about you and only provides exactly what you need, the sooner your life will become filled with peace and contentment. You can begin to move in this direction right now by doing one simple thing—accept that all is as it should be.

Don't fight against the changes that are happening around you, and don't stick your head in the sand either, because you need these experiences. Work on opening your heart and being more receptive. You are being taught to perceive things differently. You're being forced to become more flexible, so you can handle all your experiences in life more comfortably. It's all for your benefit.

The changes you're experiencing provide important lessons for the development of your consciousness. Fighting against them will only create undue stress and strain on your mind and body. By learning to fully accept what must come, you can be a beacon of hope for those who need comfort during the rapid changes ahead in the world.

When it appears society is taking a turn for the worse, do not doubt God's plan. That's the time for greater faith. You cannot say from any finite moment in time that God's plan has gone awry. In the grand scheme of things, all the necessary adjustments are occurring exactly as they should be for collective consciousness to unfold on earth. All of life is just the play and display of pure consciousness; don't be fooled by what's taking place around you.

There is nothing new under the sun—literally. Everything you are witnessing in the world today has occurred on our planet many times before. Even the most unmovable of things move. Land masses have come and gone. Vast bodies of water have appeared only to later disappear. Nation's boundaries have always changed. Peoples have shifted their locations. There's a constant ebb and flow with the tides of time, so be receptive to these changes in order to understand how they serve you.

This doesn't mean you shouldn't try to nip in the bud that which is bad in the world, however. You don't want to become fatalistic. But the events that have the momentum to exact change on our planet should not be worried over. They have come for a reason. They have come bearing gifts of greater wisdom and understanding for us all.

Life is eternal and no event at any particular point in time is so important that you should worry yourself over it. God is always aware of you and only has your best interests at heart. All the lessons you're provided are always to benefit your progress towards enlightenment. It's not always clear to us what the value is in these changes, but they have their precise purpose and the laws of nature are in complete control of them.

If you are struggling with change, ask yourself what bothers you about it. Then reflect on that reason. Try to look more deeply at what's causing you discomfort. Ask yourself what good can come from it. The value of the change rarely has to do with one person's or group of people's ideas winning over another's. It's usually much more basic than that, like the need to instill greater flexibility in our lives. It could also have to do with simply teaching people how to maintain their balance in the midst of rapid change. The superficialities usually don't matter, because the lesson is often so much more subtle than that—albeit important.

Even if you live in a volatile location where bearing witness to heinous acts is a common occurrence, know that there is a lesson in it for you. It's all God's will. In the ultimate scheme of things, it was required for you to witness. From the broadest perspective, it's exactly what you need to take the next step in your development.

Just follow your happiness and you will be doing all that is needed to help with humankind's spiritual evolution. To be happy is your only responsibility in life. Two people could be living right next door to each other in the same difficult conditions, but one is feeling completely uplifted while the other is suffering tremendously from the changes that are taking place around them.

The only difference between these two realities is the broadened perspective of the person who accepts the changes, and the limited awareness of the one who cannot see the value in what they're experiencing. If you have faith and believe that there's never a mistake in God's plan, you can maintain peace in your heart even in the midst of turmoil. If you resolve to see only peace and order in life, that will be your experience.

You might say, "But there is such decadence in the world. How can this be good?" You would not be here if you didn't need to witness decadence. It's not the refusal to see decadence that's required, because the decadence is surely present. There's a higher good that will come by your bearing witness to it.

Some of us need to learn how to remain calm while witnessing negativity. It's necessary in order to remain happy and content in any situation. It's part of our training. If you can maintain your equanimity under any circumstances, you have mastered life and will never suffer again—everlasting happiness will be yours.

The transgressors of natural law have their lessons to learn as well. They will receive the difficult lessons that inevitably must come with the performance of their nefarious acts, either in this lifetime or the next. There is no need to concern yourself over those who don't care about what's right and wrong, because they need to behave poorly. God allows them to act in this manner of their own free will, so they can learn their difficult lessons in the same way you had to.

The misery they bring upon themselves from their transgressions of natural law will be their teacher. Just go about your own life and know that they will learn their lessons just as you did. Follow your happiness, enjoy your life, and know that nothing is outside of God's awareness. He has established his laws to allow your actions to always meet with the perfect response for your ideal growth.

Be grateful when difficulties come, so you can get it out of the way and move onto something better. Nature's plan is unfolding exactly as it should. Don't doubt this. Know that your difficulties are just maya, illusion, for your soul never really suffers; the small you only imagines your misery. We all must go through trying experiences sometimes. Eventually you will learn to see through it all. This is why it's best to develop your consciousness now to limit your exposure to such false realities in the future.

You don't have to like all that's happening in the world, but to eliminate your suffering you must accept it. Those problems that cannot be immediately remedied are necessary for humankind's spiritual evolution. In time, those who participate in ugly, repugnant behaviors will receive the necessary lessons to teach them the value of participating in only righteous, uplifting ones. After immersing themselves in decadence and then reaping as they have sown, they will crave purity and only good in the future.

So don't strain against change. Embrace what must come. Everything in physical creation is ephemeral—it comes and goes. This is the nature of life. Don't partake in negativity. Choose to live a peaceful, happy life in accord with the laws of nature. Be patient. There will always be an opportunity to experience life the way you desire it to be.

Through your example of purity and poise, you will help others see their way to righteousness. Desire a peaceful, happy life and put your attention on having it. Your pure heart will guide you to where you need to be.

Be compassionate towards others. This does not mean you should accept wrong behavior, but always be compassionate and look out for others' well-being. Compassion is such an important virtue. To be compassionate is to show your heartfelt concern for another. Help others to see their way back to right behavior, but don't be attached to the results of your actions. Don't force the issue, just offer a more enlightened way when asked. If it's accepted—fine. If it's not—fine.

Just share the purity of your consciousness and always remain dignified. Regularly allow yourself to go within to experience your non-changing source in pure Being, because it will help maintain your peaceful existence whatever comes. Nothing can stop you from finding the contentment and stillness within. So transcend regularly and nature's intelligence will guide you to greater understanding and fulfillment, regardless of what's happening around you.

THE TRUTH IS NEVER LOST

If evil forces should ever amass against the truly righteous, then this will be the time to stand up and fight to vanquish evil. Although the wicked will be the first to blow their conch to initiate war, the righteous will always prevail in the end. When it's time to stand against evil, it will be obvious to those who have developed their awareness sufficiently; they will come in numbers needed to defeat the darkness. But it's impossible to fight for righteousness if the wicked are arrayed on both sides of the issue. When evil forces are fighting against one another, go your own way and enjoy your life in peace.

If you sense negative changes afoot, and the forces of good present are not adequate to stave off the darkness, then accept the inevitable changes that must come with the understanding that God requires it for your growth. There's hidden wisdom in everything. Tap this wisdom and allow it to lead you to greater peace.

Wait patiently for the rise of righteousness to come again and then ride that wave to victory as evil meets its demise. Righteousness and higher knowledge will always come again, because the Truth alone triumphs.[2] The Truth always prevails in the eyes of God, even if sometimes it doesn't seem to be the case in the physical realm of existence.

Nature will never allow pure knowledge to be completely lost. Each time throughout the ages that the Truth was nearly extinguished,

God produced an enlightened avatar to bring life on earth back in line with righteousness. The ancient Vedic literature tells us that during the current age, there are ten great avatars to come to earth. They included Lord Raam, Lord Krishna, and Lord Buddha. Each came when the times required all of humankind to be brought back into alliance with cosmic law at once.

Nine of these ten avatars have already come and gone. The last one to come during this cycle of time will be Kalki. It is said that when righteousness is on the decline, when many people no longer believe in God, and when depraved behavior is rewarded, Lord Kalki will come to destroy the lawless and bring life back into accord with righteousness.[3]

So don't worry so much over the future. Know that even an ignorant person committing unrighteous acts can be your teacher. Their unwise behavior provides important lessons about how *not* to act; witnessing their actions will help to instill the patience needed to maintain your balance in life. Trying to reason with an ignorant person about how they ought to behave is a waste of your energy. Don't offer pure knowledge to such people. Jesus said, "Give not that which is holy unto the dogs, neither cast ye your pearls before swine, lest they trample them under their feet, and turn again and rend you."[4]

If those of ill nature have taken up in your environment in large numbers, take heed. God is dropping hints that you may need to change what you expect from your neighbors, or to move on. All knowledge that is needed comes to those who are open to it, so always remain receptive.

If you find it becoming increasingly untenable to reside where you are, then begin to put your attention on the alternatives. You may find that all you need to do is change your way of thinking to maintain a happy existence right where you are. But if the demands of your environment are that you condone or participate in ignorant behavior, then it's time to think about looking for a new place to reside. You cannot halt the tide of change once it's gained enough momentum. So go with your flow in whatever direction is needed to maintain your peace and happiness.

DENIAL INHIBITS YOUR PROGRESS

Denial is one of the biggest impediments to growth. Some people want to deny change and the value of it occurring in their lives. Have you ever met someone who rejects anything new? People like this are the ones who suffer the most in life, because they cannot see that change is their salvation. They can't accept that God is trying to move them in a direction that is needed for their progress. When inevitable change comes, you must have the wisdom and foresight to witness it without losing your balance. This is the way to lasting happiness.

If you are in denial during rapid change, it causes great suffering and can often set you up to be blindsided. Those who have not prepared for it are vulnerable, because they haven't taken the time to consider the possibilities and are surprised when they arrive. Accept that change will always happen and that it is an essential part of life.

Avoid making polarizing judgments about what you experience in your day-to-day life; move towards acceptance. If you can instill greater acceptance in your awareness life will become more effortless. Progress in this regard did not come easily for me.

My karma and conditioning came together in such a way that I had strong likes and dislikes early on in life. The experience of people with strong feelings about anything is that they will necessarily find them challenged by nature. It's inevitable, because nature wants you to be able to maintain your balance no matter what comes. You can't experience peace in life if you're so attached to objects and ideas that you resist when it's time for them to change. If they're not completely evolutionary in nature, conditions will eventually arise to challenge your most inflexible beliefs.

Even if what you believe is of "some" value, it will be challenged in time. Nature will always bring circumstances to give pause to your inflexible opinions. Life is change. You must accept this. God wants you to learn to love the unseen so much that anything in the relative field of existence pales in comparison, because this is where your freedom resides. Only by repeatedly experiencing change will a love of the more subtle, unchanging, absolute field of existence settle in.

You can culture greater balance in life to maintain your peace through the direct experience of absolute Being. It will naturally adjust your perspective about the objects of your obsession. The experience of pure Being creates such lasting contentment in your awareness that you will no longer feel bound by ideas and objects of the relative field of existence. You will still choose the ideas and objects you desire, but without them having a binding influence over you.

By naturally becoming more flexible through direct experience of the transcendental field, you will no longer like or dislike anything in excess. As you develop yourself spiritually, you will become more and more aware of how to think and feel to maintain your comfort in life. With greater understanding of the absolute field of non-change comes the ability to thrive amidst change in the relative field of existence. You learn to avoid acting in a way that continually brings frustration and pain to your life.

One who is growing in consciousness begins to recognize the unproductive patterns in their life, and tries to find new approaches to eliminate the difficulties they cause. If you're a seeker of enlightenment, you don't want to be tense and agitated all the time, particularly from the same things over and over again. You want to live a harmonious life. But until you sufficiently develop your awareness, you're destined to be a victim of your circumstances, where your life seems like a football unpredictably rolling one way and then the other without you having any control over it.

When you are growing spiritually and evaluating yourself honestly, the deeper insights that come to you about how to live your life will provide you with great freedom. You will find yourself on a more even keel that will create peace in your heart. This is the way to great liberation in life.

KNOWLEDGE AND EXPERIENCE ARE THE WAY

You don't have to renounce your ideas and possessions to grow spiritually and gain fulfillment. You only need to modify your perspective about them. Your senses are constantly wandering to find lasting happiness in the physical world, but the happiness you desire can never come from objects of the senses alone. You can only find lasting happiness once your intellect gains contentment through the direct experience of the eternal nature of life. This is the way to open the floodgates to lasting fulfillment.

There's no better or quicker way to attain this state than through experience of pure Being. With the understanding of this field through *Sankya*, the intellectual means of gaining knowledge, and the direct experience of this field through *Yoga*, transcending during meditation, you will gradually develop the *resolute intellect*, which renders all pleasures of the senses insignificant compared to the eternal bliss of pure Being.[5] It establishes you in a state of eternal freedom, where your mind is no longer affected by the minor ups and downs of the physical plane of existence, because you are forever immersed in supreme happiness.

A few individuals have had brief glimpses of the field of pure Being without first culturing the knowledge and experience of It in their awareness. But this is a rare occurrence, indeed, which can only occur through a confluence of events, including a sufficiently pure nervous system and the necessary spiritual karma.

It should not be assumed that this will be the experience of everyone. In fact, those few who have had partial experiences of the field of Being, without first gaining proper knowledge or experience of It, can feel discomfort and confusion from their lack of understanding of Its nature. How would you feel if unexpectedly your awareness shifted in such a way that you began to feel yourself expanding far beyond your body, as if connected to everything in creation, and neither you, nor anyone else, understood why it was happening?

Even if one spontaneously gets a glimpse of the field of Being and then later gains some intellectual understanding of Its nature, it is still very unlikely they will be able to preserve this experience without the regular practice of meditation. It comes and goes for those who have not mastered the ability to systematically establish themselves in Being with both the knowledge and experience of Its nature. By transcending the gross fields of existence through the practice of deep meditation, you can experience the unchanging nature of absolute Being not just in flashes, but as a regular experience in your daily life.

FAILURE IS IMPOSSIBLE

Many people have high aspirations, but for one reason or another don't achieve them. This has caused much sadness and despair in people's lives for far too long. It's thought that you only have as long as your body survives to complete what you set out to do in life, and if old age should arrive first, then you have somehow failed. This feeling of limitation is a travesty to life.

Although our bodies come and go, you are always okay regardless of what happens to you, because you have an immortal soul. No matter what befalls your physical body, your soul lives on to incarnate again and again until you gain *moksha*, final liberation. Your destiny is much greater than you know. You *will* have everything you truly desire—this is a certainty. You cannot fail. You cannot lose. You cannot miss your opportunity, for it's inevitable that you eventually experience all that your heart desires.

Don't worry about whether you are doing all the right things. The right things will find you if you do what brings you the most happiness. Just enjoy the moment and everything that is needed will come to you. In the Book of Ecclesiastes it says that there is a season for everything. There is a time to be born and a time to die, a time to weep and a time to laugh, a time to mourn and a time to dance.[6] This is the natural progression of life. Everything comes in its own time.

All that you can possibly hope for will be yours. Either you will fulfill all of your desires, or you will get close enough to them to know that you really don't want them. But then grander desires will come to take their place. You have forever to be and do all that you hope to, so enjoy your life now. You don't have to wait any longer to be happy.

The material world has a transitory nature, with both a creation and a dissolution process. See life as a big motion picture with a beginning, middle, and end. You enjoy it completely as it's playing, but when it's over you leave the theater with the memories and insights you gained. Do the same with your life. All movies have to end, including the one playing out on the screen of your awareness.

Shakespeare wrote, "All the world's a stage, and all the men and women merely players."[7] This is entirely true. Enjoy the play, but know that you're just an actor playing your role in the cosmic production. This show too shall end. But the next one is sure to be even better if you will only let it. The absolute field of existence always remains the same, as does the happiness you gain from experiencing It. The Absolute is eternal bliss, so become acquainted with this level of existence to enjoy everlasting fulfillment in all the transformations of your life.

LIFE IS PERFECTLY BALANCED

Everything in life is perfectly organized. You will find that some good always comes with the bad, and you are better off for it. There is always progress even if initially it doesn't appear that way. From your trials arise fresh fecund sprouts of wisdom bearing the fruit of your greater understanding.

When you think you are losing, there's always some gain that comes as well. If you've lost a loved one, something else will come to fill the void left from your loss. There's always a balance. Nature abhors a vacuum. For example, you may become closer with someone who provides the emotional support your loved one once did, or you could find that you're actually freer and more at ease than you were when your departed one was alive. This is not an uncommon experience. Just be open to what comes.

You could find you've been provided the opportunity to develop the strength you needed to become more independent and self-sufficient, which is a requirement to progress to the next level. Always look for the gain when you feel that you've lost, because it's always there.

You will learn to recognize the balance that exists in life and how to bring yourself more in tune with it. Developing a cool head and warm heart is what's needed. You don't want your mind to burn anyone in your frenzied attempt to attain what you desire, nor do you want your heart to become cold and hardened from your difficulties. You will recognize more fully how to maintain this balance as you grow.

Even highly evolved souls experience difficulties, but they know how to maintain their grace in the midst of their troubles, because of the reservoir of joy that's always available to them. They're not overshadowed by hardship, because they have mastered life. A realized soul knows that everything they experience only brings them closer to the Truth. They know that their past actions have necessarily brought their current conditions, and they accept them for what they are.

When you can accept with contentment in your heart what is, you are on your way. You may not have done anything in the moment to cause a difficult experience to occur, but somewhere during your soul's existence you did. Accept that it is God's will: you need, for whatever reason, at the very least, to experience the emotions it has given rise to.

But, life is never as bad as you think it is. You believe your ego, the finite you, to be so important in the grand scheme of things that you toil away to protect it. That's okay, we all do it. Do yourself a favor and free your mind from the misunderstanding that you are the only one who makes mistakes or experiences difficulties.

If your error has in some way hurt another person then, yes, that person will probably take issue with you, but in most cases it's soon past and forgotten. You can make it pass even more quickly by accepting responsibility and trying to make amends with the person or persons affected. If you are not forgiven after making a genuine effort to right your wrong, then it's no longer your concern, because it was the other person's karma to receive the ill effects of your behavior. You don't want to share this with them, but know that it is true.

CELEBRATE BOTH LIFE AND DEATH

Think of the worst mistake you could possibly make. Say, for example, because of your own error in judgment you suddenly lose your life. You know what?—Halleluiah!—because you're now on your way to the Kingdom of Heaven, or whatever you choose to call it, which will provide you the freedom to enjoy your existence without a cumbersome body to lug around. In the afterlife you will find a reprieve from your bodily struggles, which will come as a huge relief.

You may be thinking, "But what about my loved ones?" You will have better experiences of your loved ones when you're out of the body than when you're in it. You will be more unbounded in nature and therefore able to experience their essence much more fully. You will be conveying to them in their dreams and quiet moments not to cry for you, because you love your new afterlife experience. Share this information with them now, so if you should die unexpectedly they will immediately know it's you that they hear and feel, and that you are alright.

When you grieve excessively for your deceased loved ones, you make it hard for them to enjoy the afterlife, because they feel your pain and suffering. Of course some grieving for your departed loved ones is natural, but don't carry on excessively. You're only making it difficult for their soul to enjoy the experience on the other side.

You may be wondering, "But what about violent death? How can anyone be comfortable with that, much less celebrate it?" The fact is, you don't suffer as you believe you would during this type of death. God created the experience of shock, an acute stress reaction, where your mind shuts down and doesn't fully experience the pain that you imagine you would under such circumstances.

Ask anyone who has had a serious bodily injury how it felt. If they're honest, they will say they didn't feel very much pain, because they went into shock. Your awareness closes down in order to avoid the suffering from such an incident, which is the same thing that happens during violent death. Through this type of experience a lot of karma is lifted from your soul, because it's a balancing of your past actions that requires you to lose your body this way.

If you die at the hands of another, the one who kills actually experiences more pain than the one who dies. When someone unjustly kills another, it haunts them until they too are able to release the karma created by their violent act. The dying is easy compared to the guilt and mental anguish the person who did the killing carries around with them. They may not experience it initially, but over time they will be worn down by guilt to the point where they must confront their feelings. It's unavoidable.

When you die, you wake up on the other side as if from a bad dream. It's exactly like waking up in the comfort of the familiar surroundings of your bedroom after a nightmare. But you happen to be on the other side. In short order you have shaken off the experience of your death to realize that you're safe and sound back in your eternal home from where you came.

I once read a story online about a little boy who was brutally murdered by his mother and stepfather. He was badly beaten and it was not a quick process; they did a number of unspeakable things to him leading up to his ultimate demise. There was actually a picture of this little boy, who I will call Joey, with the story, which is very unusual. He looked very tiny and innocent, quite similar to my own son at the time, which caused me to struggle all the more with his senseless death at the hands of those who were supposed to protect him.

I knew a lot of what I know now about life and death, but not everything. I intellectually understood the value of karma and its workings, but didn't yet fully own this knowledge. I was so angry and shaken by Joey's death that I immediately decided in my mind that I was going to hear directly from God why such a tragedy should have to occur. I was adamant that not only was I going to hear firsthand from God about why he had to die in such a horrible way, but that I was going to speak to Joey's soul to reassure him that someone cared about him.

I printed out the picture of Joey and resolved that he would not be forgotten like so much trash dumped at the landfill. I put my entire life on hold that day and sat down and closed my eyes with the intention that I was not moving until I heard from God in a manner that satisfied me about why Joey had to die this way.

As I sat, I began to insist that God tell me why this had to happen. I was steadfast in my demand and I was not stopping until I heard from Him. Nothing came initially, but I persisted. I wanted answers and to know how Joey's soul was coping after such a horrific experience. I needed to know that he was okay.

After about two hours of demanding with absolute certainty that God would explain to me why this happened, I still heard nothing. I pressed on tirelessly, insisting that I was not giving up. My mind was clear and my thoughts completely focused on Joey as I told him I loved him. I needed to understand, and I was certain that I would. On a very deep level I knew that a loving God would provide me with the information I needed to comprehend such a tragedy.

After three hours of complete focus, a very gentle but crystal-clear thought popped into my mind: "Joey's stepfather is Joey." This may seem cryptic to you, but it wasn't to me. I instantly knew what it meant, as if God had sent the thought to me in exactly the way needed for me to understand. Joey's stepfather was going to experience the same thing Joey did. Then I immediately had a vision of Joey's stepfather in a future life as a tiny, innocent child who was going to suffer the same fate as Joey had. My heart immediately went out to this small child.

My mind seemed to step back and then another thought came that someone somewhere was going to grieve as I had for a little boy who was senselessly murdered, without knowing that in a previous incarnation that child had murdered another little boy in the same way. This very clear series of thoughts about how karma plays out had an instant and powerful impact on me.

The thought then came that Joey did something similar in the past to deserve what he had experienced. Subsequent thoughts quickly ran through my mind that Joey's mother and stepfather were young and had their judgment seriously impaired by drugs and alcohol. I then had the thought that Joey may have been an overly defiant little boy who didn't know when to stop, even at the demands of two crazed and violent adults.

Nothing justifies his parents' actions, but having this series of vivid thoughts in quick succession, with all the images and emotions that accompanied them, completely diffused my anger towards them and my anguish for Joey. In a matter of a few short minutes, these thoughts had caused me to feel compassion for a child killer's soul and to understand how a young fragile boy in a past life sowed the seeds for his own violent death. I also was able to see how a young boy could behave in such a manner as to inadvertently prompt his own demise so that his negative karma could play out and be released.

As I sat and pondered what had just happened, one last thought came. The thought was that I should not grieve for Joey like this, because he is happy to be done with this karma and doesn't want to look back, but ahead to his next incarnation. With this I sat for a few minutes with what seemed like complete understanding as my heart expanded to fully accept God's plan.

I kept Joey's picture for a couple of days until I knew that I had to let it go for him to move on unimpeded by my unnecessary thoughts for his well-being. He doesn't want me to remember him this way, but as a soul that is now cleansed and healed with so many more happy and healthy lives ahead of him. I let Joey go when I disposed of his picture, but I will always hold him in my heart for the lessons that he taught me about life and death, the causes and effects of karma, and the value of the swift flowing river of perpetual change in our lives.

I have learned a lot since this experience. We are so afraid of death for ourselves and others, but really have nothing to fear. This notion of life and death is only a misperception on our part. The great avatar, Lord Krishna, said:

You grieve for those for whom there should be no grief . . .
Wise men grieve neither for the dead nor for the living.

There never was a time when I was not, nor you, nor these
rulers of men. Nor will there ever be a time when all of us
shall cease to be.

As the dweller in the body passes into childhood, youth and
age, so also does he pass into another body. This does not
bewilder the wise.

Contacts (of the senses) with their objects . . . give rise to (the
experience of) cold and heat, pleasure and pain. Transient,
they come and go. Bear them patiently . . . . That man indeed
whom these (contacts) do not disturb, who is even-minded in
pleasure and pain, steadfast, he is fit for immortality.

The unreal has no being; the real never ceases to be. The final
truth about them both has thus been perceived by the seers of
ultimate Reality.

Know That to be indeed indestructible by which all this is
pervaded. None can work the destruction of this immutable
Being.

These bodies are known to have an end; the dweller in the
body is eternal, imperishable, infinite.

He who understands him to be the slayer, and he who takes
him to be the slain, both fail to perceive the truth. He neither
slays nor is slain.

He is never born, nor does he ever die; nor once having been,
does he cease to be. Unborn, eternal, everlasting, ancient, he
is not slain when the body is slain.

One who knows him to be indestructible, everlasting, unborn,
undying, how can that man . . . slay or cause anyone to slay?

As a man casting off worn-out garments takes other new ones,
so the dweller in the body casting off worn-out bodies takes
others that are new.[8]

Don't worry so for those who have passed. We are all eternal souls and are never separate from the Creator. We actually have never been born, but only perceive it to be so when we mistake ourselves to be separate from Him in this relative field of change and diversity. We are always pure Being—nothing more, nothing less—and we will always live to see another day, regardless of the fate of these physical bodies.

Eight

I AM YOU

At the most fundamental level of our existence, we are all One. We are each an aspect of the underlying field of pure consciousness, so any problems that arise between ourselves and others are really only problems within Ourselves. Therefore, all interpersonal problems arise from the lack of awareness of our own unbounded nature.

Every part of life is connected to the Self. By expanding your consciousness, you will begin to experience a more intimate relationship with others and start to see them as an aspect of you, and you as an aspect of them. This understanding is what's needed to cultivate better interpersonal relationships with others.

LOOK AT YOURSELF FIRST

When you have difficulties with others, try to identify the source of the problem by looking at yourself first. Don't project your problems out onto others so much. See if there's something you're doing that's causing the trouble. Examine yourself thoroughly, and ask those who are close to you for their honest feedback about what may be causing your difficulties, because it's not always clear. It may even involve karma that's not directly connected with your present circumstances, in which case you may not be doing anything wrong at the moment, and just need to be patient until it passes.

By closely examining yourself, you allow for a reflective pause, which is very helpful before moving into the conflict resolution process. Many people immediately dig in and begin to reciprocate if they feel someone's causing them trouble. When faced with a conflict, they instantly take the attitude that they didn't do anything wrong and immediately start to do more of whatever caused the problem in the first place. This, of course, is of no help and only exacerbates the issue.

There are also some who will never even consider speaking about their feelings, which actually causes them to miss out on valuable life lessons. I am the type of person who always wants to know what's causing someone to act the way they do, and will often quickly ask them to share with me in this regard. But being overly direct can have its drawbacks too, because not everyone is comfortable speaking about their feelings, particularly if they are raw.

When I was younger, I would immediately try to resolve an issue when I sensed conflict, which would come across as too forthright to some people. Sometimes this approach only makes matters worse. In my desire to quickly get to the bottom of an issue, I would be so direct that it would sometimes come across as insensitive or confrontational.

Don't expect everyone to immediately want to resolve a disagreement with you by instantly offering up what's bothering them, because many people don't even know exactly what's irking them. What's more, when most people do notice from a conflict some fault that you, or they, could work on, they're typically already upset and not in the frame of mind for a quick resolution. Some people won't always tell you what's bothering them, because they are angry, scared, or don't want to be considered weak.

It's your responsibility to find your own faults and rectify them. This is why you have to honestly examine yourself to determine if there's something you may be doing that's causing your problems. As I grew as a person, I learned to consciously try to be more diplomatic when I have disagreements with others, but even today I need to sometimes watch how directly I approach them.

I honestly believe that if I wasn't trying to broaden my own awareness, I never would have realized this about myself. I would still be
stuck unconsciously following the same overly direct way of dealing
with conflict. Even the truth said in the wrong way can be hurtful. In
fact, with some people, it's the most hurtful thing you can say to them.

The main thing I've learned about communications is to avoid
crushing the fine feeling level of another. I learned this from Maharishi. You never want to hurt another person with your words or
actions. You always want to maintain their feelings even if that means
delaying discussing your concerns. It's not always easy to implement
this practice, but keep this idea of not hurting others in your awareness, to see how it can be of value in your personal interactions.

If you don't think you can handle discussing a problem with
someone without hurting them, it's better not to address it at all. The
ramifications of hurting someone are not worth the satisfaction of
trying to quickly resolve an issue. This may mean you have to refrain
from speaking at all until you can do so in a more diplomatic fashion.
You're not expected to master this skill immediately—I certainly
didn't—but it's something to aim for.

Back off for a while until you're calm. Try to reserve judgment
so as not to think the worst of the other, and just give the situation the
necessary time until you can address it appropriately. Trying to be
completely honest and to the point with others when a conflict arises
is not always helpful, even though you may feel you're open to both
giving and receiving feedback. Some people just don't operate this
way. They don't like handling conflict so forthrightly. But ignoring
the problem altogether is not helpful either.

Some people need to process how they feel about a situation
before dealing with it. A slower, gentler approach will usually gain
more ground than the let's-get-down-to-business approach. Unless
there's some compelling reason to resolve a situation immediately,
I suggest taking some time to think it through before addressing it.

SAY HOW YOU FEEL, NOT WHAT YOU KNOW

Sometimes you have no idea why another person is acting the way they are, or they don't want you to know. Either way, even if you're certain of the reason why the conflict started, it's best to be patient and approach the situation slowly without getting your emotions involved.

Sometimes *not* putting your finger directly on why a conflict occurred is best, even if you're absolutely correct in your assumptions about why it did. Some people don't want to know the exact reasons for their difficulties with others; they don't want to look at themselves so objectively. You don't want to make the other person uncomfortable or flustered, so you need to take your time.

By waiting before approaching an issue, you sometimes find the situation dissipates of its own accord, or maybe you realize that it wasn't important enough to address in the first place. You may even find it was only a misunderstanding on your part. The other person may not be upset with you at all, but rather with someone or something else. In any case, by giving yourself the necessary time to evaluate the situation, you will find that you're more settled and better able to address it, and so is the other person.

Trying to quickly show that you're not at fault, or that the other person is wrong, causes all kinds of additional problems when resolving a conflict. Insecurity about others not understanding your point of view is not a good enough reason to be hasty in addressing a disagreement. Allow yourself a moment to process the situation. If you don't know how the other person feels, then at an appropriate time simply ask.

If all parties want to resolve a conflict immediately and can do so calmly, then go ahead. But it's usually best to provide a little time for reflection. If the other person is pressuring you to discuss it right away, but you're not ready, then say so. Remember, the most important thing is to maintain the fine feelings of the other, so don't engage until you can do this. Wait until you can speak in a calm, pleasant way before engaging the other person. When you finally decide to discuss it, you need to speak the truth, but speak it sweetly.[1]

There are some conflicts where you don't even know what you did wrong or how to fix it, because the other person is not receptive to a discussion. They're just upset with you and want to remain that way without telling you why. Or, you could have a disagreement with someone you don't know, for example over the phone, or when you're traveling, who you may never see or speak to again. Even if you think you did nothing wrong, if someone is taking issue with you, it's an experience you need to have. So try to be as receptive as possible.

In situations where the other person is acting unreasonably, or not willing to consider a resolution, just try to absorb your anger and pain into your heart, without pushing back. Accept that it's your karma and try to move on without exacerbating the issue. You may find as you reflect on the situation that there *is* something you did that caused the conflict to arise.

Whatever the case, the disagreement included karma you needed to work through. Sometimes our karma involves only having to feel a particular emotion. There's no specific resolution forthcoming, because you just needed to feel that emotion. Of course you're going to defend yourself from an onslaught of abuse from another person, but try to do so as calmly as possible and without the intent to hurt them. If they are too unreasonable, then just remain silent or walk away.

There's a story from Zen Buddhist literature[2] of a young woman who was impregnated by her boyfriend. To protect his identity, she told her parents that a spiritual master who resided nearby was the father. Her parents became very angry with the master and told others in the community what they thought occurred, causing him to lose his good name.

When the baby was born, they went to his home and handed him the child. He accepted it without question. He knew that they were not ready to hear about any other reality, so he just took the child and the responsibility of caring for it as if it were his own.

A year later, the young woman confessed to her parents the identity of the child's real father. Her parents quickly went to the master to apologize profusely and retrieve the child. The master parted with it just as easily as he had accepted it. Soon his good reputation was restored and, in fact, he became even more highly regarded by the community than he had been before. Wouldn't it be nice if we could all take our troubles in stride like this, without immediately being thrown off balance by the misunderstandings we experience in our day-to-day lives?

This is an example of behavior that will diffuse any conflict, but behavior of this kind is only available to the most highly evolved souls. Those who know the most appropriate behavior for every situation are rare. But if you can begin to replicate this behavior of acceptance for even your smallest conflicts, you will experience much more peace and happiness in your life. We get so caught up in the right and wrong of a situation that we become more upset than we need to. In most cases it's better to keep the peace than to prove we are right.

There are occasions, however, when you are so upset with another that you need to try in the best way you know how to inform them of your concerns. This not only helps you to heal, but greatly helps the person who you have taken issue with to learn and grow; so try to allow for closure when you have a disagreement with another.

If you're a timid person who cannot tell others what's bothering you, it will slow down the growth of everyone involved—in the same way that being too abrasive does. If you're not comfortable resolving such issues verbally, then perhaps you can email or write a note to the other person to say that you wanted to make sure everything is okay between the two of you.

Your message to them could begin, "Hi ____, I just had a moment to think more thoroughly about the way I felt during our interaction earlier today...." Then write your concerns to the other person by using "I feel" statements: "I feel that you..."—then write what you're thinking. You don't want to assert that you know what the other person was thinking or intended at the time, because this only creates more problems. By using "I feel" statements, you will find that your words are much more easily received by the other person than if you claim to know exactly what happened.

"I feel" statements are just as helpful when communicating verbally. The other person is able to hear your words without feeling accused, which makes a resolution much more likely. It's very important to provide others the opportunity to resolve a conflict with you. It keeps everyone moving forward in life, so try to muster the strength to resolve your conflicts in order to allow for greater growth and healing. By speaking the sweet truth, most conflicts can be resolved amicably.

BALANCE OF HEART AND MIND

Some relationships can be especially challenging. For example, if your neighbor is a know-it-all and expresses dislike for you daily in both words and deeds, you could choose to reciprocate with contempt towards him or her, but it's not going to help and will only get your physiology in an uproar. Another option is to simply accept that your neighbor is a highly stressed individual who doesn't have the broad awareness needed to be happy enough to treat others with respect.

The last thing you want is to fight it out with your neighbor. More often than not, your neighbor is going to be your neighbor for a while. There's a lot of effort involved in selling a home, packing up, and moving to a new place, so it's best to try to get along.

Why not try an unexpected alternative: show your stressed neighbor some compassion and understanding. One can only treat a caring, compassionate person with anger and disdain for so long before it just falls flat from lack of reciprocation. Aggression is best dealt with by not addressing the aggression at all, but by trying to respond with friendliness and understanding. If you really want to have some fun, send your stressed neighbor a fruitcake or something with a nice note, and mean it. It will be well worth your time.

We all have a choice about how far we are willing to go to find reconciliation. If you find your efforts for resolution to be "fruit-less," then it might be time to simply end all communication with that person, even if they are a neighbor, or a family member. There's no law that states you have to maintain a relationship with a family member you can't get along with. You don't want your emotions thrown out of balance every time you interact with a person. If the relationship causes more harm than good, then it's best for all involved to end it, at least for a time.

Unfortunately, our modern society is filled with aggression, which is why our court systems are overflowing with lawsuits. Intellectual aggression in particular abounds in our communities and workplaces. It's a very common personality trait today.

Many people feel that those with a strong intellect are such valuable assets to have around, because they have quick minds and a lot of information available to them. But when you get the combination in a person of a strong intellect and a big ego, it's not an easy personality to deal with. In an advanced civilization, intelligence certainly is important, but raw, unbridled intellect that's not tempered by compassion will often be counterproductive.

Some of these people tend to become domineering and arrogant in their interactions with others. The assumption that it's necessary to have really smart people around even if they're ill-natured is not wise. Such people tend to be immersed in conflict and surrounded by those who harbor ill will towards them. They pride themselves on outsmarting others, while not stopping to think about how difficult their personalities may be to deal with.

A powerful mind should have its foundation firmly rooted in wisdom, which is a far more valuable quality than intellect alone. Wisdom is well-rounded intelligence with an abundance of knowledge, maturity, and compassion. The combination of a fine intellect and a good heart actually does exist in the world, but most of those with this personality type tend to be spiritual in nature, which has afforded them the necessary wisdom to balance out their soaring intellectual attributes. They represent the highest ideals of both heart and mind.

Great yogis have this combination very prominently established in their personalities. They have towering intellects, while remaining unbelievably humble in nature. This is a very appealing combination and creates great magnetism in those who possess it, which is why they often have many admirers and followers. Yogis who possess this personality type effortlessly command respect, even while maintaining the innocence of a child. It's really quite a magnificent thing to witness.

You want to aim for the expression of these same qualities in your interactions with others. There are so many aggressive intellects out there stirring up bad feelings today that every good person of intelligence should desire to be something more. Strive to be both smart and compassionate. This is how to become a gem among the masses, since there are so few who fully represent this harmonious balance in life. It's a blessing to meet someone who is both humble and sweet natured, but who also has a high IQ. They stand out as a point of refinement in a crowd.

I've been lucky enough to learn from a number of people who embody these qualities. They are individuals who have devoted their lives not only to gaining mastery over their occupations and fields of study, but to gaining full enlightenment. You should know that behind the scenes there are many enlightened souls in the world today. You cannot always recognize them by appearance, but there are more enlightened souls behind the scenes than there are in the public eye.

Our most enlightened personages uplift the world through their mere presence on our planet. While much of the world focuses on trying to turn small ideas into big money, the highest souls tend to avoid such diversions. They don't waste their time dealing with such trivialities. Many are blissfully content keeping a low profile while putting their attention on helping humankind in the most significant manner possible—by assisting in the development of global consciousness.

They are humble in their wisdom and compassionate, because they understand that the purpose of every action that one takes, even the unwise actions of a highly ignorant person, is ultimately to experience greater happiness. They know that even those who repeatedly perform bad actions are attempting to gain fulfillment, but are just acting from a level of ignorance.

Try not to be overly judgmental of others. Instead, bring the light to dispel darkness. Don't grope for a solution in the dark, but rather bring the light of your refined consciousness to bear on the problem. Keep yourself moving forward in a way that provides lasting happiness, while not counting on anyone to behave in a particular way.

When I was young, it seemed that I was surrounded by those who thought very much like I did. But as you get older and begin to interact with different kinds of people and experience new situations, you don't always find yourself in circumstances where your thoughts and behaviors are exactly in sync with those around you. With the pace of change and the speed at which new information is produced in the world today, divergent ideas and perspectives will necessarily continue to grow.

But know that everyone is just trying to find greater happiness and that this desire will ultimately guide their actions, whether good or bad, based upon their level of consciousness. Don't expect the next person to act according to your standards or expectations. We all view life through our own colored spectacles, so be receptive to variations in perspective in your interactions with others.

Until you know another person well, you should speak from a

broad and diplomatic perspective so that your words are not misunderstood. This will assist you in your day-to-day communications with others. It will also allow you to avoid any unnecessary conflict and to become more patient with others. Most people are not intentionally trying start trouble.

Don't let your spiritual development make you feel you know more than the next person. Being on the pathless path is so valuable and helpful to your well-being, but it's important to understand that it's an extremely rare incarnation who knows everything. There is just too much to know. As soon as you think you know it all, nature will humble you with circumstances in which you are not well versed. So don't push your ideas on others, and always be receptive to new and better ways of doing things.

It's easy to have a breakthrough in your personal growth and believe that you can conquer the world. But if you really understand all that higher knowledge has to offer, you will understand that humility is an essential aspect of a more fulfilling life. Try to be innocent and open to the next person's good ideas.

Never talk down to others with lofty platitudes. There is no quicker way to get someone to challenge your perspective than to be condescending. It will only bring conflict to your door. Sweet-natured humility will win the day every time, because your environment will be open and receptive to you and your ideas.

The meek really will inherit the earth, as described in the *New Testament*.[3] Meek doesn't mean weak, but rather moderate and reserved in nature. A meek person is someone who recognizes that the environment will be more receptive if they are both unassuming and wise. Even being perceived as overly proud or privileged could be considered by some as aggressive. To avoid unduly ruffling the feathers of those in your environment, try to be more understated. Don't strain to gain these qualities, because your insincerity will be obvious. Just have these ideas in your awareness and gently try to implement them in your day.

As your consciousness grows, you will begin to more easily recognize your own missteps in life. This will allow you to imbibe more of these good qualities into your nature. Modesty is a sign of your advancing spiritual development and evidence of the growth of wisdom. Others won't overlook your intelligence just because you are more reserved. On the contrary, they will be all the more drawn to your thoughts when you express them.

THE GOLDEN RULE

Always treat others as you would like to be treated. This is the Golden Rule as lauded by Christians in the West.[4] It's an old tenet of behavior that has been passed down for generations, and it's based upon sound wisdom. Don't overlook its value just because you've heard it so many times before. It is an invaluable guideline to use in your interactions with others, particularly when you're having trouble in your relationships.

The Golden Rule is based upon a deep principle that can be found in many religions. It can even be found in the ancient Vedas, which predate religion. In the *Mahabharata* it says, "One should never do that to another which one regards as injurious to one's self."[5] This maxim of reciprocity should be taken very seriously by all.

We all hail from the one field of pure consciousness. Therefore, treating others as you would like to be treated is actually treating "yourself" as you would like to be treated, because you're one and the same at the subtlest level. This is the reality of life, and as your consciousness grows, this idea will become much more real to you in every way.

You may think that your interactions with others are good, but everyone has moments of difficulty in their relationships. At such times, ask yourself if you are treating the other person exactly as you would like to be treated. Really think about it, and ask yourself if there's anything that you would want done differently if the tables were turned. Many people are not sufficiently aware to pinpoint exactly where the rub is in their relationships, even if they know they're not going well.

You would think that someone with boorish behavior would know exactly why they are having relationship issues, but often they don't. As mentioned earlier, if you're not sure why you are having such troubles, it might be helpful to ask a mature friend for their honest feedback. Listen closely to the feedback you receive to better understand how you might adjust your behavior to improve your interactions with others.

Meditation will make this whole process so much easier for you. By practicing real meditation for a few minutes in the morning and evening, you will naturally become more self-aware.[6] With each passing year of your practice, your relationships with others will improve.[7] There is a lesson in the Vedas that goes as follows:

Richo akshare parame vyoman
Yasmin deva adhi vishwe nisheduh,

The hymns of the Veda exist in the collapse of fullness in the transcendental field in which reside all the impulses of creative intelligence, the laws of nature responsible for the whole manifest universe.

yastanna veda kim richa karishyati
ya it tad vidus ta ime samasate.

He whose awareness is not open to this field, what can the verses accomplish for him? Those who know this level of reality are established in evenness, wholeness of life.[8]

This verse clearly expresses the value of regularly practicing meditation. Through your practice, you contact the transcendental field, the unbounded field of pure consciousness, and unlock in your own awareness the wisdom required to live a life in everlasting fulfillment.

COMMUNICATION STYLES DIFFER

Each of us has a unique communication style. Some of us are very forthright and others are extremely shy. The rest of us fall somewhere in between. Men are typically more forthright than women, but not always, because women have become more direct today than they once were. Regardless of how forthright you are, everyone is capable of being hurt. Women tend to be more open about showing when they are hurt by expressing their feelings more readily, whereas men, often unknowingly, hide their true feelings by expressing contrary emotions.

When a man is hurt, it may not always be obvious, because they often show anger to hide their pain. This is usually an unconscious behavior that has been conditioned into them. It prompts a tough facade whenever they feel scared or hurt. Emotional energy has to be expressed in some way, so when fear and pain are suppressed, it often shows up as agitation or anger. If you have a man spouting off in anger, it may well be that he's hurt in some way. Some of the angriest men are the most sensitive. Only as I've grown spiritually have I allowed more of my own emotions to show through. I try to let others know when I've been hurt by verbalizing my feelings, which I think is helpful for the healing process and the resolution of conflict.

Many women are often able to talk through their emotions during a conflict in order to feel better. They don't always need a particular resolution. The expression of their feelings is often more valuable to them than what is said. Most men, on the other hand, want to know the reason for a conversation about a conflict before they will fully engage in a lengthy dialogue. They need to know early on what the goal is—Where is it all going?

Of course, these are just general descriptions of how many men and women react during a conflict. It goes without saying that there are both men and women who express behaviors completely opposite to those described above. But for the sake of providing helpful insights, generalizations are sometimes needed.

The point I am really trying to make here is to be open to different communication styles if you want to improve your relationships. Many of your most important lessons in life are gleaned from interactions with other people, so try to understand where they are coming from. People are forever coming and going in our lives with valuable lessons for us, so it's important to learn all that we can from them.

I believe our interactions with other people to be so important that if I do have a conflict with someone, particularly if it's serious, when it's resolved, I will often thank them for the lessons they brought me. You are not accepting fault by doing this. You're merely being grateful for the positive impact that your exchange has had on your life. Any difficult situation is an opportunity to learn something about yourself, so pay attention. Acknowledge the value of your interactions with other people by showing gratitude for the lessons they bring you, even if it's simply acknowledging to yourself the value of what you gained from them.

FORGIVENESS HEALS YOU

Practice forgiveness in your life. A forgiving heart allows the healing process to begin. There is no need to go up to a person who you feel transgressed your good nature to say you forgive them, because in reality you only get what you deserve. Yes, that person may have chosen to treat you poorly, but in your heart you need to take responsibility for how others behave towards you. This allows you to heal, but also makes it easier for you to forgive them for their misbehavior.

In those situations where you can see that another person is suffering because of how they have hurt you, it's helpful to forgive them in person. But forgiveness is not so much for the other person as it is for you. By forgiving another, you are clearing your heart of stress and restricted energy.

At the same time, also try to get in the practice of saying you're sorry to those who you have hurt. Wounding other people's feelings, intentionally or unintentionally, is often what causes conflict to come to you in the first place. Saying you are sorry also allows you to forgive yourself.

For conflicts from long ago that still remain unresolved, it's helpful to write the person's name down on a piece of paper followed by what you would like to say to them. Write a sentence or two about what you want to express to that person to clear your heart and resolve the situation in your mind. After you write what was difficult for you using "I feel" statements, and what you want the other person to know, then be sure to write what you gained from the situation, and what you are grateful for. This last step may be difficult, but it is very important to create closure. It's particularly helpful to perform this exercise for conflicts that you no longer can resolve in person.

This will help you free yourself from the pain you are experiencing. Write both how the other person hurt you, and also how you may have hurt them. Probe deeply into your awareness and be totally honest with yourself to find a balance between what you lost and what you gained from the situation. Always be grateful for what you learned, because that's the reason you had the experience in the first place. This exercise will allow you to free yourself from any residual anger or pain you have not been able to let go of.

If an incident requires more than a few sentences, then write a note or letter as if you are going to send it to the other person involved. Research has found that you don't even have to deliver your letter of gratitude to the other person to gain the emotional benefits of writing it. The act of writing a letter of gratitude of any kind is considered by researchers as a valuable tool to increase your happiness, sometimes even for weeks afterwards.[9]

Remember you always receive exactly what you deserve—no more and no less. This is the inevitable law of karma in action. Harboring animosity for another person's actions only hurts you, which is why you need to release these feelings. You need to forgive the other person in order for your own healing to begin. If you can find it in your heart to do this, a great wave of healing energy will begin to well up inside of you. As this happens, tremendous gratitude will flow into your awareness about how perfect God's plan is for you.

If you don't let your pain go by forgiving others, you can become stuck for years or even lifetimes before finally letting it go. Anyone who has participated in wrongdoing against you will be provided an equal and opposite reaction for what they have done—you can be certain of this. Equal and opposite does not mean that bad behavior will bring good behavior. Rather, bad behavior will create behavior in kind, but traveling in the opposite direction with the same intensity as the behavior committed.

All wrongdoers at some point have to resolve their own karma. Divine justice is exacting in this way. Try not to worry if punishment is not immediately forthcoming to someone who has done you wrong, because it will always be provided at the right time and in the most effective manner possible.

Don't wish harm upon another. People perform wrong actions to learn and grow. You only inhibit your growth by holding onto ill will towards others. Wish instead for them to gain understanding about their wrongdoing. This realization will be hard enough for them to endure.

Try to learn to accept and act in a way that shows gratitude towards God for your blessings. He's always sending you solutions to your problems. He wants you to find fulfillment. Happiness is always there for you whether you're experiencing it or not. It's only because of the free will God has granted us to make our own mistakes that there is ever any reason to experience difficulties in our lives. Difficulties come to you for your highest learning, so accept them, be grateful for them, and move on.

Pay homage to God for your lessons. Pay your respects for everything you experience in life, since it's all needed for your progress towards enlightenment. Say that you are grateful for the opportunities you've been provided to develop yourself. Say it aloud or in your head to Him often. Your words of appreciation are freeing to your soul, because they show your recognition of His Divine plan.

YOUR DIFFICULTIES WILL SET YOU FREE

Your problems only come because you have transgressed natural law and need to be shown the proper way to proceed. By accepting this truth, you will be able to handle any difficulties that come your way much more easily. Some people even find joy in their difficulties. This is not a contradiction in terms, nor is it advocacy of any type of masochism. You can learn to feel peace even during moments of suffering, because peace is always present within you for the taking. You just have to choose peace over suffering.

I have had moments where life seemed excruciatingly difficult, when suddenly my awareness expanded to understand that I was able to step outside of my suffering to see that I had a choice to feel good or bad. I learned it was up to me to determine what my experiences were going to be. It's really just a choice. In every moment you make a decision about how you want to perceive your life.

At a time when nothing seemed to be going right in my life, I sometimes would get the feeling that I didn't want my difficulties to end, because I intuitively sensed I was learning and being purified by these experiences. I even found myself at times asking for more, for God to give me more of the same, so that I could experience greater growth. These were moments when I was able to glimpse the underlying workings of cause and effect in my life, which has grown as I've developed myself spiritually.

Many of our most difficult moments in life involve issues with others. These experiences allow your ego to dissolve and free you from your petty misunderstandings about being treated unfairly. You're never treated unfairly. It's just an illusion that you're participating in. All of life is just the play and display of pure consciousness.

But how you perceive it makes all the difference. Your pain is not real. Your bound awareness has only allowed you to experience pain, but in time, through your personal development, you will learn to be at peace even during the most severe pain.

For example, we can worry over our impending death, or we can feel the joy of soon being liberated from our finite body. It's all a choice. The more you understand that you can choose how you feel, the more you will be able to feel good all the time. When your time comes for death, tell those who are mourning your body's demise not to weep, for you are going to a place far more charming, without all the suffering of this earthly plane. Tell your loved ones that you actually grieve for them being left behind.

A DIAMOND REQUIRES PRESSURE

You are only able to incarnate into a human body after many previous incarnations as lower life forms. It is said that you have to incarnate eight million times before you are given the opportunity to incarnate as a human being,[10] which provides you with the only physiology on earth capable of allowing you to find your way back to your source in God. Think about what it would be like if you just began your first incarnation in a human body and had no difficulties of any kind to speak of. Everything you did was lauded and praised by all.

But let's say the actions you were performing while being praised were not good actions, but bad actions for both you and your environment. Would you learn anything from this type of life? How would you know what right behavior is, since no indication is being provided by your environment? This type of life wouldn't provide the necessary contrast to show you how to improve yourself. Your growth would be stunted if everyone only said good things about you, which would deprive you of the lessons needed to grow as a person. Be thankful for your difficult lessons in life, whatever form they come in.

I remember seeing a rich and famous person on television exercising really poor judgment in their behavior without a word of reprimand from anyone. It seemed this person was able to do anything they wanted, regardless of how ignorant it was, without anyone taking issue with them. We often give the rich and famous a pass for their poor judgment, because of all their other appealing qualities. But getting a pass for poor behavior is not helpful, because it doesn't allow you to learn from your mistakes. Fortunately, the laws of nature allow one to get away with bad behavior for only so long. In time, the necessary experiences come to show us a better way to live our lives.

The beautiful diamond is created from coal placed under the pressure of the earth's weight. You sometimes need to feel pressure from your wrong actions to develop into a diamond. Some may be able to act irresponsibly for a time, but nature eventually will help them right their wrongs through pressure of one kind or another. In fact, some famous people who transgress natural law may be having horrible dramas play out in their private lives without any of us even knowing.

Rest assured that those who seem to never have to take responsibility for their actions eventually do have to pay the piper. Otherwise, they would never grow. If someone is taking advantage of their good fortune in life, know that they will eventually reap the consequences of their selfish behavior, either in this lifetime or a subsequent one. By developing your consciousness in earnest, you can avoid experiencing the bad karma that you have set in motion.

The rich and famous have their fair share of difficulties. You may think going to work on a bad hair day is hard, but what if you're a famous person with a bad hair day for all your fans to see? You think having to suffer through acne in youth is difficult, but what if you had fans, reporters, and television cameras constantly focusing on you? This could make your skin problem seem far greater than it really is. You may think going bankrupt as a private citizen is difficult to handle, but think about experiencing it as a famous person where the media is talking and writing about it every day.

Rich and famous people have personal agonies just like the rest of us. A common stressor for rich people involves how to protect their money. Wealthy people think about this all the time. When you own a lot, you worry a lot about it. Let me give an example of a lottery winner.

We all have heard about people who won large fortunes in the lottery. I remember hearing one of them say during a radio interview that as soon as he learned his was the winning ticket, he immediately locked all the doors and windows in his house. The stress of ownership of all that money began immediately, even before he had it in his possession. Attachment and fear were instantly created as soon as he knew he had the winning ticket, which he had not experienced even one minute earlier. He now had something that needed protecting, first with the winning ticket and soon thereafter with all the money he was going to receive.

Some wealthy people drive themselves crazy thinking about how to protect their money and who they can trust to help them do so. Just think about how stressful it would be to hire a new accountant, financial planner, or lawyer if you were wealthy, since you count on their help to keep your money safe. Few wealthy people have the time or know-how to oversee their fortunes themselves. You would be concerned whether the accountant you hired was honest. Many wealthy people have been taken advantage of by those helping them care for their money. What a burden to life it would be to have to worry about this all the time.

How about the generous, compassionate soul who happens to have a lot of money? This person is constantly being nagged by their own conscience to help those in need. This may be a laudable desire, but it takes a lot of time to make sure your large gifts to charity are distributed and used correctly. Do you think wealthy people just donate large sums of money here and there without thinking through the details about how to make sure it's done properly? Maybe some wealthy people don't concern themselves with such things, but most pay attention to the details just like the rest of us.

This would get tiring after a while, particularly if you really felt deeply about the needs of others. How many families with dying children could you help with their medical bills? If you help just one, what about the thousands of others around the world who could use the same assistance? When do you say no? Can you say no? How do you decide?

Or think about the last time you went to a quaint café and had a nice private meal with a friend or loved one. What if you were too famous to ever have a quiet, spontaneous meal in public with friends and family? This would make your life very constrained.

Fortunately growing in enlightenment lightens every load, even those larger loads of the rich and famous. By developing your consciousness, you will begin to see freedom where before you saw none.

The lesson to learn about your possessions is not to be attached, because attachment only creates worry and stress. You can't enjoy what you have if all you think about is how to maintain possession of it. The fact is, you really don't own what you have. You merely are the overseer of it while here on earth. You can't keep it when you drop the body. You literally can't take it with you when you go. Material possessions don't go over so well on the other side.

It's just your soul that transmigrates to the afterlife. There's no need for material possessions, since your soul can manifest the likeness of what you desire with thought force alone. We are only the custodians of our physical possessions while here on earth, so it's necessary to learn how to enjoy them properly. What a waste of life it would be if you own so many valuable and beautiful things, but don't know how to really enjoy them. As your consciousness grows, you will naturally begin to lose your mental attachment to your possessions, allowing you to enjoy them without worry.

GOOD THOUGHTS, GOOD LIFE

You are the creator of your reality. Even if you find yourself in the company of those who are devoid of good qualities, you can still choose a better experience for yourself. If the people around you express negativity, you can choose to focus on what is positive. You always want to put your attention on what is good and uplifting to life, even if you are in the midst of what is bad. Doing this allows you to keep your mind in a happy place.

There's a story in India about a holy man who would only allow his mind to dwell on positivity.[11] He would only see the good in everything. One day, a very pessimistic man, who didn't believe it possible to always be so positive, invited him to dinner. His plan was to lead the holy man down a street where a dead dog lay rotting. It apparently had a very bad smell and was a quite a gruesome sight to behold.

As they approached the macabre scene, the pessimist gestured to the dog and said how repulsive it looked. He thought the holy man would cringe in disgust. The wise man's only response was to say, "But look at its clean white teeth." He only focused on the pearly white teeth of the dog, which was really the only positive aspect of the situation. It is so beneficial to try to emulate the uplifting behavior of such great incarnations in our own lives.

You have the ability to craft the life you want to live, because ultimately you determine how you're going to experience it. Begin today, no matter what your circumstances, to try to find the positive in everything you see and do. It will allow you to find good in places where you never knew it existed before, to create your experiences as you want them to be. Believe you can live a positive, happy, uplifting life and it will begin to be your reality. You can enjoy a fresh oasis of positivity where others only see a dry, harsh desert of negativity, if you choose to.

LOVE IS INSIDE US ALL

If you have been alone for a time and want a new love relationship, then be deliberate in your desire to find a companion. Think constructively about what you desire and begin to manifest it through the power of your attention. Those who want a love relationship, but are having difficulty finding one, are unconsciously pushing it away. You need to love yourself before anyone else can love you. You're not separate from others on the level of pure consciousness. The only separation that exists is in the limitations of your awareness.

By developing your consciousness, you will begin to break down the barriers that separate you from others. More and more you will begin to express from within very positive qualities that even you can appreciate about yourself. Once this happens, others will soon appreciate them too. These changes will naturally increase the affection others feel towards you. Similarly, as you develop your awareness, an affinity for others will increase within you as well. By expanding yourself in this way, you will be expanding your capacity for love.

To receive more love, you need to love yourself more. To love yourself more, you need to love others more. Either approach will bring more love into your life. But the most important one to love is the One that gives rise to all others. Love God. By deepening and broadening your awareness, your affection for Him will naturally begin to increase. You will experience yourself loving all aspects of His creation more and more—including yourself and others.

Likewise, when you are always critical of others, you will also be overly critical of yourself. And when you are overly critical of yourself, you will also be overly critical of others. Again, both behaviors produce the same result, which is a lack of appreciation for your own essential nature. By becoming more expansive in your perspective, you will naturally become more easy and loving towards everything, causing everything, in turn, to become more easy and loving towards you.

So expand your consciousness to expand the boundaries of your heart and unbounded love will be yours. As you are developing yourself, use positive, uplifting thoughts and actions to expand these qualities in your nature. Say to yourself, "I love others and they love me." Don't strain, just gently let these thoughts radiate out from your heart into your environment with the intention of encompassing all that is with your love. These easy, comfortable thoughts of love will bring in-kind feelings back to you. Anyone who can learn to love more can bring more love and affection into their life.

THE INVINCIBLE YOU

If others are making you feel small and dejected, ask yourself how this experience serves you. Work through this difficult experience by quietly showing your detractors that such behavior will never overshadow who you really are. Try to avoid feeling sorry for yourself, because whatever you get from others, you have given to others in the past. Your acceptance of this fact will mitigate your difficulties tremendously.

Regardless of how you're treated, you are never going to be less than whole. The real You is expansive, and untouched by such things. Politely ignore those who are causing you trouble and soon they will lose interest. You don't need to lash out with excessive pain and anger at them, even if their treatment causes you embarrassment. Being embarrassed is not going to wreck your life, because there's an invincible You that's untouched by these experiences.

The real You is resilient and has the ability to handle anything that comes your way. It is said that "time heals all wounds," but time is not required to heal your wounds. You're already healed. You just want to believe that time is needed for you to feel better. You don't think you deserve to be healed and whole right now. But you already are.

Say to yourself, "Everyone likes me, and I am healed." Visualize this reality in your life. You actually are healed now, because the real You was never hurt. It's only the illusory you, your ego, that's hurt. The real You is always pure and untouched by it all. Put your attention on being healed now and this reality will be yours.

If you still are having doubts about yourself and feeling tormented, think about something that makes you feel better in order to shift your awareness to a more enjoyable state of mind. Think about anything that makes you feel good. You need to lighten up during difficult times and put things in perspective; sometimes that requires doing something to immediately make you feel better. When I was a young boy, and afraid of the dark, I would think about cartoons to forget about my fears.

Once when my brother and I were visiting our cousins' home, a big, old house that was quite spooky at night, I invented the cartoon technique. One evening I had to sleep in a separate room away from everyone else because of the way the bedrooms were arranged. There was me, one of my brothers, and our four cousins to accommodate in the upstairs bedrooms.

To a young boy, the bedrooms seemed to be really far apart and the old wood floors creaked when you walked on them in certain areas, which made it seem really spooky when it was dark. It was a nice home, but this didn't help when I had to sleep in a secluded bedroom all alone in this unfamiliar house. It wouldn't have been so bad if the entire morning wasn't spent with my cousins creating a haunted house in the basement, which we used to terrorize the neighborhood kids as they toured through. Then in the evening, just before bed, one of my cousins, who was several years older than my brother and me, told us horror stories until it was time to go to bed.

It was very dark in the house at night, and there were all these really deep closets in the bedrooms with real doors on them. I don't know about you, but real doors with doorknobs on closets in bedrooms scared me when I was little. They seemed like doors that things could happen behind without you knowing, like the opening and closing of secret hatches. Something could hide behind them without being detected.

Regular, skinny louver doors on closets were not so scary to me, since they're flimsy and normal and what you would expect on a small closet. You could hear the labored breathing of a monster in a small closet with skinny louver doors and know to run for your life. But these were not small closets with skinny louver doors. They were deep, dark ones that had real doors with real doorknobs on them.

The ceilings in the bedrooms were really high, with lots of dead space up there—enough for ghosts to fly around. There also seemed to be a lot of dark empty spots throughout the hallway at night—you know the way old houses have a lot of inefficient dead space in them. There was one stairwell in the front coming up to the top floor, which everyone frequented, but there was another really dark stairwell that went down the back of the house that no one ever used. It had a door to the outside at the bottom of the first flight, and another set of stairs after the landing down to the basement door, the haunted-house basement door!

The bedroom I slept in was right near this back stairwell, with no other rooms as a buffer between me and what seemed like a good stairwell for someone, or something, to use to snatch a little kid from his bed. I was terrified. I wasn't sure I was going to make it through the night, but I was too proud to tell anyone how scared I was. It was going to be a long night, so I covered everything but my eyes with the blankets and pillows.

My imagination began to spin out of control. Every little noise heightened my senses and put me on alert. That night would have been much worse if it hadn't been for all my many years of watching cartoons. When I was on the verge of descending into pure terror, I started to visualize scenes from my favorite cartoons in my mind—*Bugs Bunny, The Road Runner, The Flintstones*, even *Scooby Doo*—but only the funny scenes with no ghosts or ghouls. If it wasn't for these funny memories, I'm certain I wouldn't have slept a wink that night.

This is a lighthearted example of what to do when times get really tough. Don't just wallow in your scary, depressing thoughts about what may or may not happen. Think instead about something lighthearted or funny. Develop your own cartoon technique. Do whatever it takes to occupy your mind with something that's uplifting and takes your attention away from your difficulties. In mildly difficult circumstances, you should be able to just think good thoughts and make your way through, but in the most difficult circumstances you may need to literally block your bad thoughts with something uplifting.

Another thing to do when dealing with difficult experiences is to try to remember the last time you were in a similar predicament, because you almost certainly have a number of incidents from your life where you thought at the time you would never make it through, but you did. You learned from these experiences that you can always move past your difficulties, and you will again.

Try to remember how you initially worried over these experiences, only to realize later that you didn't need to. You have probably heard the saying, "What doesn't kill you only makes you stronger." These sayings stick around because they're for the most part true. But their logic always breaks down at some point, and this one is no exception—even if an experience did kill you, it still would make you stronger, because your soul learns from every experience, including those that literally kill you!

Use any uplifting technique you have at your disposal to push through your difficult moments, until you're stronger spiritually, which will sustain you in any situation. As you grow, you will find that your increasing wisdom bolsters you during even the most difficult times. Developing your consciousness and gaining higher knowledge removes a lot of fear from your awareness.

If you start to feel stagnant, you know it's time to redouble your efforts to gain more knowledge. As you seek higher knowledge, higher knowledge will make itself more available to you. Little awakenings from new things you learn are what keep you moving forward in your spiritual evolution.

When you are really growing rapidly, you may find yourself choosing the documentary over the movie and the lecture over the ballgame. It's as if you become a sponge for knowledge. You may even begin to prefer talk radio over listening to music on occasion, because the knowledge you need comes from these informational media more readily. Take it all in and enjoy your growth. When you're intending to grow spiritually, all of life will become interesting and full of lessons and value for you.

God wants you to grow in wisdom, because it will sustain you through thick and thin. Over time you will find yourself longing for new knowledge if you haven't gained any in a while. As you put your attention on having it, God will send it your way. This is how He supports your spiritual development. God provides some of His most powerful insights to you through spiritual knowledge.

As your consciousness develops, even old spiritual lessons will continue to come back to bring greater understanding, because you will fathom deeper truths in these spiritual principles over time. This is the beauty of higher knowledge: it can be understood on many different levels. It's like peeling away the skin of an onion to find ever deeper and more powerful wisdom the farther you go.

The spiritual pearls of wisdom in Maharishi's commentary on the *Bhagavad-Gita* are more like this than any knowledge I have ever read. His commentary comprises the first six chapters, which contain the kernel of the *Bhagavad-Gita's* wisdom. There are more commentaries on this book than any other ever written. There's such profound knowledge available within its pages that it has inspired lovers of Truth throughout the ages to try to describe it in their own words.

I feel that Maharishi's commentary is really extraordinary, because he clarifies many misinterpretations that have been made over the past several hundred years. You can witness firsthand the amazing thought processes of a great sage by following along verse by verse as he expounds on the knowledge of the ages. Maharishi describes the *Bhagavad-Gita* as the highest spiritual knowledge understandable by humans, and if you are lucky enough to read it, you will see why.[12]

Maharishi's *Bhagavad-Gita* commentary is not just another spiritual book to read. You need to have the necessary karma to approach this one. It's not so much a book that you read, but one that reads you. It's the only book I know of that you can't just pick up and read whenever you want to. It seems to choose when you will read it. Only when it's the right time for you to take in more of its immense knowledge will it make itself available to you.

The first few times I read it, I asked myself, "Why don't I read this book every day? This is the book of all books." But I eventually realized that I could only read it when I was ready to uncover wisdom that had been previously missed or incomprehensible to me.

I believe that his commentary is the most important spiritual work in hundreds of years, and it's the only book I know that edits itself while sitting on the shelf. You can read it one time and then go back later to find it takes on a whole new meaning, particularly if you're rapidly growing in consciousness. Maharishi explains in minute detail how Lord Krishna quickly raises Arjuna up to full enlightenment. It's a book that should not be missed by any genuine seeker of the highest knowledge.

I remember watching Maharishi answer questions live via satellite video several years before he took his *mahasamadhi,* or consciously departed the physical plane, in 2008. At the time you were able to email in real time any questions you wanted to ask and they would be read to him on air so he could answer them live. Questions were coming in from around the world, and some people were asking about issues regarding the pros and cons of war and military service, since it was in the early years of the Iraq war. He was asked if fighting for a righteous cause exonerates you from the karma of killing another person in war.

These questions appeared to be coming from some serious-minded people, perhaps some of them serving in the military at the time. They were not taking one side or the other in the conflict, but they seemed to be genuine questions about the karma incurred by fighting for a good cause. Some of the questioners were referring to Maharishi's commentary on the *Bhagavad-Gita* as a reference. I remember thinking, as it seemed the questioners were, that you would not incur sin by fighting for a righteous cause.

But Maharishi, without even a pause after the question was read, replied, "Killing is a sin no matter who is killed." I thought this was strange, and I am sure those asking the questions felt the same, because it seemed they were just trying to get verification of what they already knew to be the answer. I was puzzled, because I thought I knew the answer to this question as well, since nearly the whole of the *Bhagavad-Gita* is devoted to bringing Arjuna to enlightenment in order to more effectively fight to protect righteousness, even if that meant killing others.

I opened my *Bhagavad-Gita* concordance and tried to find all the places where he may have said this in his commentary, which had been written nearly 40 years earlier. After a few minutes, I found exactly the same words that he used during the satellite transmission to answer this question. I was surprised that I had not noticed this point in his commentary before.

The words he used for his answer were the same words written so many years earlier: "The act of killing does not produce life-supporting influences for anyone at any time. Killing is sin for all time. No matter who is killed, killing is sin."[13] He didn't elaborate further, because perhaps he knew that those asking the questions needed to hear only this aspect of the knowledge.

But if you read on in his commentary, in a later chapter he makes it perfectly clear that this only applies to the unenlightened. You can overcome the binding influence of your actions to gain invincibility by becoming established in Yoga (union), "whereby the intellect... will be eternally established in the oneness of life, in the oneness of absolute Being, the eternal liberation in divine consciousness here and now."[14] He says this is the way to avoid all sin.

I found this experience very inspiring, and it reminded me of something that Dr. Bevan Morris had mentioned a few years earlier. Dr. Morris is a leader in Maharishi's worldwide organization and has spent many years with him. He once said that when Maharishi repeats a phrase in exactly the same words as he has in the past, he is not simply remembering what he said and then reiterating it again. He is actually cognizing it at the moment he's saying it, as if for the first time.

He said this is how an enlightened sage communicates pure knowledge. He is established in Being and expresses it from that level each and every time anew. I found that fascinating and saw its proof in Maharishi's answer to this question, some four decades after writing these same words.

THE PURPOSE OF PAINFUL MEMORIES

You may occasionally have memories come to mind from your past that are painful to remember. Some of these memories may remind you of hurtful conflicts you have had with others. You probably would like to forget these events completely, but for some reason they keep coming back to nag at you again and again. This happens so you can learn the lessons from these difficult experiences that you have refused to fully look at.

Sometimes we don't understand the lessons that are being provided when the initial experience occurs. That's why memories of it come back to us over and over again, because as we grow we can look more deeply and honestly at it to learn what we need. It comes back to refine our awareness into a fully polished diamond.

You need the proper understanding of these experiences to move on to the next level. Your most difficult experiences don't come back just to cause you pain. On the contrary, they come back for you to learn how to relieve your pain. By gaining the correct understanding of these experiences, you can quickly let them go forever.

Don't be afraid to take a fresh look at your difficult memories, so you can learn what is needed and get on with your life. If you don't know what the lesson is, then just take responsibility for what you have experienced and be done with it. Submit yourself to God by accepting what has happened to you.

Even if you were not the one who started the trouble, by taking responsibility you will feel God's healing power begin to release you from your pain. In time, what you needed to understand will become clearer to you. But if you take responsibility now, you will no longer be haunted by the memories of these events because the healing process will have begun.

Memories like these come to help expose the part of you that feels the need to defend itself. In time this process will allow you to discover the real you, your higher Self, so you can once and for all see that you are not tarnished by your experiences, and don't have to hide from these memories.

Just accept that you mistook another aspect of your Self—a person or thing—as something separate, which caused you to feel like a victim. Try to accept all your experiences. It doesn't matter if you didn't do anything in this life to deserve what happened to you, just take responsibility for it. The higher wisdom that comes from your acceptance will afford you great relief.

Once you take responsibility, you can go on with your life in serenity. Often just contemplating how to take responsibility for your difficulties will allow you to see what you couldn't before. It sometimes allows you to quickly focus in on the lessons you were missing. Once you're able to acknowledge responsibility for all your difficulties in life, they will cease to be difficulties and your anguish will subside.

Try to see your painful memories as humorous, because they're really not as serious as you think. You will realize this as you begin to release your pain and then look back on them. View these memories as silly slapstick comedies from your ignorant past. Don't beat yourself up over them. Allow yourself to "look at them and then release them. Hiding from the reality of these memories only perpetuates your pain.

Don't let your painful experiences cripple you. Be easy with yourself about your past. You may have done something stupid that caused a difficult situation to arise, and you're reluctant to accept how foolishly you behaved, because of what you think it will say about you. But this makes no sense, because we all sometimes make unwise choices in our lives. Don't be afraid to accept responsibility for yours.

Everyone, even the most successful and dignified among us, have had difficult moments in their lives that evoked feelings of insecurity and inadequacy. Just learn the lessons being offered and let them roll off your back. They are just the diversified images you are projecting onto the screen of your awareness. The real You cannot be touched by them—no matter how bad they may seem.

Our past experiences are nothing to be overly concerned about. What happens to your body is not what happens to you. In actuality, you are the ever-fulfilled, silent witness, uninvolved with the experiences of the body. Your past doesn't say anything about you now. It may say a little about you then, but who cares because it's over and done with and you have learned from it.

Again, you are not sullied or degraded by your experiences. Regardless of what happened, it was needed to provide you with important insights. Just pull yourself back into the moment and start enjoying your life again—remember, there's no past, there's no future, there's only now. Now is all that matters.

For those who perceive themselves as living a life of destitution with no apparent way out, know that you're just fine. For those who are lonely and yearning for companionship, you're fine too. For those who are suffering from illness with death knocking at the door, you're perfect, because there's never an end to your immortal soul. You will come back again and again to enjoy and accomplish beyond your wildest dreams. It's all exactly as it should be to provide for your greatest understanding. Try to look past your pain and suffering to perceive this truth.

I was told Maharishi once said, "Everyone thinks that death is the end, but it's only the beginning." We are only experiencing the surface waves of our nature in our relative lives, which find their origin in the vast ocean of pure consciousness. We imagine ourselves separating from the Source, but we're never really separate at all. For just behind the scenery of this physical world is the reality of your infinite, eternal nature.

Begin to develop your consciousness so that you can have this experience in your daily life. Develop your awareness so you can wake up to the reality that your essence is pure bliss consciousness. You have only been entranced by the lights and shadows of material existence. Your mind and body possess all the resources necessary to experience the divine Totality—and the awareness that you are me, and I am you. Choose the status quo if you want to continue to struggle, or choose to develop your consciousness and live a life in lasting fulfillment. The choice is yours.

Nine

YOUR SEQUENTIAL AWAKENING

You understand now that your greatest fulfillment can only come from doing that which comes naturally and easily to you. This is the only way of living a happy life. Don't worry so much over your problems. Don't worry so much over society's problems. Take care of yourself, of course, but don't worry so much about yourself. Go in the direction of least resistance and the rest will just take care of itself. There is a natural flow to life, and you need to tap into it in order to progress in the quickest and easiest manner possible.

Don't wrestle with what is. Accept what is, but keep your attention on that which is more uplifting and brings the most happiness. If things are not as you would like them to be, find something else to put your attention on that brings the fulfillment you desire. Don't strain to live your life. If you are experiencing difficulties, stop to recalibrate yourself to the moment, and put your attention on something that's more uplifting to you.

YOU'RE THE CENTER OF THE UNIVERSE

Don't let negative thoughts infringe on the happiness that you've created for yourself. Understand that you are a growing, fully self-sufficient aspect of the Almighty. There's nothing you must do but that which brings joy to you each and every day, because your ultimate purpose in life is to be happy.

Even if no one else is doing what you want to do—do it anyway. If you are happy thinking and working on your own, do it. If you are happy working with others, do it. You are that important. Believe that you are the center of the universe and everything in life revolves around you. All of creation exists for your pleasure. You are flawless no matter what you do, even if it turns out you're doing it all wrong, because you will learn from your errors. As long as you are happy and your actions are uplifting to you and your surroundings, you are in the natural flow of life. Be conscientious and try to play your role well—this will help bring peace to your heart.

When you feel yourself tensing up, insecure, or agitated, you're no longer in line with your purpose. You have lost touch with the simplicity of life. When you begin to worry over things, it's only because your life has become more complicated than it needs to be. There should always be an ease to your life. It should not entail undue stress and strain.

I know this may sound unrealistic and grandiose to some of you, but if you can just move in the direction of greater comfort and enjoyment, you will feel so much more contentment. It will allow more joy to naturally well up inside of you, and your life to become so much simpler and more successful.

Think what it would be like to forever be in love with your life. Think what it would be like to forever be in love with those around you. Think what it would be like to forever be in love with yourself. This state of love does not come from having everything go your way. It comes from pursuing what makes you happy, but accepting what comes.

There is no bigger waste of your energies than choosing to fight against what life brings you. Don't worry if everyone around you is behaving in a way you're not comfortable with. Just choose to do what makes you happy, which may include changing how you view what bothers you. I know this is easier said than done, particularly if you're only trying to attain this state from the level of your thoughts. It's far easier to achieve by transcending to expand your awareness and naturally arriving at this way of thinking.

Anger, frustration, agitation, jealousy, etc., are not pleasant emotions to experience. If you are experiencing negative emotions on a regular basis, maybe you need to go someplace where you don't have them. It may take some effort initially to change your thinking or your environment, but try you must.

What you put your attention on grows. If you put your attention on bad things, you will feel bad. If you put your attention on good things, you will feel good. Turn your TV off if what you're watching is making you feel bad, or at least turn it to a station that portrays life in a more uplifting manner. Stop doing whatever you're doing if it makes you unhappy. Many people are so ready for this change. They are longing to feel better. Just make the decision to do it and start on your way.

You can begin to live a happy life right now, or you can push it out over many lifetimes. But eventually you have to be happy. All your experiences in life are exactly what you need at exactly the time you need them. Life doesn't miss a single opportunity to give you what you need for your greatest growth. Once you accept this truth, you are on your way to a better life.

Allow yourself to believe that you are perfect in your imperfections. God has ordained you in consciousness as a soul worthy of a human body. You have come so far to have achieved this status. You're at the pinnacle of earthly existence. You have so little to go to reach complete fulfillment. Enlightenment is at hand. Believe this, because it's true. You have gone through so many life forms and now you have the quintessential body to gain enlightenment. Don't ever allow yourself to feel inferior or insignificant. Immediately cauterize these thoughts from your mind when they come. Know that you are Divine in every way.

TO STRUGGLE IS TO DIGRESS

If someone is treating you poorly, ask if there is something you can do to make their life more comfortable. If it's something simple and dignified then just do it, so you can get on with enjoying your life. It's not worth the struggle to do otherwise. Don't waste your time struggling to stop what you don't like from happening around you. If you can't correct it without unnecessary strain, then it's not worth your energy.

You can reduce many of the difficulties in your life in this way, but don't expect to eliminate them completely, because some of them will choose you due to your past actions. But you don't have to struggle with them, and you definitely don't have to create more for yourself. You don't want to bring more hardship to yourself by choosing to do that which creates more difficulties. If you don't know what causes your suffering, remove the stress from you physiology that's blocking you from seeing it.

Lasting happiness comes to those who consciously focus their attention on it. Broadening your awareness to better understand this truth is the way forward. All other methods have failed again and again. If it were as simple as thinking our way to a happy existence, we would all have done it long ago. You need to tap the source of your happiness to regularly experience it.

Only by developing your consciousness can the deeper values of human existence be fully understood and lived in daily life. This is the Truth today, and it will be the Truth 10,000 years from today. The commonly accepted methods for achieving lasting fulfillment have proven unsustainable, because they are based upon incomplete knowledge.

It's because of this lack of knowledge that people are now longing for the Truth. They are longing for a way to attain lasting fulfillment in their lives. By repeatedly experiencing only that which is bad, we begin to develop a desire for what is good. This is the nature of life.

The reason why people continue to act out of accord with nature is that they are trying to find lasting fulfillment in their lives, but don't know how. They have incurred so much stress in their mind and body that it blocks their ability to see what's needed to bring fulfillment to their lives. They keep trying new and different ways to find it, but to no avail.

It's a failure of society's institutions when people cannot find lasting happiness in life. It's a failure of leadership. When people behave poorly and society begins to decline, it's because of a shortcoming in the leadership of the nation. But out of decay comes new life. Maharishi has said that we are indebted to the sinful, because their actions are what prompt God to bring life back into accord with righteousness.[1]

You only need to uplift yourself spiritually to find your way back to happiness. This alone will do far more good for society than fighting against negativity could ever do. By increasing your individual capacity to act rightly, you gain personally and add to the upliftment of society. Spend time developing yourself and your influence will bring far greater benefit to humanity than any political activism could ever accomplish.

Focus on what's good for you and good things will manifest for you. This is the principle of the second element that Maharishi so often referred to: bring the light to remove darkness. Do not focus on what you don't want, the darkness. Rather focus on what you want, the light, which naturally removes darkness.[2]

The more you put your attention on negativity, the more negativity you will experience in your life. By constantly focusing your attention on what is bad, the more malefic things will develop around you. If society would spend more time focusing on the good things in life, our planet would begin to grow and flourish and the bad would quickly fall away.

ABOUT DOING EVERYTHING

Until you read this book, you may have thought what many people do, that meditation is just sitting quietly with eyes closed doing nothing. But meditation is in fact about sitting quietly with eyes closed doing everything. Meditation allows you to experience the source of life from where all thoughts and actions arise. This experience guides you to what will bring the greatest success in life. There's no better time spent than practicing meditation, because using the infinite intelligence of nature to achieve more success is all you could possibly ask for.

The repeated experience of pure consciousness during meditation allows you to increasingly experience spontaneous right action.

There's nothing more valuable to life than the development of your consciousness through deep meditation. Continued practice facilitates higher states of consciousness, broadened awareness, and greater success in all you do.

Meditation allows you to gain deep rest for both your mind and body, removing the stresses that impede the effective functioning of your nervous system.[3] The removal of these blockages provides the broadened awareness,[4] enhanced thought force,[5] and physical dynamism needed to perform highly effective action in your day-to-day life.[6]

The U.S. Centers for Disease Control attribute up to 90 percent of all doctor visits to stress-related problems.[7] Taking a few minutes a day to practice meditation to remove stress from your physiology is well worth the time.[8] It's a simple, natural way to maintain better health[9] and develop your full potential.[10] It will also allow you to grow towards enlightenment in the most efficient manner possible.[11]

We are not meant to struggle and strain to complete our daily activities. Slow down and be quiet on occasion by learning how to meditate. Be still and know that you are God.[12] You're not just some small, insignificant part of God's creation. You are an intelligent aspect of Him, with complete access to His infinite potential through the transcending process.

Your individual soul is a finite aspect of the unbounded field of pure Being. But each individual aspect of this field has access to the intelligence of the entire field. Each point is fully self-referral to its infinite source. Two elementary particles on opposite sides of the universe provide a perfect example of this underlying, self-referral field of pure intelligence in action. When one changes its spin, it instantly communicates with the other, which simultaneously changes its spin to match its partner.[13]

There's a continuous feedback loop between the parts and the whole of the unbounded field of pure consciousness, which is how the field remains fully awake to Itself. In this same way, you, as an aspect of pure consciousness, have the capacity to access the full creative intelligence of God, and you will increasingly do so as you expand your awareness.

We are just scratching the surface of what's possible in life. As we grow in consciousness, our thoughts will take on greater power and coherence. A physics professor once explained an experiment to me: a ball is placed in the middle of a room and participants are asked to go into the room one at a time to move it one foot away from where they found it to try to get the ball as far away from its original position as possible.

The participants can't see the various placements of the ball before they enter the room. If the researcher tells 100 participants to enter the room one at a time to each move the ball one foot, when the experiment is completed the ball will have moved on average ten feet from its original starting point. This type of experiment is representative of individuals in the normal waking state of consciousness who cannot see all the knowledge that's currently hidden from them.

But if an experiment was set up where 100 participants were to go into the room one at a time and move the ball one foot away from the place they found it, knowing where the ball started, they could very easily move the ball exactly 100 feet from its starting point. This is possible because they have expanded knowledge of where the ball started, which makes them more coherent in their actions than the previous group. This is similar to the actions of those who have developed higher states of consciousness, and gained access to more knowledge for greater progress in life.

By developing your awareness, you expand the container of knowledge, which gives access to solutions you didn't even know existed. Meditation pushes out the envelope of your awareness to allow for greater understanding, so your thinking becomes more powerful and efficient, allowing you to do less and accomplish more.

THE CYCLES OF TIME

The Vedas tell us that there are different *yugas* or cycles of time that our planet progresses through. They are four in number: a dark period of ignorance and low intelligence, called *Kali-yuga*; a period of discovery of the invisible forces of nature, including the advent of electricity, called *Dwapara-yuga*; a period of advanced intelligence and comprehension of nature's subtlest energies through the increased power of the mind, called *Treta-yuga*; and finally a golden period of all knowingness, an age of enlightenment, called *Sat-yuga*.[14] Some consider these cycles to be very long periods of time, the shortest of which is the Dark Age or Kali-yuga period, which is 432,000 years in duration.

According to these calculations, we have completed just over 5,100 years of the 432,000 Kali-yuga period. This sounds a little scary, since it means we have just begun an unbelievably long period of darkness. But others say there are much shorter yuga periods, which provide tastes of each of the four yugas within a 12,000-year time frame. I happen to believe that shorter yuga cycles exist, because I think it's unlikely that humankind would survive 432,000 years of unabated ignorance and darkness. What this shorter yuga system indicates is that each of the four yuga periods come and go in sequence as follows: Kali-yuga, 1,200 years; Dwapara-yuga, 2,400 years; Treta-yuga, 3,600 years; and Sat-yuga, 4,800 years.

Swami Sri Yukteswar, who was the guru to Paramahansa Yogananda, calculated these smaller cycles and described them as having an ascending 12,000 years in the sequence of Kali-yuga, Dwapara-yuga, Treta-yuga, and Sat-yuga, and then a 12,000 year descent in the following sequence: Sat-yuga, Treta-yuga, Dwapara-yuga, to Kali-yuga. The ascent and descent comprise 24,000 years in total. This is more representative of the history of humankind, since it includes both good and bad yuga periods within a more reasonable time frame.

Sri Yukteswar explained that we are currently on the ascending side of the 24,000-year cycle, a little over 300 years into the Dwapara-yuga period. This has allowed us to discover the subtler forces of nature, including electricity, which brought the advent of the industrial age, and has now progressed into the era of technology. We have a little over 2,000 years to go to complete the Dwapara-yuga period before beginning Treta-yuga.

The preceding, smaller Kali-yuga period would have ended around 1700, which corresponds closely to the broader historical descriptions of when the Dark Ages ended. This was an uncivilized period in history where war was common and humankind was too base to grasp the concept of the subtler forces of nature. Life has improved significantly on our planet over the last several hundred years. The masses are no longer living in a constant state of poverty or engaged in a perpetual state of hand-to-hand combat as they were in earlier centuries.

The Dwapara period we find ourselves in will culminate in the complete expression of all things electronic and technological as a prelude to the 3,600-year Treta period, which will entail a great expansion of our mental faculties. We can even see glimpses of these immense powers of the mind being utilized by some of the geniuses of today, but they will become even more prevalent in the future. Look to the children and you will find an increasing expression of these mental capabilities.

We are also seeing more people beginning to establish themselves in higher states of consciousness than ever before in recorded history. These achievements of both mind and spirit are going to become much more common. Humankind's consciousness will continue to increase throughout the Dwapara and Treta periods, culminating in the Sat-yuga period, or Age of Enlightenment. In Sat-yuga, we will not only express our full mental capabilities, but also use our maximum spiritual capacities. There are no limits to what we are going to achieve over the next several thousand years.

We are moving upwards to better times for the world. There are very good things to come with regard to human life on our planet. We are going to experience a rise in consciousness in coming centuries that will allow life to be lived more and more in accord with natural law. This is why there are increasing opportunities for people to develop themselves spiritually, which will continue unabated for many, many generations to come.

I hope this instills some optimism in you concerning our planet's future. I believe this description of the yuga cycles to be accurate, since I feel God would not doom humankind to 432,000 years of darkness without a reprieve. It would make no sense. We are moving into a time of higher knowledge and greater spiritual development for all, even if there are still a few hiccups along the way.

THE FRICTIONLESS FLOW

We are going to see great progress on our planet even in the next few decades, which is why our spiritual growth is speeding up. It's as if a videotape is running on fast-forward, speeding ahead faster and faster as it gets closer to the end. In our case, we are speeding up humankind's progress towards unlocking our full potential. We are gaining more knowledge and accomplishing greater things as we ascend towards higher levels of human development.

The rate of growth of human consciousness is expanding very quickly now. Once we reach a critical mass of people who are experiencing higher states of consciousness, improvements in the world will come even faster across the globe towards an ideal way of life for us all. What we are witnessing now in regard to gaining knowledge is just the beginning. In the not too distant future, we are literally going to take a quantum leap in our ability to gain knowledge, which will continue to expand at a faster and faster pace for thousands of years.

But there are smaller steps to be taken first, including many more technological innovations to make life easier and more efficient for us all. In order to move information around the globe quicker and easier, our technology has to improve. You will know we have made great progress when the way we disseminate this information no longer includes the use of print media. But our computer and Internet technology will have to make great gains in this regard before people become comfortable with the complete elimination of paper.

I have spent nearly my entire adult life regularly using a computer both at work and at home. I have also had a cell phone, website, and several email addresses for much of this time. But I really don't like the effects of spending so much of my day using electronic devices, particularly the wireless ones, because of the electromagnetic radiation that they expose me to. When I am overexposed to these energies, it makes me feel gray, both physically and mentally.

I am fairly sensitive to the energy that flows through many of our technological devices, and cannot be around them for long periods of time without it agitating my physiology. The most disconcerting part is that although anyone who is near these devices for long periods is receiving the same negative side effects that I am, most people are unaware of it.

The energies that flow through many of these devices make them unhealthy when overused. Wireless technologies in particular are of great concern because of the greater risks. There is a growing body of research indicating that the electromagnetic radiation from these products is harmful to your health. The radiation emitted by wireless technology will not burn you, but it's strong enough to give scientists great concern about it causing biocellular damage or even cancer. This, according to Dr. George Carlo, who oversaw the largest research program to date on the dangers of wireless technology, with over 200 physicians and researchers involved in a total of 56 studies, and peer review participation by the Harvard School of Public Health.[15]

You don't have to stop using these devices, but you do need some time away from them each day to maintain good health and to experience your own power without interference from technology. There's no need to live an austere life to get away from these items for a portion of your day. I reserve time every day to be completely away from anything having to do with technology, just to free myself from their subtle energies.

Today I still prefer to receive many forms of information via paper products. For example, I like to hold a book, magazine, letter, or even a marketing piece in my hand when I'm reading it. Not that I have enough room to keep all of these materials around for future reference, so all of it, except the books, eventually wind up in the recycling bin.

But even though I prefer reading a newspaper to surfing the Web for my news, I have been getting almost all of it online for years now. I just suffer through it, since it's so much faster and easier than sitting down and paging through a large format newspaper. The uses for technology are only going to expand, so we just have to keep making them healthier and more comfortable to use.

Our interfaces with these technologies have to be improved before we all become seriously ill from overexposure. My eyes have taken a beating since the advent of computer technology, which I'm sure many of you have experienced as well. The research is in and it shows very clearly that staring at a computer monitor all day causes eye problems. Computer Vision Syndrome (CVS) is a growing epidemic,[16] and data from the National Institute for Occupational Safety and Health indicates that 88 percent of those using computers for more than three hours a day suffer from eyestrain.[17]

But the way we access information online via computers is going to greatly improve, and the harmful energies that run through these devices is going to continue to be reduced. Microchips and other components will continue to get smaller, faster, and more efficient, which will reduce the warm energy fields they emit. In the not-too-distant future, we will have massive amounts of information coming to us at mind-boggling speeds, but through far healthier technologies. Gaining knowledge is going to become quicker and easier than even the most strident technology advocate can imagine today.

As far as paper materials go, soon we will be receiving the information we currently get through this medium from interfaces that are much more appealing. Many products that used to be found on paper are now being viewed on browsers and other customized interfaces like those used for e-books, for example. But in the near future you may well find all information, including what's currently only available on paper, accessible without your even having to sit in front of a monitor. If the technology continues to advance and drop in cost, and the safety concerns surrounding lasers are reduced,[18] you will be viewing this information via holographic technology.

Viewing a 3D holographic image that has the same vibrancy and color as a printed piece would be amazing. Great advances still need to be made, but I feel the excitement around holography will continue regardless of the hurdles that need to be overcome, particularly since it greatly mirrors the way in which humans create their own physical reality in consciousness. New technologies are not just created to make life easier for humankind, but to open our own awareness to the potential that's within us already.

As technology advances, so must our own human capacity to keep up with it. For this reason more than any other, I believe that holographic technology will find its place in mainstream applications. It's a near-exact replica of our own ability to view the field of pure consciousness in the ever-changing phenomenal forms that we do. We literally project physical creation into existence in the form of a hologram. We are not aware that we do this, but in the future we will learn how to do it *consciously.*

The field of science has started to describe the existence of this holographic reality in the combined research of the eminent physicist David Bohm and Stanford neuroscientist Karl Pribram.[19] But much greater breakthroughs are yet to come. This is why I feel that the only way we would skip this phase of technology is by developing our own inner ability to physically manifest anything we wish, which would render the development of holographic technology unnecessary.

If this technology ever becomes commonplace for displaying information in homes and businesses, initially the format will likely resemble that used by paper products, probably starting with the standard format sizes we have today. Not because it has to be these sizes, but because in the same way that the width of roads and cars was determined by the width of the covered wagon, holography will probably start this way when being introduced in the forms of books, magazines, marketing materials and the like, to make the transition more palatable.

You will probably be able to view these materials in a similar fashion to the way you do print media today, with the option of viewing two sides to simulate turning a page. But it will be a hologram you're manipulating instead of paper. If holography ever becomes a usable technology, it will have to include all the color you currently get from a printed piece, but with the added benefit of taking up nearly no space in your environment. Vast amounts of this information could be stored digitally, and imagine all the trees that will be saved when paper is no longer needed for moving and storing information.

Think about the information that comes to you now via your mailbox. This could instead come to you via holographic technology, but directly into your home with the added feature of you being able to quickly scan through these items for relevance. What's not relevant could be quickly and easily deleted.

Information coming to you via technology in the future will be much easier to read and far less stressful on the eyes. I am still reluctant to read e-books using the latest custom interfaces. It's just too uncomfortable for me to look at yet another electronic screen for long periods of time, but they are improving. What's great about holographic technology, if done correctly, is that it will be healthier, because it uses three dimensions as opposed to two, which is far easier on your eyes than the screens that we currently use.

When a holograph can come to you in informational formats that resemble books, magazines, and newspapers, with the readability of paper products, and without the negative side effects of our current technologies, you will learn to love it. Some of us may be dragged kicking and screaming into the future, but once we get there, we will be glad we are. In the future, technology will not only be a valuable tool, but a comfortable aid that you will enjoy using every day of your life.

We're not going to allow ourselves to become more and more inundated with monitors, gadgets, and gizmos that are unhealthy for us. It is all going to get much better. The technology of the future will become so good that it will seem like it's not even there, which will help to provide the necessary silence needed in our lives. Greater efficiency and silence are the goal, because it's required for our spiritual growth.

As the time it takes to acquire information continues to decline, the more refined our human capacity to gain knowledge is going to become. Through our technological advances, we acclimate ourselves to taking in information faster and faster, but we are only at the beginning stages of how efficiently knowledge will be gained in the years to come. By developing our consciousness, the rate at which we access information will increase to the speed of light.

In the future we are literally going to *jump conduit* to gain knowledge without the need for a device of any kind, at least not an electronic one. This leap ahead will include capturing information via direct apprehension into our own biocomputer, our human brains. All information already resides in the field of consciousness anyway. We only need to tap it directly via the expansion of our own awareness to eliminate the need for technological devices of any kind.

There's no computer more powerful than our own astonishingly exquisite gray matter. We are currently using only a small percentage of our brain's capacity. Once we manage to unlock its full potential, we will be able to gain knowledge instantaneously.

This is already being done by a small segment of the population in a very limited way. For example, researchers at the University of California, Irvine have documented six cases of *hyperthymesia*, a condition where a person displays superior autobiographical memory. If you provide these people with any date from their past, they can instantly tell you the day of the week and exactly what they were doing on that day.[20] It's as if they were experiencing it as it happened all over again, including the emotions attached to the events of that day.

Those who have this ability say the information just comes to them as if being downloaded into their awareness. It comes before they can consciously think about how to obtain it. They don't use a mnemonic (memory) device to recall this information. It just appears in their mind once they settle upon the day they want to remember. The ability to instantly access data in this manner can only come by pulling it from the infinite reservoir of knowledge within the field of consciousness. In the future, people will be able to do this with any knowledge they desire.

Our increased capacity to gain knowledge won't just include the intake of more trivia from some finite data server somewhere. It will involve accessing all knowledge available within the vastness of our infinite awareness. This will allow us to take in not only incredible amounts of information, but to attain huge amounts of pure knowledge as well.

We are rapidly moving into a time where all knowledge is going to simply be downloaded from the cosmic server directly into our minds. Our ability to do this has already been scientifically demonstrated with over 25 years of Remote Perception Research in hundreds of documented experiments at Princeton University.[21] We don't need to become some kind of human-computer cyborg, where we're part human and part machine like in the movies. Our technology is currently a very crude representation of what our own awareness and biological systems are capable of accomplishing. What's more, having a lot of electronics attached to our bodies would be extremely unhealthy.

As humankind progresses, technology will begin to reflect more and more our own biology by adapting to and mimicking organic systems. We will learn to create new and better technologies that are nearly, or even completely, biological in nature. But in the years to come, the need for typing and manually manipulating data with our hands will disappear, because the last, most advanced stages of technology will be controlled with our thoughts alone. There has been quite a bit of Pre-Stated Operator Intention research with humans manipulating machines already, indicating that this can be done now in a rudimentary way.[22]

Eventually, we will go beyond technology to access all information via the medium of our own pure awareness, without the need for outside help of any kind. Technology will climax with the realization that we can instantaneously create everything we need from within our own consciousness. No wires, no buttons, no receivers will be needed, just our own magnificent human physiology.

This will entail using our enormous human capacities to not only gain any knowledge we desire, and manifest any object we wish, but to create any state of happiness we choose. Humankind has very exciting times ahead—we should feel blessed to be able to look forward to such an unbounded future for ourselves. If you choose to be, you can be present during the full expression of these outstanding abilities in human life. Have your attention on it and develop your consciousness in order to be worthy of incarnation during the full realization of these natural human gifts.

TO BE OR NOT TO BE

Maharishi, in his *Apaurusheya Bhashya*, has described how all of creation comes out of pure consciousness through the sequential unfoldment of the sounds of the *Rk Veda*, the foundational document of Vedic literature.[23] He said that the verses of *Rk Veda* represent consciousness creating from within itself to give rise to all of material creation. He explains that the first syllable, Ak, is the starting point that then gives rise to all of the diversity of relative existence. The first sound of the first syllable, "A," pronounced with wide-open throat (Ahhh), is representative of infinity, which then comes to a complete collapse of the throat in "k," (ka) the fully closed point value of the second sound of the first syllable.

He explains that the first *richa* or verse containing nine words— *Agnim ile purohitam yagyasa devam ritwijam hotaram ratna dhatamam* —is just an elaboration on the first syllable, Ak, and that the whole of the Vedic literature is an elaboration on the first richa. The sounds of the *Rk Veda* represent the actual sequential unfoldment of creation being produced from within the silent gaps of pure consciousness between the syllables. In this way, every fragment of creation is lively with the totality of natural law and always self-referral back to its source in pure consciousness.

All the knowledge you could possibly want or need is already available within your own consciousness, as expressed in the first syllable of the *Rk Veda* from A to k. The rest of the *Rk Veda* is simply an elaboration on the full range of the first syllable from infinity to point, or from unmanifest consciousness to the manifestation of all the diversity of creation. This is why you are never without pure knowledge, because it's always available to you within your own self-referral awareness.

Our own human body arises in the same way that other aspects of creation come out from the invisible gap of pure consciousness.

The human body is created by your soul's intention to manifest from within the field of pure consciousness. The intelligence that gives rise to the structure of your physiology resides within the unmanifest gaps of your DNA.

Pure consciousness provides the intelligence for your DNA to create your body within the womb of your mother. It may seem unusual to some that your body is created within this confined space, now that you understand it's actually unbounded pure consciousness that gives rise to human bodies. You might ask, "Why don't bodies just fall out of the air, since they don't need anything but pure consciousness to produce them?" Although this may seem like a more unbounded perspective, it is actually more limited because of your illusion of the solidity of your mother's body.

The human physiology seems finite to the unaided eye, with its outer edges providing a fleshy outline to the body. But if you were to look closer with a powerful microscope, you would see that looking at the body is very similar to looking into outer space with a telescope. The human body consists primarily of the invisible intelligence within pure consciousness, with very little physical matter to speak of, much like the fragmented consistency of galactic space.

Physical objects viewed in this way have confirmed that even what appears to be solid to the naked eye is mostly just empty space, with a few vibrating subatomic waveicles filling in the void so that we see what appears to be solid matter. You will recall that the actual substance of an object is only a fraction of what it appears to be to the human eye; the rest is composed of the invisible intelligence of nature. This is the reality of our phantom bodies.

Everything in physical creation at its basis is pure energy, with a few smatterings of dense matter where it seems to have crystal-lized. The mother's body and the baby in her womb are no exception. Consciousness coagulates into grosser and grosser levels of physical reality by adjusting its vibration to create what appears to be matter. These increasingly manifest energy fields are what we see as material objects, and in this case the flesh and bones of mother and child.

A mother appearing to give birth to a newborn baby is nothing more than one intelligent concentration of energy giving rise to another intelligent concentration of energy—or the field of pure conscious-ness creating and giving birth from within itself. Viewed in this way, the mother's womb, being the location where conception and birth take place, makes perfect sense. This is where the creative impulses for making babies happen to exist in the field of consciousness. From within your mother's womb, your soul's intention to manifest a body is acted upon in the most amazing manner to sequentially give rise to an embryo, then a fetus, and finally your fully developed body as a newborn baby.

As discussed previously, Maharishi had some of the world's most important scientists and thinkers visit and talk with him. The story of one of these visits was conveyed to me by a much older, longtime student of Maharishi. Many years ago, while meeting with a world-renowned scientist, and discussing the nuances of human biology, Maharishi told this scientist that DNA can be altered at the level of your own consciousness to heal a sick body simply by means of a new intention. This famous scientist, expressing some frustration, was unable to comprehend how it could be done, since all of his training had been in the field of objective science.

But shortly after completing his conversation with Maharishi, his son, a scientist himself, visited Maharishi to ask how to do it and quickly grasped the idea. He has been a student of Maharishi's ever since. Once it is understood that your physiology is created completely from pure consciousness, it necessarily follows that you can change any aspect of it with a new intention, in the same manner that you created it in the first place. You are the creator of your reality in every respect, including your own body.

IMMORTALITY OF THE FLESH

You have only forgotten your vast powers through your conditioning. In fact, you are always renewing your body. Due to the illusion of time, you have allowed your body to age, but there is really no need for this process to occur. Your cells, organs, and bones are constantly being recreated, such that what appears to be your static body is actually a continuing cycle of renewal and regeneration from within the intelligent field of pure consciousness.

You only age because you think that with the illusion of time you are supposed to. On a very subtle level of your awareness, your physiology is being recreated as you believe it should be. You think you should grow older, so you do. But the aging process does not have to occur, since you can also provide the intention to your DNA not to age. You can begin the process at any time to consciously intend your body to become healthier and more youthful.

There is a jellyfish—*Turritopsis nutricula*—that has cell *transdifferentiation* capabilities that allow it to revert itself back into an infant jellyfish at will. This ability has made scientists believe it to have the potential for immortality.[24] But a jellyfish, as with everything else in creation, gains its creative abilities from cosmic intelligence just the way you and I do. We can also tap this most fundamental field of intelligence to set into motion the regeneration of our own body's cells in such a way that we become younger or older as we wish.

Babaji, the great *param-paramguru* (guru to his guru) of Yogananda, is claimed to still be walking the earth after hundreds of years of life in a human body. Yogananda had a portrait drawn of him in which Babaji appears as a young man in his twenties even though he's centuries old. According to Yogananda, Babaji continues to live on, century after century, to help the spiritual teachers of the world fulfill their roles here on earth.[25]

It's only a matter of cleaning the lens of our own consciousness to master this technique. Once you develop your consciousness to the point where you are able to believe beyond any doubt that you can live in your physical body forever, it will become a reality. The question is—Will you want to? You may prefer to incarnate elsewhere in order to bring greater variety to your existence. As mentioned earlier, there are many options available to your soul after growing to enlightenment. Upon your body's death, you can choose between many dimensional realities to continue your existence. Jesus said, "In my Father's house are many mansions."[26]

There is no reason why you cannot do anything you wish to, since all that's needed is a powerful enough intention. By learning to tap into deeper and more powerful aspects of nature's intelligence, you can master doing and being all that you desire in life. In coming years, humankind will learn to perform miraculous feats with a mere intention, even gaining the ability to re-grow damaged or lost limbs like the salamander.

The celebrated physicist, James Jeans, said:

The old dualism of mind and matter . . . seems likely to disap-

pear, not through matter becoming in any way more shadowy or insubstantial than heretofore, or through mind becoming resolved into a function of the working of matter, but through substantial matter resolving itself into a creation and manifestation of mind.[27]

All possibilities exist within our own creative intelligence. Some people are even orchestrating their own spontaneous remission from malignant cancers by having the intention at a very subtle level of their awareness to heal themselves. There are now a number of such documented cases. These experiences are difficult to explain using object-oriented science, because phenomena of this sort are given rise to within the subjective field of consciousness, which is beyond the scope of objective science. Experiences like these will become more common as the collective consciousness of our planet rises.

The Nobel Prize winning quantum physicist, Max Planck, said:

I regard consciousness as primary. I regard matter as derivative from consciousness.[28]

CREATED IN THE IMAGE OF GOD

When you begin to experience how simple and easy it is to bring your life into alliance with natural law, you will understand the immense possibilities that are available to you. The 3-in-1 structure of pure consciousness gives rise to all of creation through the interaction of the qualities of knower, known, and process of knowing. From the self-interacting dynamics of pure consciousness, all of creation comes out. As you develop your consciousness within, cosmic intelligence becomes increasingly familiar to you.

Sometimes your awareness is as if a wave on the ocean of pure consciousness, but at other times it subsides back into the ocean. By developing yourself spiritually, you will one day control the nexus between the wave and the ocean of pure consciousness, expanding your reign to encompass the vastness of the entire universe. Eventually you will evolve into a universe of your own. That's right. You will be a living and breathing universe where your greatest pleasure comes from creating within yourself another planet or galaxy.

There should be no surprise why outer space looks strikingly similar to inner space. This has been explained in the wisdom of some of our oldest cultures. For example, the ancient Egyptian *Emerald Tablet* says, "As above, so below. As within, so without." Scholars believe these words were first written down between 200 and 500 AD.[29] This idea of "As is the macrocosm so is the microcosm" was later carried on by the Greeks.

As you extend the reach of your awareness, you will realize that as is the universe, so are *you*. You too can expand to the vastness of the universe. There are ever-new potential universes bubbling up from within the field of pure consciousness. You are one of them. As your awareness increases, you will not only become a universe, but someday the God of a universe. In fact, you already are considered to be God by the cells in your body.

From within your own awareness the same creative process is occurring that gave rise to our physical universe. The sounds of the Veda sprang forth in order to create you just as they did to create the universe. You too can develop into a universe and beyond. There is no reason to believe that the words, "As is the macrocosm, so is the microcosm," are not meant to be a literal statement in every sense that its words imply. The rishis of old said, *Yatha pinde tatha bramande*, "As is the atom, so is the Universe; as is the body, so is the Cosmic Body."[30]

Most people believe these words to mean that we in some non-specific, ancillary way are similar to the Cosmic Body—to God. But these statements mean more than that. They mean not only that we are like the cosmos, but that the cosmos is like us. What if the cosmic body is no different than our own, with head, arms, and legs? Perhaps life consists of a huge nesting doll of one life form inside of another. With NASA scientists using the Chandra X-Ray Observatory to peer out at the offspring of colliding galaxies, some of which have striking similarities to our own human fetuses, while also monitoring their galactic heartbeats,[31] one should not be surprised at such a proposition.

We believe the invisible laws that govern our planet to be God, but earth feels the laws that govern the galaxy to be its God. The galaxy in turn thinks the same of the universe. But the reality is that all these conceptions are of the same God. They are only separated by the constraints on our awareness. If a planet thinks its orb shape is all that it is, then it will feel that something greater still is its God. If a galaxy feels that all the planets it encompasses are all that it's comprised of, then it will feel that something greater is its God. The broader your awareness, the more expansive You become: human, planet, galaxy, universe, and beyond.

We think that we have a God outside of us because of our limited awareness of our larger Self. We believe that the unmanifest intelligence underlying our world to be God, but in reality it's only the Self. The "mistake of the intellect" (or pragyaparad) has simply covered over the Truth—that *you* are God. Jesus said, "I and my Father are one."[32] We are the person, we are the planet, we are the galaxy, we are the universe, and we are God. They are all the Self.

Swami Vivekananda explained it this way:

> *What we call God is really only the Self, from which we have separated ourselves and which we worship as outside us; but it is our true Self, all the time, the one and only God.*[33]

As your awareness grows, you eventually will gain the capacity to know yourself as God, because your consciousness will encompass all that is. The world is God, the galaxy is God, the universe is God, and they are all You. Jesus also said, "Is it not written in your law... Ye are Gods?"[34] Everything is God regardless of how you compartmentalize it, but as long as there is something larger that you don't recognize as yourself, it will be considered your God and worthy of worship as such. What will you worship when you awaken to the ultimate reality that nothing exists other than You?

REDISCOVERING A UNIFIED REALITY

When I was a child, I used to enjoy creating a very simple design on paper. I would do it when I was passing time or when I needed a quick project for an elementary school art class. It involved simple bands or layers growing from the sides of the paper to finally end in the outline of a distinct shape of a person, animal, tree, etc. The bands would become smaller and smaller until they would surround and outline the object they replicated. I sometimes would start from the image and grow the bands outward as well.

I always found creating these designs very comforting and fascinating to look at. They appealed to me intuitively, because I was much more in harmony with natural law as a child. But it wasn't until I was much older and far more knowledgeable spiritually that I understood why that was. It's because they mirror the structure of nature.

The bands emerge from infinity until an object precipitates out of them. The final image in the center of the drawing appears as if a crystallization of the unmanifest field. There are gaps between each band, which is where the invisible intelligence of creation resides at each level of nature's functioning to orchestrate the manifestation of an object, or to allow it to dissolve back into the field of pure consciousness.

Nature exists in layers, with only the grossest levels finally appearing to us as solid matter. Going in the opposite direction, you can delve deeply into matter to arrive at the level of subatomic particles. If you dive even deeper still, you discover non-localized waves of energy, which are fluctuations in the vacuum state at the superunified level of all the laws and forces of nature.

The level of superunification represents the smallest time and space differentials that exist in creation. Here we arrive at the unified field, the field of pure consciousness, which is beyond time and space, eternal and infinite. This is the subtlest level of nature's functioning, where all possibilities exist. Here is where the total potential of natural law underlying and giving rise to all of physical creation resides.

John Hagelin, a renowned Harvard-educated physicist, who developed one of the leading grand unified theories known as Flipped SU(5),[35] describes the unified field as follows:

As one's attention is brought to the most fundamental level of nature, there is a transition in the structure of natural law. From this most basic standpoint, it is possible to see that the apparent laws of nature at more superficial levels are the result only of an approximate and fragmented viewpoint. At the level of the unified field, nature is completely abstract but infinitely energetic and dynamic, and within that level of infinite energy all the laws of nature are found united. Out of this most fundamental level of nature's functioning arise all the laws of nature which uphold the functioning of the more superficial and complicated levels. The unified field is thus highly abstract, but very real. From there, all the laws of nature originate.[36]

The laws of nature at this most fundamental level represent pure consciousness interacting within itself. The unified field is the name the scientific community has given to the field of pure consciousness, first witnessed by the ancient rishis. We see physical objects as something other than our own pure consciousness with our eyes, but at every level of their development, in reality, they are composed of nothing more than Us.

Both realities exist—the reality of our own consciousness and the reality of matter—but only as differentiated by the limitations of our awareness. With finite awareness you witness the world of objects, with no knowledge of pure consciousness. But through the development of your awareness, you can once more gain access to the unified reality of life to witness everything as nothing more than fluctuations of your Self.

Maharishi explains the benefits of accessing this unified reality through deep meditation in this way:

In Transcendental Meditation, the conscious mind comes to a state of self-referral awareness, which is the simplest form of human awareness where consciousness is open to itself. This self-referral state of consciousness is the ground state of all the laws of nature—the unified field of natural law.

The supersymmetric unified field theories of physics have glimpsed this state of unity, which, in its own self-interacting dynamics, expresses itself as diversified forms and phenomena in creation.

The complete knowledge of the unified field of natural law is available in Vedic Science, which provides the technology for human consciousness to harness the total creative potential of natural law. Through practice of Transcendental Meditation, the conscious mind identifies itself with the unified field, and human awareness is open to its own full potential, the infinite potential of nature's intelligence.[37]

To know the unified field, one must transcend the relative field of existence to directly experience pure Being. This can be achieved in a systematic way through the practice of meditation. There's so much more to life than many of us have ever allowed ourselves to imagine. By developing your consciousness, you can wake up to this blissful reality within your own awareness. The pathless path to enlightenment is a magnificent one, which entails all the happiness your heart could possibly desire.

Imagine feeling very happy. Then imagine feeling a million times happier still. The great yogis have spoken about the experience of transcendental bliss consciousness in these terms,[38] and you can have this experience most rapidly by systematically developing your awareness. As you proceed towards higher states of consciousness, much more significant levels of human development will sequentially unfold for you, and living a life in supreme happiness will be your reward.

Ten

FULFILLED

Life is magical and you will experience this magic as you begin to grow towards enlightenment. I remember the famous magician Doug Henning saying he once asked Maharishi if there is any real magic in life. He said Maharishi assured him that there was, and that you can experience it by fully developing your awareness.

Your soul has an infinite capacity to create anything it wishes. All you need to do is put your attention on it and watch it grow. Don't miss another moment to develop the full potential of your consciousness, so that you can experience all the magic life has to offer.

You are taking in this knowledge now because you know there's more to life than meets the eye. You know that somewhere deep inside you is the ability to be and to do anything that you could ever dream of. You just needed to be reminded of your immense power. Your soul is eternal, with a tremendous capacity to create again and again all that you desire in life. It's inevitable that you eventually create to your heart's content. It's inevitable that you be fulfilled. Put your attention on it and do not vacillate about what you want, and it will be yours.

GRACED BY LIFE

Be grateful for your human existence. Know that you may have created some difficulties for yourself, but be thankful for them all. They provide exactly what you need to learn and grow. You know there are no mistakes, only lessons. I didn't always understand this. Early on, some of my mistakes felt like serious transgressions that I didn't know I could recover from. But you can recover from any error, which is why you make them in the first place. They allow you to know how to do it better next time.

I tried from a very young age to take responsibility for my mistakes in life. That's not to say I always immediately owned up to them all, because I surely didn't. I did my share of pushing responsibility for my troubles out onto others. But once alone with myself I eventually did own up to them and accept them. I thank God for this quality. Taking responsibility for your life is a requirement of waking up to the Truth that you are an eternally growing soul with infinite potential.

I once knew a young man who frequently sabotaged his own happiness, and sometimes that of others. He didn't intentionally do this, but he did it all the same. I actually only knew him vaguely, however, because that man was the unaware me. As I write these words, tears well up in my eyes for the trouble my actions have sometimes caused. But they are quickly pushed aside by larger tears of joy that come from my gratitude for what I've learned from my mistakes. Grateful tears of joy have flowed often during the writing of this book.

My mistakes, like yours, allowed me to grow. But life doesn't have to be so hard. We are so lucky to have easy access to the age-old wisdom of the masters to unlock our full potential. This knowledge is capable of lifting anyone out of even the deepest and darkest of ignorance. It can take many, many painful lessons to get it right, but with this timeless wisdom you can get it right in this lifetime. If I can be taken from where I was to where I am now in one lifetime, so can you.

I was allotted many opportunities to develop myself, as we all are. I am thankful for my trials, because without them I would not know what I do today. My difficulties were the blessings that allowed me to see my way Home, to find the knowledge for my awakening. They helped me understand how to do everything better. The blue-hot fire of pure knowledge burns through even the most deep-rooted ignorance to reveal how effortless a life in lasting fulfillment can be.

Honestly examine your life to be sure you're allowing yourself to move forward towards greater understanding. If you want to be happy, you need to be honest about why you're not. You must look at those things that need to change to allow happiness to be expressed in your life. I was determined as a young man to recapture the innocent joy I experienced as a child. This unwavering desire forced me to look at some things that I didn't want to see in myself. But I had to, because I knew that was the way forward.

Taking responsibility for your life in this way allows every experience to become a lesson for your highest learning. If you can look through the rationalizations that you contrive to avoid taking responsibility for what happens in your life, you can progress quickly. Be willing to question your thoughts and behaviors to gain the pearls of wisdom that are always available to you. This is the way to Self-mastery.

Denial and avoidance are not an option on the pathless path to enlightenment. Sooner or later you will be forced to look at yourself, because you will not allow yourself to continue suffering as you do. Once you remove the veil of the imaginary you to step outside of your illusion, you will see that God is always there guiding you.

The complexities in our lives get created when we try to avoid looking at ourselves, but as you push through them to discover the simpler reality of your existence, you will see your way Home. Uncovering the Truth is natural and innate to human life. If only you will stop covering up and hiding from your Self, it will be yours. Your acceptance of what life has dealt you is your savior, because it will allow for your greatest growth and healing.

Humble acceptance of your circumstances will allow the higher knowledge you need to be revealed to you. At first, my awakening came slowly, a little at a time. With each passing year the mirror became a little clearer to allow me to see who I really was, and how I was getting in my own way.

But then, all the complexity I had been clearing away from my life over the years allowed for a flood of knowledge to come pouring into my awareness all at once. It coalesced into my understanding about how to maintain my greatest happiness for all times. In one stroke, all the pieces I had learned over the years about how to gain fulfillment came together. The ideas in this book are the basis of that understanding.

THE TRUTH IS YOURS

Meditation is the most rapid way to cultivate spontaneous right action in your life. Its practice allows you to see clearly what will bring you the greatest happiness. It allows you to attain a state of awareness where all you choose to do is only uplifting to life. It lets you awaken to the ideal you.

You are ready to take the next big step in your spiritual growth. Your awareness is expanding. Only when you are ready do you get the knowledge you need. You are increasingly exploring spiritual knowledge now, because your consciousness is vibrating at a higher frequency. You are ripe for a great expanse in your spiritual evolution.

You were born to be enlightened. The pure knowledge that is now flowing to you is familiar. You knew of it while residing in the gap between your many incarnations, and are unconsciously reminded of it in the gap of the sleeping state of consciousness when your soul roams free. You may have even glimpsed it during transcendental moments in your daily life, in the spaces between your thoughts. You are never far from it.

The wisdom of the Veda is not foreign to you. It is all there is and all there ever will be to completely lift humankind out of darkness. The immemorial wisdom of the Veda predates all religions and traditions. The underlying principles of this eternal knowledge have either consciously or unconsciously inspired all good things in life. All streams of knowledge that lead one closer to God find their source in this wisdom. The Veda is part of all our ancestries.

Enlightenment is available to all of us now. Maharishi's one-pointed focus has made it a possibility for everyone in this lifetime. He clarified the many misunderstandings of the past about this knowledge. There's no need to strain or to renounce the world to become enlightened. Enlightenment is for everyone, including energetic people living and working in the world.

You don't have to live in poverty or squalor to obtain it. Enlightenment is gained in your own awareness, so no particular deprivation is required. Misunderstandings like these are what caused the destruction of society, and we are only now pulling ourselves out of deep ignorance after thousands of years of decline. You can live a comfortable and dignified life as you gain higher states of consciousness.

Strong and successful people from all walks of life, for their own sake and for the great benefit of society, need to embrace this wisdom and with it bolster the underpinnings of their own belief systems.

Maharishi has made it crystal clear that meditation is the first step to gaining union with God, not the last. It has been commonly misunderstood for far too long that *samadhi*, union with pure consciousness, is the last step of the yoga system, when in fact it is the first. He said you cannot gain samadhi by simply attempting to conform to codes of right behavior and action, which have generally been thought to be the first steps of the yoga system. Rather, he said, ideal behavior comes from first practicing meditation to experience union (yoga) with God in pure consciousness.[1]

He presented this wisdom in such a profoundly simple manner that one could not miss the value to be gained from using it to live a life in everlasting peace and happiness. There are saints in India who believe Maharishi was the greatest exponent of the wisdom of enlightenment in thousands of years. The immensity of his work was recognized and lauded by some of the highest among us.

I have been fortunate to have met so many enlightened souls whose mission on earth it is to uphold the purity of this wisdom. We should be so thankful that Maharishi spent his life not only reviving, organizing, and sharing this knowledge in its completeness with humankind in our generation, but that he trained so many dedicated souls to be the custodians of this wisdom after he was gone. We should also be grateful to those who preceded Maharishi to soften the hard rocks of ignorance so that he could have such a profound effect on the spiritual development of the world. We should be thankful to them all.

IT'S NEVER TOO LATE FOR FULFILLMENT

It's never too late to be fulfilled, because the happiness you desire is never out of your reach. Through right knowledge and correct practice, you too can experience great fulfillment in life. Whether you want more success or greater peace and happiness, the eternal wisdom of the Veda is the most direct means by which to attain it.

Only this moment here and now matters. There's no time like the present to begin to transform your life into what, deep down, you always knew it could be. Just set your trajectory in the direction of greater happiness and put your attention on having it. You cannot fail using this time-tested knowledge. This is the ancient, unchanging wisdom of lasting happiness. Start now to live your life in complete fulfillment: seize the moment—*carpe diem!*

Time appears to pass as the objects of the world come and go, but what humankind seeks is always the same—fulfillment. The formula to have it is simple: develop your consciousness, grow towards enlightenment, and attain everlasting happiness in life. You can take the long path, or you can follow the pathless path of least resistance by heading straight for it. Learn to meditate, stay in the moment, think positive thoughts, follow your happiness, and it will be yours.

There is no other way to attain the lasting fulfillment you seek. Don't put off your spiritual growth until tomorrow. No pursuit is more necessary and more practical to life than this one. To do otherwise is to live a life of never-ending obsession over the objects of the senses, which can never bring the fulfillment you desire. Break the cycle now to attain lasting happiness in this lifetime.

This beautiful knowledge is not owned by me or anyone else. It does not belong to any one country or faith. It belongs to all of us. The need of this age is to implement this knowledge on a global scale to bring human existence back into accord with natural law. This is our collective destiny. The cycles of time will not have it any other way.

Let us begin now so all our highest collective desires can be achieved in this lifetime. Put your attention on it. Your purpose in life is to attain the vast expanse of your heart's desires, so stop thinking so small. You don't want this or that—you want it all. You can have it all. The process is simple and you incarnated into a human body to partake of it, so start now to live the life you were meant to live, a life in everlasting freedom and happiness, a life forever fulfilled.

ENDNOTES

One: You are Happiness

[1] Matthew 6:33, *New Testament*, King James Version.

[2] **First Reference:** Alexander, C. N., et al. Effects of the Transcendental Meditation program on stress-reduction, health, and employee development: A prospective study in two occupational settings. *Anxiety, Stress, and Coping: An International Journal* 6: 245–262, 1993.

Second Reference: Eppley, K. R., Abrams, A. I., and Shear, J. Differential effects of relaxation techniques on trait anxiety: A meta-analysis. *Journal of Clinical Psychology* 45: 957–974, 1989.

[3] The author uses the male gender when referring to God, since his teacher did the same. But God is both male and female and, therefore, can accurately be referred to in the female gender as well. This is evidenced by some of the major religious traditions of the world referring to God as male, female, or even as free of gender.

Two: Spaceless-Timeless Wisdom

[1] **First Reference:** DeWitt, B. S. Quantum theory of gravity. I. The canonical theory. *Physical Review*. 160 (5): 1113–1148, 1967.

Second Reference: Folger, Tim. Newsflash: time may not exist. *Discover*, June, 2007: http://discovermagazine.com/2007/jun/in-no-time

[2] **First Reference:** Simons, D. J., and Chabris, C. F. Gorillas in our midst: Sustained inattentional blindness for dynamic events. *Perception* 28 (9): 1059–1074, 1999.

Second Reference: Simons, D. J. Monkeying around with the gorillas in our midst: Familiarity with an inattentional-blindness task does not improve the detection of unexpected events. *i-Perception* 1 (1): 3–6, 2010.

[3] **First Reference:** Szabo, Richard, J. *An Introduction to String Theory and D-Brane Dynamics*. Imperial College Press, London, England, p. 5, 2004.

Second Reference: Tegmark, M. Parallel universes. Not just a staple of science fiction, other universes are a direct implication of cosmological observations. *Scientific American* 288 (5): 40–51, 2003.

[4] *Bhagavata Purana* 10.87.41: http://vedabase.net/sb/10/87/41/

[5] Einstein, Albert. Zur Elektrodynamik bewegter Körper. *Annalen der Physik* 17: 891, 1905; English translation: Perrett, W., and Jeffrey, G. B. *On the Electrodynamics of Moving Bodies*. Dover Publications, New York, NY, 1923.

[6] Maharishi Mahesh Yogi. *Maharishi Mahesh Yogi on the Bhagavad-Gita: A New Translation and Commentary, Chapters 1–6*. Penguin, New York, NY, II, 24, 1969.

[7] von Mayer, J. R. Remarks on the forces of inorganic nature. *Annalen der Chemie und Pharmacie* 43: 233, 1842.

Brief History: The idea that energy is conserved was first stated by Julius Robert von Mayer in 1842; it was also independently discovered by James Prescott Joule in 1843. Hermann Helmholtz's definitive 1847 declaration of the conservation of energy credited both von Mayer and Joule. The law of the conservation of energy states that the total amount of energy in an isolated system remains constant over time. This led to the First Law of Thermodynamics, which states that energy can neither be created nor destroyed. It can only be transformed from one state to another. In 1860, in works of Rudolf Clausius and William Thomson, there initially were two established *principles* of thermodynamics. But by 1873 the principles turned into "laws" when Willard Gibbs, in his *Graphical Methods in the Thermodynamics of Fluids*, clearly stated that there were two absolute laws of thermodynamics, a first law and a second law. In 1905, Albert Einstein's theory of special relativity also showed that energy and mass are one and the same, and that neither one appears without the other. In a closed system, both mass and energy are conserved separately, but particles of matter can be converted to non-matter forms of energy, such as light, or kinetic and potential energy, such as heat. This does not affect total mass, because non-matter energy still retains its mass.

[8] **First Reference:** Dillbeck, M. C. Meditation and flexibility of visual perception and verbal problem solving. *Memory & Cognition* 10 (3): 207–215, 1982.

Second Reference: So, K. T., and Orme-Johnson, D. W. Three randomized experiments on the longitudinal effects of the Transcendental Meditation technique on cognition. *Intelligence* 29: 419–440, 2001.

[9] **First Reference:** Alexander, C. N., et al. Effects of the Transcendental Meditation program on stress-reduction, health, and employee development: A prospective study in two occupational settings. *Anxiety, Stress, and Coping: An International Journal*, 6: 245–262, 1993.

Second Reference: Eppley, K. R., Abrams, A. I, and Shear, J. Differential effects of relaxation techniques on trait anxiety: A meta-analysis. *Journal of Clinical Psychology* 45: 957-974, 1989.

[10] Maharishi Mahesh Yogi, *Historic Lecture Series: Maharishi's Keynote Address at the Annual Convention of the American Association of Higher Education 1973* (Chicago, IL). Maharishi International University Press, Fairfield, IA (Videotape), 1974.

[11] Maharishi Mahesh Yogi. *Maharishi Mahesh Yogi on the Bhagavad-Gita: A New Translation and Commentary, Chapters 1–6.* Penguin, New York, NY, IV, 39, 1969.

[12] **First Reference:** *Chandogya Upanishad*, 6.12.

Second Reference: Egenes, Thomas and Reddy, Kumuda. *Eternal Stories from the Upanishads*, Smriti Books, New Delhi, India, p. 11. 2002. (with English Translation)

[13] **First Reference:** Jarosik, N., Bennett, C. L., Dunkley, J., Gold, B., Greason M. R., Halpern, M, Hill, R. S., Hinshaw, G., Kogut, A., Komatsu E., Larson, D., Limon, M., Meyer, S. S., Nolta, M. R., Odegard, N., Page, L., Smith, K. M., Spergel, D. N., Tucker, G. S., Weiland, J. L., Wollack, E., and Wright, E. L. Seven-year Wilkinson Microwave Anisotropy Probe (WMAP) Observations: Sky maps, systematic errors, and basic results. *Astrophysical Journal Supplement Series* 192 (2): 14, 2011. (See page 39 of original 42-page version for cosmological parameters summary: http://arxiv.org/pdf/1001.4744v1.pdf)

Second Reference: Wollack, E. J. What is the universe made of? *Universe 101, Our Universe.* NASA/WMAP Science Team, National Aeronautics and Space Administration, 2010: http://map.gsfc.nasa.gov/universe/uni_matter.html

[14] Planck, Max. *Das Wesen der Materie* [The Nature of Matter]. Speech presented in Florence, Italy, 1944. (From Archiv zur Geschichte der Max-Planck-Gesellschaft, Abt. Va, Rep. 11 Planck, Nr. 1797)

Three: The Attention of the Creator

[1] Sheldrake, Rupert, *Dogs that Know when their Owners are Coming Home, and Other Unexplained Powers of Animals*, Three Rivers Press, New York, NY, pp. 48–49 & 125–128, 1999.

[2] Paramahansa Yogananda, *Man's Eternal Quest.* Self-Realization Fellowship, Los Angeles, CA, p. 90, 1975. (Collected Lectures)

[3] Mark 11:23, *New Testament,* King James Version.

[4] de Armas, Frederick A. Tracking the path of transcending: The source of creativity in Lope de Vega's El ganso de oro. *Modern Science and Vedic Science* 10 (1): 42, 2000. (Quoting a reading of the *Bhagavad-Gita*, IX, 8, by Maharishi Mahesh Yogi)

[5] **First Reference:** Radin, D. I., and Nelson, R. D. Replication in random number generator experiments: Meta-analysis and quality assessment. Human Information Processing Group, *Technical Report*, Princeton University, 1987.

Second Reference: Radin, D. I., and Nelson, R. D. Meta-analysis of mind-matter interaction experiments: 1959–2000. In Jonas, W., and Crawford, C., eds., *Healing, Intention and Energy Medicine.* Harcourt Health Sciences, London, 2003.

[6] Maharishi Mahesh Yogi, *Science of Being and Art of Living.* Signet, New York, NY, p. 34, 1968. (Paperback)

[7] *Taittiriya Upanishad,* 2.6.

[8] Social psychologists have identified a field-independent cognitive style associated with positive social behavior:

First Reference: Gelderloos, P., Lockie, R., and Chuttoorgoon, S. Field independence of students at Maharishi School of the Age of Enlightenment and a Montessori school. *Perceptual and Motor Skills* 65: 613–614, 1987.

Second Reference: Nidich, S. A study of the relationship of the Transcendental Meditation Program to Kohlberg's Stages of Moral Reasoning. *Dissertation Abstracts International* 36: 4361A–4362A, 1975.

[9] **First Reference:** Alexander, C. N., et al. Transcendental Meditation, self-actualization, and psychological health: A conceptual overview and statistical meta-analysis. *Journal of Social Behavior and Personality* 6: 189–247, 1991.

Second Reference: Ferguson, P. C., and Cowan, J. C. Psychological findings on Transcendental Meditation. *Journal of Humanistic Psychology* 16: 51–60, 1976.

[10] **First Reference:** Travis, F. The TM technique and creativity: A longitudinal study of Cornell University undergraduates. *The Journal of Creative Behavior* 13: 169–180, 1979.

Second Reference: Jedrczak, A., et al. The TM-Sidhi programme, pure consciousness, creativity and intelligence. *The Journal of Creative Behavior* 19: 270–275, 1985.

[11] **First Reference:** Woolley, J. D., Boerger, E. A., and Markman, A. B. A visit from the Candy Witch: Factors influencing young children's belief in a novel fantastical being. *Developmental Science* 7 (4): 456–468, 2004.

Second Reference: Wang, Shirley. The power of magical thinking: Research shows the importance of imagination in children's cognitive development. *The Wall Street Journal* December 22, 2009: http://online.wsj.com/article/SB10001 424052748703344704574610002061841322.html

[12] **First Reference:** Nidich, S., Ryncarz, R., Abrams, A., Orme-Johnson, D. W., and Wallace, R. K. Kohlbergian cosmic perspective responses, EEG coherence, and the Transcendental Meditation and TM-Sidhi program. *Journal of Moral Education* 12: 166–173, 1983.

Second Reference: Lyubimov, N. N. Electrophysiological characteristics of mobilization of hidden brain reserves. Abstracts, the International Symposium *Physiological and Biochemical Basis of Brain Activity* (St. Petersburg, Russia: Russian Academy of Science, Institute of the Human Brain): 5, 1994.

[13] **First Reference:** Warner, T. Q. Transcendental meditation and developmental advancement: Mediating abilities and conservation performance. *Dissertation Abstracts International* 47 (8): 3558B, 1987.

Second Reference: Dixon, C. A. Consciousness and cognitive development: A six-month longitudinal study of four-year-olds practicing the children's Transcendental Meditation technique. *Dissertation Abstracts International* 50 (3): 1518B, 1989.

[14] **First Reference:** Nidich, S., Seeman, W., and Dreskin, T. Influence of Transcendental Meditation: A replication. *Journal of Counseling Psychology* 20 (6): 565–566, 1973.

Second Reference: Seeman, W., Nidich, S., and Banta, T. Influence of Transcendental Meditation on a measure of self-actualization. *Journal of Counseling Psychology* 19 (3): 184–187, 1972.

Third Reference: Hjelle, L. A. Transcendental Meditation and psychological health. *Perceptual and Motor Skills* 39: 623–628, 1974.

[15] Maharishi Mahesh Yogi. *Maharishi Mahesh Yogi on the Bhagavad-Gita: A New Translation and Commentary, Chapters 1–6.* Penguin, New York, NY, IV, 38, 1969.

[16] **First Reference:** Orme-Johnson, D. W., and Farrow, J. T., eds. *Scientific research on the Transcendental Meditation program: Collected Papers, Vol. 1.* MERU Press, Rheinweiler, W. Germany, 1977.

Second Reference: Chalmers, R. A., Clements, G., Schenkluhn, H., and Weinless, M., eds. *Scientific Research on Maharishi's Transcendental Meditation and TM-Sidhi Program: Collected Papers, Vol. 2.* MVU Press, Vlodrop, The Netherlands, 1989.

Third Reference: Chalmers, R. A., Clements, G., Schenkluhn, H., and Weinless, M., eds. *Scientific Research on Maharishi's Transcendental Meditation and TM-Sidhi Program: Collected Papers, Vol. 3.* MVU Press, Vlodrop, The Netherlands, 1989.

Fourth Reference: Chalmers, R. A., Clements, G., Schenkluhn, H., and Weinless, M., eds. *Scientific Research on Maharishi's Transcendental Meditation and TM-Sidhi Program: Collected Papers, Vol. 4.* MVU Press, Vlodrop, the Netherlands, 1989.

Fifth Reference: Wallace, R. K., Orme-Johnson, D. W., and Dillbeck, M. C., eds. *Scientific Research on Maharishi's Transcendental Meditation and TM-Sidhi Program: Collected Papers, Vol. 5.* MIU Press, Fairfield, IA, 1990.

Sixth Reference: Dillbeck, M. C., ed. *Scientific Research on Maharishi's Transcendental Meditation and TM-Sidhi Program: Collected Papers, Vol. 6.* MVU Press, Vlodrop, The Netherlands, 2011.

Seventh Reference: http://www.mum.edu/tm_research/welcome.html

Eighth Reference: http://www.truthabouttm.org/truth/TMResearch/TMResearch Summary/index.cfm

[17] **First Reference:** Nagel, Ernest. *The Structure of Science: Problems in the Logic of Scientific Explanation.* Harcourt, Brace, and World, New York, NY, p. 3, 1961.

Second Reference: McGee, W. J. The science of humanity. *Science* VI (142): 418, 1897.

[18] Einstein, A. Physics and reality. *Journal of the Franklin Institute* 221: 349–382, 1936.

[19] **First Reference:** http://www.tm.org/national-institutes-of-health

Second Reference: http://nccam.nih.gov/recovery/IRmindbody.htm

[20] Miskiman, D. E. The treatment of insomnia by the Transcendental Meditation technique, Graduate Department of Psychology, University of Alberta, Edmonton, Alberta, Canada, In Orme-Johnson, D. W., and Farrow, J. T., eds. *Scientific research on the Transcendental Meditation program: Collected papers, Vol. 1.* MERU Press, Rheinweiler, W. Germany, pp. 296–298, 1977.

[21] Oates, Robert, Jr. *Celebrating the Dawn.* G. P. Putnam's Sons, New York, NY, p. 90, 1976. ("Knowledge is structured in consciousness" was a phrase often used by Maharishi Mahesh Yogi. Sourced from a response to a question asked by the author to Maharishi about a lecture he had just given at Banares University in India.)

[22] Maharishi Mahesh Yogi. The seven states of consciousness. *Science of Creative Intelligence: Knowledge and Experience.* MIU Press, Los Angeles, CA, 1972. (Videotape)

[23] Paramahansa Yogananda. *The Divine Romance.* Self-Realization Fellowship, Los Angeles, CA, p. 406, 1992. (Collected Lectures)

[24] Maharishi Mahesh Yogi. *Maharishi Mahesh Yogi on the Bhagavad-Gita: A New Translation and Commentary, Chapters 1–6.* Penguin, New York, NY, IV, 34, 1969. (Paraphrased)

[25] Maharishi Mahesh Yogi. *Maharishi Mahesh Yogi on the Bhagavad-Gita: A New Translation and Commentary, Chapters 1–6.* Penguin, New York, NY, II, 41, 1969.

[26] Frawley, David. *Gods, Sages, and Kings: Vedic Secrets of Ancient Civilization.* Passage Press, Salt Lake City, UT, p. 23, 1991.

[27] **First Reference:** Luke 2:42, *New Testament,* King James Version.

Second Reference: Luke 3:23, *New Testament,* King James Version.

[28] Notovitch, Nicolas. *The Unknown Life of Jesus Christ.* Rand, McNally & Co., pp. 8–9, 1894.

[29] Swami Abhedananda, *Journey into Kashmir and Tibet* (the English translation of *Kashmir 0 Tibbeti*), Ramakrishna Vivekananda Math, Calcutta, India, pp. ii–v, 1987.

[30] http://www.truthabouttm.org/truth/IndividualEffects/IsTMaReligion/Religious Leaders/index.cfm#Top

[31] Nader, Tony. *Human Physiology: Expression of Veda and the Vedic Literature.* Maharishi Vedic University, Vlodrop, The Netherlands, p. 5, 2000.

Four: Walking the Pathless Path

[1] Maharishi Mahesh Yogi. *Maharishi Mahesh Yogi on the Bhagavad-Gita: A New Translation and Commentary, Chapters 1–6*. Penguin, New York, NY, II, 47–48, 1969.

[2] Maharishi Mahesh Yogi. *Maharishi Mahesh Yogi on the Bhagavad-Gita: A New Translation and Commentary, Chapters 1–6*. Penguin, New York, NY, II, 48-50. 1969.

[3] Berra, Yogi, and Kaplan, Dave. *When You Come to a Fork in the Road, Take It!* Hyperion, New York, NY, p. 20, 2001.

[4] Oates, Robert, Jr. *Celebrating the Dawn*. G. P. Putnam's Sons, New York, NY, pp. 198–200, 1976. (Book includes excerpts of conversations with professional athletes Joe Namath, Larry Bowa, Del Unser, and Willie Stargell about experiences from their practice of Transcendental Meditation.)

[5] **First Reference:** Waitley, Denis. *The Psychology of Winning*. Penquin Group, New York, NY, p. 92, 1979.

Second Reference: http://deniswaitley.com

[6] *Yoga Sutras* 1.4.

[7] Raymond, Bradley, Dir. *Tinker Bell*. Exec. Prod. John Lasseter. Writers. Jeffrey Howard and Bradley Raymond. Perfs. Mae Whitman. Walt Disney Pictures, 2008.

[8] Maharishi Mahesh Yogi. *Maharishi Mahesh Yogi on the Bhagavad-Gita: A New Translation and Commentary, Chapters 1–6*. Penguin, New York, NY, II, 57-58, 1969.

[9] Jefferson, Thomas, et al. *United States Declaration of Independence*, Second Section, Preamble, July 4, 1776.

[10] Diener, E., Ng, W., Harter, J., and Arora, R. Wealth and happiness across the world: Material prosperity predicts life evaluation, whereas psychosocial prosperity predicts positive feeling. *Journal of Personality and Social Psychology* 99 (1): 52, 2010.

[11] http://www.ilo.org/global/about-the-ilo/press-and-media-centre/press-releases/WCMS_005291/lang--en/index.htm

[12] http://www.americanprogress.org/issues/2010/01/three_faces_report.html

[13] Luke 11:34, *New Testament,* King James Version.

[14] Matthew 7:7, *New Testament,* King James Version.

[15] Pasricha, Prem, *The Whole Thing, The Real Thing: A Brief Biography of Shri Gurudeva*. Delhi Photo Company, New Delhi, India, pp. 59–65, 1977. (A translation of the Rameswar Twari version by the same title.)

Five: Balance with the Cosmos

[1] Newton, Isaac. *The Mathematical Principles of Natural Philosophy, Volume 1.* London, England, p. 20, 1687.

[2] Maharishi Mahesh Yogi. *Maharishi Mahesh Yogi on the Bhagavad-Gita: A New Translation and Commentary, Chapters 1–6.* Penguin, New York, NY, IV, 17, 1969.

[3] Matthew 27:46, *New Testament,* King James Version.

[4] Sin, N. L., and Lyubomirsky, S. Enhancing well-being and alleviating depressive symptoms with positive psychology interventions: A practice-friendly meta-analysis. *Journal of Clinical Psychology: In Session* 65: 467–487, 2009.

[5] Paramahansa Yogananda. *Journey to Self-Realization.* Self-Realization Fellowship, Los Angeles, CA, pp. 8–9, 1997. (Collected Lectures)

[6] Mark 11:24, *New Testament,* King James Version.

[7] *Dasadhyayi*, 1.3. (The text referred to is quoted in the *Dasadhyayi* from even a more ancient Sanskrit text titled J*ataka Samgraha.*)

[8] Paramahansa Yogananda. *Autobiography of a Yogi.* Self-Realization Fellowship, Los Angeles, CA, pp. 192–193, 1946. (Paperback)

[9] Maharishi Mahesh Yogi. *Maharishi Mahesh Yogi on the Bhagavad-Gita: A New Translation and Commentary, Chapters 1–6.* Penguin, New York, NY, III, 8, 1969.

[10] Maharishi Mahesh Yogi. *Maharishi Mahesh Yogi on the Bhagavad-Gita: A New Translation and Commentary, Chapters 1–6.* Penguin, New York, NY, IV, 23, 1969.

Six: Cleaning the Lens

[1] **First Reference:** Walsh, C. J., Luer, C.A., Bodine, A. B., Smith, C. A., Cox, H. L., Noyes, D. R., and Gasparetto, M. Elasmobranch immune cells as a source of novel tumor cell inhibitors: Implications for public health. *Integrative and Comparative Biology* 46: 1072-1081, 2006.

Second Reference: http://www.mote.org

Third Reference: Handwerk, Brian. Do sharks hold secret to human cancer fight? *National Geographic News,* August 20, 2003: http://news.nationalgeographic.com/news/2003/08/0820_030820_sharkcancer.html

[2] **First Reference:** Black, W. C. Overdiagnosis: An underrecognized cause of confusion and harm in cancer screening. *Journal of the National Cancer Institute* 92 (16): 1280–1282, 2000.

Second Reference: Black, W. C., and Welch, H. G. Advances in diagnostic imaging and overestimations of disease prevalence and the benefits of therapy. *New England Journal of Medicine* 328 (17): 1237–1243, 1993.

Third Reference: Harach, H. R., Franssila, K. O., and Wasenius, V. M. Occult papillary carcinoma of the thyroid: A 'normal' finding in Finland: A systematic autopsy study. *Cancer* 56 (3): 531–538, 1985.

[3] Pereyra, F., et al. The major genetic determinants of HIV-1 control affect HLA Class I peptide presentation: The International HIV Controllers Study. *Science* 330 (6010): 1551–1557, 2010.

[4] Wallace, R. K. Physiological effects of Transcendental Meditation. *Science* 167: 1751–1754, 1970.

[5] **First Reference:** Blank, M., ed. Electromagnetic fields (EMF) special issue. *Pathophysiology* 16 (2-3): 67–250, 2009.

Second Reference: http://www.bioinitiative.org/report/index.htm

[6] **First Reference:** Pelletier, K. R. Influence of Transcendental Meditation upon autokinetic perception. *Perceptual Motor Skills* 39: 1031–1034, 1974.

Second Reference: Frew, D. R. Transcendental Meditation and productivity. *Academy of Management Journal* 17 (2): 362–368, 1974.

[7] **First Reference:** Wallace, R. K. The physiology of meditation. *Scientific American* 226 (2): 84–90, 1972.

Second Reference: Miskiman, D. E. The effect of the Transcendental Meditation technique on compensatory paradoxical sleep, Graduate Department of Psychology, University of Alberta, Edmonton, Alberta, Canada, In Orme-Johnson, D. W., and Farrow, J. T., eds. *Scientific research on the Transcendental Meditation program: Collected papers, Vol. 1.* MERU Press, Rheinweiler, W. Germany, pp. 292–295, 1977.

[8] Cohen, D. A., Wang, W., Wyatt, J. K., Kronauer, R. E., Dijk, D. J., Czeisler, C. A., and Klerman, E. B. Uncovering residual effects of chronic sleep loss on human performance. *Science Translational Medicine* 2: 14ra3, 2010.

[9] **First Reference:** Tucker, A. M., Whitney, P., Belenky, G., Hinson, J. M., Van Dongen, H. P. A. Effects of sleep deprivation on dissociated components of executive functioning. *Sleep* 33 (11): 47–57, 2010.

Second Reference: Alhola, P., and Polo-Kantola, P. Sleep deprivation: Impact on cognitive performance. *Neuropsychiatic Disease and Treatment* (5): 553–567, 2007.

[10] **First Reference:** Gangwisch, J. E., Malaspina, D., Boden-Albala, B., and Heymsfield, S. B. Inadequate sleep as a risk factor for obesity: Analyses of the NHANES I. *Sleep* 28 (10): 1289–1296, 2005.

Second Reference: Taheri, S., Lin, L., Austin, D., Young, T., and Mignot, E., Short sleep duration is associated with reduced leptin, elevated ghrelin, and increased body mass index. *Public Library of Science Medicine* (3): e62, 2004.

[11] **First Reference:** Gottlieb, D. J., Punjabi, N. M., Newman, A. B., et al. Association of sleep time with diabetes mellitus and impaired glucose tolerance. *Archives of Internal Medicine* 165 (8): 863–867, 2005.

Second Reference: Spiegel, K., Leproult, R., and Van Cauter, E. Impact of sleep debt on metabolic and endocrine function. *The Lancet* 354 (9188): 1435–1439, 1999.

Third Reference: Goes, F. S., Zandi, P. P., Miao, K., et al. Mood-incongruent psychotic features in bipolar disorder: Familial aggregation and suggestive linkage to 2p11-q14 and 13q21-33. *American Journal of Psychiatry* 164 (2): 236–247, 2007.

[12] Cranson, R. W., Orme-Johnson, D. W., Gackenbach, J., Dillbeck, M. C., Jones, C. H., and Alexander, C. N. Transcendental meditation and improved performance on intelligence-related measures: A longitudinal study. *Personality and Individual Differences* 12 (10): 1105–1116, 1991. (The university participating in this study with students practicing meditation was Maharishi University of Management in Fairfield, IA, formerly known as Maharishi International University.)

[13] Chandler, H. M. Transcendental Meditation and awakening wisdom: A ten-year longitudinal study of self development. *Dissertation Abstracts International* 52, 1991.

[14] Wallace, R., Benson, H., and Wison, A. A wakeful hypometabolic physiologic state. *American Journal of Physiology* 221 (3): 795–799, 1971.

[15] Paramahansa Yogananda. *Man's Eternal Quest.* Self-Realization Fellowship, Los Angeles, CA, p. 79, 1975. (Collected Lectures)

[16] Matthew 7:14, *New Testament*, King James Version. (Paraphrased)

[17] Maharishi Mahesh Yogi. *Science of Being and Art of Living.* Signet, New York, NY, p. 63, 1968. (Paperback)

[18] *Shantipath, Kena Upanishad*, 5.1.1. (This is part of the introductory verse to several Upanishads.)

[19] Luke 17:21, *New Testament*, King James Version. (Paraphrased)

[20] Kamath, M. V. *Gandhi: A Spiritual Journey.* Indus Source Books, Mumbai, India, pp. 68–70, 2007.

[21] Center for Science in the Public Interest (CSPI). Chemical Cuisine: Learn about Food Additives: http://www.cspinet.org/reports/chemcuisine.htm

[22] **First Reference:** Davis, D. R., Epp, M. D., and Riordan, H. D. Changes in USDA food composition data for 43 garden crops, 1950 to 1999. *Journal of the American College of Nutrition* 23 (6): 669–682, 2004.

Second Reference: Mayer, A. M. Historical changes in the mineral content of fruits and vegetables. *British Food Journal* 99 (6): 207–211, 1997.

Third Reference: Stephey, M. J. Eating your veggies: not as good for you? *Time*, Feb 18, 2009: http://www.time.com/time/health/article/0,8599,1880145,00.html

[23] **First Reference:** http://www.localharvest.org

Second Reference: http://locavores.com

[24] Smith, S. Organic foods vs supermarket foods: Element levels. *Journal of Applied Nutrition* 45: 35–39, 1993.

[25] Heaton, S. Organic farming, food quality and human health: A review of the evidence. *Soil Association Organic Standard*, Bristol, UK, pp. 7 & 50, 2001: http://www.soilassociation.org/LinkClick.aspx?fileticket=cY8kfP3Q%2BgA%3D&tabid=388

[26] Maharishi Ayurveda Products International: http://www.mapi.com

[27] Ibid.

[28] Ibid.

[29] Ibid.

[30] Levi, J., Vinter, S., St. Laurent, R., Segal, L. M., Gratale, D. F as in Fat: How obesity threatens America's future 2010, a report from the Trust for America's Health and the Robert Wood Johnson Foundation. 2010: http://healthyamericans.org/reports/obesity2010/

[31] Lewis, G. D., et al. Metabolic signatures of exercise in human plasma. *Science Translational Medicine* 2: 33ra37, 2010.

[32] **First Reference:** Framson, C., Kristal, A. R., Schenk, J. M., Littman, A. J., Zeliadt, S., and Benitez, D. Development and validation of the Mindful Eating Questionnaire. *Journal of the American Dietetic Association* 109 (8): 1439–1444, 2009.

Second Reference: Kristal, A. R., Littman, A. J., Benitez, D., and White, E. Yoga practice is associated with attenuated weight gain in healthy, middle-aged men and women. *Alternative Therapies in Health and Medicine* 11 (4): 28–33, 2005.

[33] National Institutes of Health, National Center for Complimentary and Alternative Medicine: http://nccam.nih.gov/health/yoga/introduction.htm

Seven: The Swift-Flowing River

[1] Ashby, Hal, Dir. *Being There*. Exec. Prod. Jack Schwartzman. Prod. Andrew Branunsberg. Perfs. Peter Sellers. Warner Brothers, 1979. (Adapted from the 1971 novel by Jerzy Kosinski.)

[2] *Mundaka Upanishad* 3.1.6.

[3] *Agni Puran*, 16.

[4] Matthew 7:6, *New Testament*, King James Version.

[5] Maharishi Mahesh Yogi, *Maharishi Mahesh Yogi on the Bhagavad-Gita: A New Translation and Commentary, Chapters 1–6*. Penguin, New York, NY, II, 41, 1969.

[6] Ecclesiastes 3:1 & 3:4, *Old Testament*, King James Version. (Paraphrased)

[7] Shakespeare, William, *As You Like It*, Act II, Scene VII, Lines 136-166, 1623.

[8] Maharishi Mahesh Yogi. *Maharishi Mahesh Yogi on the Bhagavad-Gita: A New Translation and Commentary, Chapters 1–6*. Penguin, New York, NY, II, 11-22, 1969.

Eight: I Am You

[1] *Manu Smrti*, 2.161. (Paraphrased)

[2] Reps, Paul, and Senzaki, Nyogen. *Zen Flesh, Zen Bones: A Collection of Zen & Pre-Zen Writings*. Tuttle Publishing, North Clarendon, VT, p. 22, 1957.

[3] Matthew 5:5, *New Testament*, King James Version. (Paraphrased)

[4] **First Reference:** Matthew 7:12, *New Testament*, King James Version.

Second Reference: Luke 6:31, *New Testament,* King James Version. (Paraphrased)

[5] *Mahabharata*, Book 13, Anusasana Parva, CXIII, 8.

[6] **First Reference:** Travis, F. Patterns of EEG coherence, power, and contingent negative variation characterize the integration of transcendental and waking states. *Biological Psychology* 61: 293–319, 2002.

Second Reference: Travis, F., and Miskov, S. P300 latency and amplitude during eyes-closed rest and Transcendental Meditation practice. *Psychophysiology* 31: S67 (Abstract), 1994.

[7] **First Reference:** Turnbull, M. J., and Norris, H. Effects of Transcendental Meditation on self-identity indices and personality. *British Journal of Psychology* 73: 57–68, 1982.

Second Reference: Nidich, I. S., Seeman, W., and Dreskin, T. Influence of Transcendental Meditation: A replication. *Journal of Counseling Psychology* 20: 565–566, 1973.

[8] *Rk Veda*, 1.164.39. (English translation: Maharishi Mahesh Yogi, *Celebrating Perfection in Education, Dawn of Total Knowledge*, Maharishi Vedic University Press, Holland, p. 59, 1997.)

[9] Toepfer, S. M., and Walker, K. Letters of gratitude: Improving well-being through expressive writing. *Journal of Writing Research* 1 (3): 181–198, 2009.

[10] **First Reference**: *Brihadaranyaka Upanishad* 6.2.

Second Reference: *Chandogya Upanishad* 5, 3-10.

Third Reference: Paramahansa Yogananda, *Man's Eternal Quest,* Self-Realization Fellowship, Los Angeles, CA, p. 277, 1975. (Collected Lectures)

Fourth Reference: Paramahansa Yogananda, *Journey to Self-Realization,* Self-Realization Fellowship, Los Angeles, CA, p. 255, 1997. (Collected Lectures)

[11] Maharishi Mahesh Yogi. *Science of Being and Art of Living*. Signet, New York, NY, p. 226, 1968. (Paperback)

[12] Maharishi Mahesh Yogi. *Maharishi Mahesh Yogi on the Bhagavad-Gita: A New Translation and Commentary, Chapters 1–6*. Penguin, New York, NY, IV, 1, 1969.

[13] Maharishi Mahesh Yogi. *Maharishi Mahesh Yogi on the Bhagavad-Gita: A New Translation and Commentary, Chapters 1–6*. Penguin, New York, NY, I, 36, 1969.

[14] Maharishi Mahesh Yogi. *Maharishi Mahesh Yogi on the Bhagavad-Gita: A New Translation and Commentary, Chapters 1–6*. Penguin, New York, NY, II, 38–39, 1969.

Nine: Your Sequential Awakening

[1] Maharishi Mahesh Yogi. *Maharishi Mahesh Yogi on the Bhagavad-Gita: A New Translation and Commentary, Chapters 1–6*. Penguin, New York, NY, IV, 7, 1969.

[2] Maharishi Mahesh Yogi. *Maharishi Mahesh Yogi on the Bhagavad-Gita: A New Translation and Commentary, Chapters 1–6*. Penguin, New York, NY, II, 45, 1969.

[3] Eppley, K. R., Abrams, A. I., and Shear, J. Differential effects of relaxation techniques on trait anxiety: A meta-analysis. *Journal of Clinical Psychology* 45: 957–974, 1989.

[4] Seeman, W., Nidich, S., and Banta, T. Influence of Transcendental Meditation on a measure of self actualization. *Journal of Counseling Psychology* 19: 184–187, 1972.

[5] Cranson, R. W., et al. Transcendental Meditation and improved performance on intelligence-related measures: A longitudinal study. *Personality and Individual Differences* 12: 1105–1116, 1991.

[6] Frew, D. R. Transcendental Meditation and productivity. *Academy of Management Journal* 17: 362–368, 1974.

[7] Murphy, L. R., and Schoenborn, T. F., eds. *Stress Management in Work Settings*. U.S. Department of Health and Human Services, Center for Disease Control, p. 70, 1987.

[8] Alexander, C. N., et al. Effects of the Transcendental Meditation program on stress-reduction, health, and employee development: A prospective study in two occupational settings. *Anxiety, Stress, and Coping: An International Journal* 6: 245–262, 1993.

[9] **First Reference:** Orme-Johnson, D. W., and Herron, R. E. An innovative approach to reducing medical care utilization and expenditures. *The American Journal of Managed Care* 3: 135–144, 1997.

Second Reference: Haratani, T., and Hemmi, T. Effects of Transcendental Meditation (TM) on the health behavior of industrial workers. *Japanese Journal of Public Health* 37 (10 Suppl.): 729, 1990.

[10] **First Reference:** Orme-Johnson, D. W., and Hayes, C. T. EEG phase coherence, pure consciousness, creativity, and TM-Sidhi experiences. *International Journal of Neuroscience* 13: 211–217, 1981.

Second Reference: Dillbeck, M. C., Orme-Johnson, D. W., and Wallace, R. K. Frontal EEG coherence, H-Reflex recovery, concept learning, and the TM-Sidhi Program. *International Journal of Neuroscience* 15: 151–157, 1981.

[11] **First Reference:** Travis, F. Patterns of EEG coherence, power, and contingent negative variation characterize the integration of transcendental and waking states. *Biological Psychology* 61: 293–319, 2002.

Second Reference: Travis, F., and Miskov, S. P300 latency and amplitude during eyes-closed rest and Transcendental Meditation practice. *Psychophysiology* 31: S67 (Abstract), 1994.

[12] Psalm 46:10, *Old Testament*, King James Version. (Paraphrased and altered)

[13] **First Reference:** Aspect, A., Grangier, P., and Roger, G. Experimental realization of Einstein-Podolsky-Rosen-Bohm Gedankenexperiment: A new violation of Bell's inequalities. *Physical Review Letters* 49 (2): 91–94, 1982.

Second Reference: Aspect, A., Dalibard, J., and Roger, G. Experimental test of Bell's inequalities using time-varying analyzers. *Physical Review Letters* 49 (25): 1804–1807, 1982.

[14] **First Reference:** Swami Sri Yukteswar. *The Holy Science.* Self-Realization Fellowship, Los Angeles, CA, pp. 7–20, 1949.

Second Reference: Paramahansa Yogananda. *Autobiography of a Yogi.* Self-Realization Fellowship, Los Angeles, CA, pp. 193–194, 1946. (Paperback)

[15] **First Reference:** Crofton, Kerry. *Wireless Radiation Rescue: Safeguarding Your Family from the Risks of Electro-Pollution.* iUniverse, Bloomington, IN, pp. 26–31, 2009.

Second Reference: http://radiationrescue.org (This website includes a list of research describing the risks associated with radiation emitted from wireless devices.)

[16] Yan, Z., Hu, L., Chen, H., and Lu, F. Computer Vision Syndrome: A widely spreading but largely unknown epidemic among computer users. *Computers in Human Behavior* 24 (5): 2026–2042, 2008.

[17] Anshel, Jeffrey. *Visual Ergonomics Handbook.* Taylor & Francis Group, Boca Raton, FL, p. 3, 2005.

[18] **First Reference:** Johnston, Sean F. *Holographic Visions: History of New Science.* Oxford University, London, England, pp. 190 & 442–444, 2006.

Second Reference: Bjelkhagen, H. I., and Mirlis, E. Color holography to produce highly realistic three-dimensional images. *Applied Optics* (4): A123–A133, 2008.

[19] **First Reference:** Bohm, David. *Wholeness and the Implicate Order.* Routledge & Kegan Paul, London, England, pp. 182–186, 1980.

Second Reference: Pribram, Karl H. Brain and Perception: *Holonomy and Structure in Figural Processing.* Lawrence Erlbaum Associates, Hillsdale, NJ, pp. 22–27, 1991.

[20] Parker, E. S., Cahill, L., and McGaugh, J. L. A case of unusual autobiographical remembering. *Neurocase* 12 (1): 35–49, 2006.

[21] Dunne, B. J., and Jahn, R. G. Information and uncertainty in remote perception research. *Journal of Scientific Exploration* 17 (2): 207–241, 2003.

[22] Jahn, R. G., Dunne, B. J., Nelson, R. D., Dobyns, Y. H., and Bradish, G. J.

Correlations of random binary sequences with pre-stated operator intention: A review of a 12-year program. *Journal of Scientific Exploration* 11 (3): 345–367, 1997.

[23] Nader, Tony. *Human Physiology: Expression of Veda and the Vedic Literature.* Maharishi Vedic University, Vlodrop, The Netherlands, pp. 56–57, 2000.

[24] **First Reference:** Piraino, S., Boero, F., Aeschbach, B., and Schmid V. Reversing the life cycle: Medusae transforming into polyps and cell transdifferentiation in Turritopsis nutricula (Cnidaria, Hydrozoa). *Biological Bulletin* 190 (3): 302–312. 1996.

Second Reference: Bavestrello, G., Sommer, C., and Sarà, M. Bi-directional conversion in Turritopsis nutricula (Hydrozoa). *Scientia Marina* 56 (2-3): 137–140. 1992.

[25] Paramahansa Yogananda. *Autobiography of a Yogi.* Self-Realization Fellowship, Los Angeles, CA, pp. 345–355, 1946. (Paperback)

[26] John 14:2, *New Testament,* King James Version.

[27] Jeans, James. *The Mysterious Universe.* Cambridge University Press, Great Britain, p. 137, 1930.

[28] Planck, Max, quoted in: *The Observer,* London, England, January 25th, 1931.

[29] Abel, Christopher R., and Hare, William O. *Hermes Trismegistus: An Investigation of the Origin of the Hermetic Writings.* Holmes Publishing Group, Sequim, WA, p. 7, 1997.

[30] Maharishi Mahesh Yogi. *Maharishi's Absolute Theory of Government.* Age of Enlightenment Publications, New Delhi, India, p. 237, 1995.

[31] **First Reference:** See pictures of Antennae Galaxy at: http://chandra.harvard.edu/photo/2010/antennae/

Second Reference: http://www.spitzer.caltech.edu/news/1066-feature10-03-Spitzer-Detects-the-Heartbeat-of-Star-Formation-in-the-Milky-Way-Galaxy

[32] John 10:30, *New Testament,* King James Version.

[33] Swami Vivekananda. *Inspired Talks.* Ramakrishna-Vivekananda Center, New York, NY, p. 31, 1958.

[34] John 10:34, *New Testament,* King James Version.

[35] Anderson, Christopher. Hagelin & Quantum Theory: Holding on by a super-string. *Nature* 359 (6391): 97. September 10, 1992.

[36] Oates, Robert M. *Permanent Peace.* Institute of Science, Technology, and Public Policy, Fairfield, IA, pp. 111–112, 2002.

[37] Maharishi Mahesh Yogi. *Scientific Research on the Maharishi Technology of the Unified Field: The Transcendental Meditation and TM-Sidhi Program, One Program to Develop All Areas of Life.* Maharishi International University, Fairfield, IA, p. 1, 1988.

[38] Paramahansa Yogananda. *Journey to Self-Realization.* Self-Realization Fellowship, Los Angeles, CA, p. 7. 1997. (Collected Lectures)

Ten: Fulfilled

[1] Maharishi Mahesh Yogi. *Maharishi Mahesh Yogi on the Bhagavad-Gita: A New Translation and Commentary, Chapters 1–6*. Penguin, New York, NY, Preface: pp. 14–16, 1969.

ACKNOWLEDGEMENTS

I would like to thank first and foremost my wife and two children for affording me the time to complete this project. In some ways this was a family effort, because we all had to be in agreement about Dad's time if this book was ever going to see the light of day. Thank you for your patience and assistance. I love you all so much for what you contribute to my life on a daily basis.

I would also like to thank Neil Dickie for his refined literary counsel and light-edit approach to the manuscript of this book. You were just the right hand to maintain the integrity of the work. In addition, I am grateful to Evelyn Perricone for her valuable proofing suggestions.

Finally, I give deep thanks to Maharishi Mahesh Yogi for his magnificent insights into the processes for developing human awareness, and for explaining in such simple terms what enlightenment really is. Without his wisdom and techniques for the development of consciousness, this book would never have been written. All glory to His Holiness Maharishi Mahesh Yogi and his legacy of enlightenment.

ABOUT THE AUTHOR

Jay Gardner has spent nearly 30 years studying higher knowledge for the development of consciousness. He has long immersed himself in the wisdom of the great enlightened masters, and along the way has increasingly gained familiarity with God and the pathless path to lasting fulfillment.

Gardner has a BA in Government, an MBA in Management, and an MA in the Science of Creative Intelligence (Vedic Science).

He has a wealth of experience in business, with special expertise in the areas of marketing, sales, and operations management. Gardner has participated in a consulting role with some of the world's largest and best-known corporations.

Jay Gardner is currently President of ATS, Inc., which strives to make higher knowledge in all its manifestations available to the public. (For questions and comments about *Forever Fulfilled*, email info@ jaygardner.us)